GLORY DAYS

GLORY DAYS

THE STORY OF SOUTH SYDNEY'S GOLDEN ERA

ALAN WHITICKER

This edition published in Australia in 2015 by
New Holland Publishers (Australia) Pty Ltd
Sydney • Auckland • London

The Chandlery Unit 009 50 Westminster Bridge Road London SE1 7QY United Kingdom
1/66 Gibbes Street Chatswood NSW 2067 Australia
5/39 Woodside Ave Northcote, Auckland 0627 New Zealand

Copyright © 2015 New Holland Publishers (Australia) Pty Ltd
Copyright © 2015 in text Alan Whiticker
Copyright © 2015 in pictures Ian Collis

All rights reserved. No part of this publication may be reproduced, stored in
a retrieval system or transmitted, in any form or by any means, electronic,
mechanical, photocopying, recording or otherwise, without the prior
written permission of the publishers and copyright holders.

Front flap photos, top to bottom: Souths legend Bob McCarthy; Dual international
Jim Lisle and mascot; John Sattler is chaired from the field after winning the 1970
grand final against Manly playing with a broken jaw.

A record of this publication is held at the National Library of Australia.
ISBN: 9781742578002

Publisher: Diane Jardine
Publishing Manager: Lliane Clarke
Production Manager: Olga Dementiev
Project Editor: Rochelle Fernandez
Designer: Celeste Vlok
Cover image: Celeste Vlok
Printer: Everbest Printing Co Ltd, China
10 9 8 7 6 5 4 3 2 1

For Kevin Longbottom, Jim Lisle, Jim Morgan, John O'Neill, Clive Churchill and Ivan Jones

ACKNOWLEDGEMENTS

My sincere thanks to all the Souths players who consented to be interviewed for this book, especially Bob Honan, Gary Stevens and Brian James for lending me their playing scrapbooks. Thank you to the team at New Holland ... Fiona Schultz and Lliane Clarke, for their faith and support in this project; Rochelle Fernandez and Jessica McNamara for their editing, and Celeste Vlok for her wonderful design. Thank you also to Brad Ryder, Jeremy Monahan and Shane Richardson at South Sydney for their help with contacts; Grant Vendenberg and Russell Crowe for their generosity; Ian Collis for his brilliant photos; uber-Souths collector Phil Laws for allowing me to access his memorabilia; Vance Rennie, the Secretary of the Brisbane chapter of the Men of League; Wayne Stevens, who may not have played in a first grade grand final, but who remains a Souths legend; and Stuart Mullins and Tom Berry on the Gold Coast. Lastly, thank you to Lisa Bolger and my wife, Karen, for their help with interview transcriptions.

CONTENTS

FOREWORD 9
INTRODUCTION 11
PART 1. HIGH TIDE AND GREEN GRASS (1967–68) 17
John Sattler (1967–71) 26
Eric Simms (1967–71) 39
Bob Honan (1968–71) 51
Elwyn Walters (1967–70) 65
Arthur Branighan (1968, 1970) 76
The Class of '67 Kevin Longbottom, Jim Lisle,
Ivan Jones, Alan Scott and Greg Norgard 86
PART 2. YOU CAN'T ALWAYS GET WHAT YOU WANT (1969) ... 97
Ron Coote (1967–71) 106
Michael Cleary (1967–70) 119
Bob Grant (1968–71) 132
Brian James (1967–69) 142
Bob Moses (1967–69) 155
Denis Pittard (1968–71) 164
PART 3. LET IT BLEED (1970–71) 177
Bob McCarthy (1967, 1969–71) 186
Paul Sait (1969–71) 199
Gary Stevens (1970–71) 209
Ray Branighan (1970–71) 222
George Piggins (1971) 235
Not to forget ... Jim Morgan, Kerry Burke, Keith Edwards
and Clive Churchill 249
PART 4. FORTY LICKS (1972–2011) 261
Remembering John O'Neill (1967–71) 270
In search of '21' 283
EPILOGUE 297
RECORDS AND STATISTICS 301

FOREWORD

My connection to South Sydney begins in the back streets of Beaconsfield. My Dad ran a multi-fit muffler shop on Botany Road. My first solid Souths memory is, unfortunately, losing the 1969 grand final, the only glitch in the last 'Golden Era' of 1967 to 1971.

It was the great names of that era who fueled my backyard, back street and local park football fantasies—one day I was Bob McCarthy, the next I was Eric Simms and, if I was feeling particularly brave, I'd be Gary Stevens. Every time I see Ron Coote I still remember the disbelief that I felt the day I heard he was leaving Souths to go to the Roosters. How was that possible? My young mind just couldn't comprehend it.

Given Souths' patchy finals record ever since, it is still these names Souths fans draw on for comparison to any young player that comes along. That era still defines Souths for many of us, and it is that type of team we are always looking to build. Who knows? Perhaps in this era of Roy Asotasi, Sam Burgess, Dave Taylor, Issac Luke, Chris Sandow, John Sutton, Nathan Merritt and Greg Inglis, we might finally feel the resurgence on the field that all Rabbitohs diehards have dreamt of since 1971.

—Russell Crowe, 2011

INTRODUCTION

For the generation of baby boomers, the 1960s was a great time to be alive ... the era of The Beatles and The Rolling Stones, glorious black and white TV, and the explosion of youth culture. Rugby league in the late 1960s was full of drama and great theatre – champion players, villainous referees and last minute victories It was also a time of incredible change. Dominated by two champion clubs, St George and South Sydney, the 1960s saw Rugby League introduce the limited tackle rule, and in 1967, the promotion of new clubs Cronulla-Sutherland and Penrith. This is where I came in. While my cousins and schoolmates were Saints and Souths fans, I took the view that if you were Penrith born and bred, as I was, then you were pretty much fated to be a Panthers supporter. By the time the 'Chocolate Soldiers' were promoted into the NSWRL in 1967 the once great St George team may have been on the wane – Penrith's 24-12 win over the defending premiers in April that year remains a cherished memory – but a great Souths' era was on the way.

Those matches against Souths remain as vivid today as the day I sat on the hill with my father and sundry friends more than 40 years ago – being thrashed by the Rabbitohs 39–0 in our debut season; taking on the defending premiers at the SCG in Penrith's first 'match of the day' in 1968; Eric Simms kicking six goals and five field goals in 1969; Bobby McCarthy diving over in the corner, close enough for me to touch him, in 1970; Ray Branighan breaking our hearts with a winning goal in 1971. I was never a Souths supporter, even when they were playing in all those grand finals (except against Manly) but I was a fan of what the champion team stood for – brilliance, toughness, flair and finesse.

When I was old enough to travel to Redfern Oval by train with friends, and staunch Souths supporters, we knew we were in 'Rabbitoh' territory before we even got to Redfern Station. The roofs of the train yards in Everleigh Street were painted red and green and the letters that spelt out 'SOUTHS' were painted twenty feet high in white paints on the side of the sheds. Walking into Redfern Oval was like walking into another universe for Western Sydney kids – the Redfern matrons adorned in their knitted red and green cardigans sitting in the club's modest stand, and the mob on Baker's Hill made sure we knew we weren't welcome. I can rarely recall making the long train trip back to Penrith with a winning feeling, but being a Panthers supporter back then you were used to that.

Founded on 17 January 1908, South Sydney is the oldest rugby league club competing in the NRL premiership – but then Souths have always been at the forefront of rugby league history. A proud club formed in the game's inaugural year, the 'Rabbitoh men' won the first ever premiership title in 1908. The following year, they won the premiership on forfeit after allegedly pulling out of a deal with the Balmain Club to boycott the 1909 final because it had been programmed as a curtain-raiser for a Kangaroos versus Wallabies match. Souths also won the first premiership played under the four tackle rule, in 1967, and the six tackle rule, in 1971, to complete a unique trifecta of premierships under different playing conditions. Sensationally axed from the NRL Premiership in October 1999, Souths resisted the financial lure of a merger (unlike fellow foundation clubs Balmain, Wests and Norths) and became the only club to fight their way back into the competition.

This was 'people power' at its finest. Today, Souths remain the code's most successful club, with 21 first grade titles to their credit.

Introduction

If the St George Dragons were the rugby league equivalent of The Beatles, with hit year after hit year in the early part of the decade, then South Sydney were surely The Rolling Stones. Where St George had been the glamour team of the Sydney premiership, Souths, with their working class origins, were the opposite. And just as The Rolling Stones usurped The Beatles on the world stage, South Sydney assumed the mantle of Sydney premiers and produced their own 'Golden Era' from 1967 to 1971. The club's 'Dream Team', which was announced in 2004, contained nine of players from that era: Clive Churchill, Harold Horder, Herb Gilbert, Paul Sait, Ian Moir, Jim Lisle, Bob Grant, John Sattler (captain), Elwyn Walters, John O'Neill, George Treweek, Bob McCarthy, Ron Coote. (Reserves) Greg Hawick, Ray Branighan, Ian Roberts, Les Cowie. Jack Rayner (coach).

When I started writing about rugby league in the 1980s, I interviewed many of the players I had watched play as a kid in the 1960s and 1970s. I first talked to John Sattler more than 20 years ago for a book I was writing on the history of grand finals. My wife and I caught up with 'Satts' some years later at the launch of Graeme McNeice's video That's Rugby League in 1995 and he recalled our interview, and such is the charm of the man, he spoke to us as if we were lifelong fans. I once interviewed Ron Coote late one night as he worked the night shift at his Kings Cross McDonalds. Coote, a thorough professional, still found the time to talk to me about the game he loves. At the book launch for The Encyclopedia of Rugby League Players in the early 1990s, my co-author Glen Hudson brought along Bobby McCarthy, and I think for the first time in my life I was actually lost for words.

The South Sydney players from that golden era were superstars and remain so in the minds and memories of the game's fans.

What happened to that elite group of players who starred for Souths in five consecutive grand finals? Incredibly, only 25 players appeared in those five grand finals from 1967 to 1971, and four have passed away, as has premiership-winning coach Clive Churchill. Perhaps, through the players' eyes, we can gain an insight into rugby league in that era, and how the club let such a champion team slip away. How did life fare for the hardy bunch of 'Rabbitohs' after fulltime was called on their careers … was there further successes, further glory?

Tracking down the surviving members of Souths' last golden era was made easier with the assistance of the club's enthusiastic historian Brad Ryder. John Sattler and Bob Honan live on the Gold Coast, Kerry Burke is in Brisbane and Elwyn Walters on the NSW side of Tweed Heads. Greg Norgard lives in Newcastle and Ron Coote on the NSW South Coast, but the remaining players are spread over Sydney. All agreed to be interviewed for this book – Bob McCarthy, genial and a natural story-teller; Michael Cleary, guarded and straight to the point; Brian James, quietly-spoken and reflective; Eric Simms, unassuming and humble. The Branighan brothers were wonderful hosts, as was Gary Stevens at nearby Malabar, and Bobby Moses in the western suburb of St Clair. George Piggins was generous with his time and his opinions while Paul Sait, recovering from knee surgery, was a late call-up thanks to the intercession of Wayne Stevens. While Kerry Burke proved as elusive now as he was in his days as a promising centre for Parramatta and Souths, a last minute call from Denis Pittard resulted in one of those rare interviews of which writers dream.

I trust the reader enjoys this book as much as I did piecing it together over the summer of 2010–2011. Meeting so many legends willing to share 'war stories' from their careers could only be described as a labour of love for any true rugby league fan. This 2015 edition, which highlights the club's success in the 2014 grand final, completes the proud South Sydney story … for now.

To paraphrase an old Rolling Stones song, 'I know, it's only rugby league, but I love it.'

— Alan Whiticker, 2015

Introduction 15

PART 1: HIGH TIDE AND GREEN GRASS (1967–68)

It may have been the 'Summer of Love' in the Northern Hemisphere, with The Beatles releasing their landmark album *Sergeant Pepper's Lonely Hearts Club Band* in 'Swinging England' and hippies flocking to San Francisco's Haight Ashbury district searching for free love and peace, but in the Australian winter of 1967 it was the beginning of a new era in rugby league and for the South Sydney Club. After six decades of the 'unlimited tackle' rule, where a team could hang onto the ball for the entire match if they were good enough, the International Rugby League Board of Control in England introduced the 'four tackle' rule. Now both teams had an equal chance to win the ball with a scrum set after every four tackles in possession. The era of 'bash and barge' was over, hastening an end to St George's 11-year reign as Sydney premiers.

South Sydney had a new club president in Dennis Donoghue, a new secretary in Charlie Gibson and a new coach with the return of favourite son, Clive Churchill. Soon the Rabbitohs would have a new captain in John Sattler, and a new winning attitude. At year end Souths reclaimed the Club Championship and first grade premiership title it had surrendered to Saints in the mid 1950s.

The four tackle rule succeeded in making the game 'more spectacular, faster and more entertaining' and crowds increased from 1.37 million in 1966 to 1.84 million in 1967. It also evened out the NSWRL competition. Eleven-time premiers St George, with its ageing players and inexperienced front row, came back to the pack of contenders but still had enough talent in its ranks to secure the minor premiership. Souths knocked Balmain out of finals contention when Simms potted a 'glorious 50-yard field goal' to snatch an 11-10 win in the final round match at the SCG. Canterbury, victors over Norths, and a resurgent Easts team under the coaching of Jack Gibson, made up the top four.

When Souths defeated Saints for the second time during the competition, journalist Mike Gibson wrote: 'Old Father Time and a team of Rabbits from South Sydney yesterday made bunnies of

St George.' It was no different in the major semi-final, with Souths winning 13-8. St George scored two tries to one but a combination of speed, strength and great goal-kicking from Eric Simms (4) and Kevin Longbottom (1) took Souths into the grand final. Many keen judges correctly predicted that Saints were on the way out, and when Canterbury defeated the defending premiers 12-11 in the final, St George's premiership reign was over.

After the chaos of the 1965 grand final where fans scaled the walls to see the match between Souths and St George, organisers now ensured rugby league's big day was an 'all ticket' affair. 50,000 tickets were quickly snapped up—$1 for grandstand seating for an adult and 20 cents for children, and 60 cents for adults in the outer and 10 cents for children and pensioners, with no reserved seating. In the week leading up to the grand final the NSWRL came to an agreement with the four Sydney television channels, for a fee believed to be between $6,660 and $8,000, and the 1967 grand final became the first shown live on television—on all four channels simultaneously. This decision, and the inclement weather, kept the grand final crowd down to 56,385.

Minor premiers and defending premiers in reserve grade, Souths' were beaten by Balmain in the grand final, 11-7. George Piggins was one of three players sent from the field in a fiery semi-final loss to Balmain the fortnight before. (Piggins may not have been eligible for the grand final anyway because he had not played the requisit number of reserve grade matches.) Souths defeated Parramatta in the preliminary final to set up a rematch with Balmain in the grand final, but the Tigers were too strong on the day. Souths' reserve grade team was: Colin Dunn (c), Wayne Stevens, Ray Branighan, Arthur Branighan, Alan Heiler, Greg Norgard, Bob Grant, Paul Sait, Gary Stevens, Steve Lawrence, Dennis Lee, Ted Payne and Chris Armstrong.

In first grade, Canterbury's George Taylforth and Eric Simms traded penalty goals before John O'Neill barged over from dummy half to give Souths a 5-2 lead. The 'Berries' held an 8-5 advantage after two more goals and a towering field goal from Ron Raper and were attacking the Souths line minutes before half-time when the unthinkable happened. All year Souths tactics had been to fan their forwards outward from the ruck and play Bob McCarthy inside the winger, giving them an overlap in the centres. It was almost their undoing in the grand final. As Canterbury switched play and Les Johns looked to come into the backline, McCarthy found himself stranded as the widest defender. Hooker Col Brown threw a lofted pass which McCarthy intercepted and sprinted 80 yards to score underneath the posts. No other forward could have scored that try because no-one but McCarthy stood as wide in a match or had the pace to finish the job. Simms' conversion gave Souths a 10-8 lead at the break and effectively turned the tide of the grand final.

Canterbury equalised with a penalty goal nine minutes into the second half and for the next 30 minutes the grand final was in the balance at 10-all. Kevin Longbottom missed with three long-ranged penalty goals during the match and with 17 minutes remaining, referee Col Pearce disallowed what was later determined to be a fair goal. The ball hit the left upright about a yard above the crossbar and skewered inside the posts. With one touch judge ruling a goal and the other no goal, Pearce had to disallow the goal because, he admitted to me in an interview conducted twenty years later, he had lost sight of the ball in the sea of faces in the crowd. A penalty goal from a scrum infringement four minutes from fulltime gave Simms a shot from 40 yards out, which he duly converted. Fulltime: Souths 12 Canterbury 10.

John Sattler, who moved to prop after Jim Morgan broke a rib in the final round of competition, was selected on the 1967-68 Kangaroo Tour hours after completing the lap of honour with his team. Ron Coote, Souths' 'stilt-legged lock', was considered an automatic selection while hooker Elwyn Walters, who appeared in just eight games that year (four in first grade), was a shock inclusion.

But there was no room for grand final hero Bob McCarthy or a bevy of other Souths' stars with undeniable claims. St George, the fallen premiers, supplied six players for the tour.

Two days after the grand final, a squad of 34 South Sydney players and officials sailed to Perth on the Oriana for a mini tour (the club's reserve and third grade squads had to settle for Coolangatta). The South Sydney team that defeated Western Australia 37-12 was: Kevin Longbottom, Mike Cleary, Bob Moses, Eric Simms, Brian James, Jim Lisle, Ivan Jones, Steve Lawrence, Alan Scott, Bob McCarthy, John O'Neill, Tom Craigie and Dennis Lee. Wayne Stevens, Bob Grant and Alan Heiler (reserves).

Eric Simms, naturally, won a goal-kicking dual against the best goal-kickers the West had to offer from all the football codes and Brian James won a 110 yard sprint. Both players received wrist watches for their efforts. The Souths' contingent flew home on 7 October, ending a record-breaking year.

In 1968 Australia hosted the four-nation, World Cup competition for the first time since 1957. As reigning premiers, Souths could have expected to supply several candidates, but when the first NSW team was announced in May, the club's sole representative was Brian James. The speedy winger beat his NSW Country counterpart Don Pascoe for a place in Australia's 19-man squad but the only other Souths' representatives were Ron Coote and Eric Simms. While James appeared in one World Cup match, against France in Brisbane, Coote scored tries in all four matches, including the 20-2 win over France in the final. Eric Simms, who got his chance in the rep teams when Les Johns broke his jaw in the City versus Country fixture, was quickly becoming a phenomenon in the game. The top point-scorer in the World Cup competition with 50 points from 25 goals in four appearances, Simms turned the two-point field goal into a deadly attacking weapon. He landed a record 29 field goals in 1968, sometimes kicking two or three in a match. Although many others tried, no other player so exploited this attacking option under the new limited tackle rules.

The big news for Souths fans in 1968 was the arrival of former Western Suburbs five-eighth Denis Pittard. After making his first grade debut as a teenager with the Magpies in 1965, a contractual dispute saw him travel to England in the 1967-68 off-season. He came to terms with Souths after his return to Sydney and made his debut for the club midway through the season. Souths' committee, mindful that former dual international Jim Lisle was coming to the end of his career, offered Pittard an $8,000 contract—almost twice the benchmark set by Bernie Purcell back in 1964 for international players. Although the signing added to the inflationary pressures the club would experience as more players earned international status, Pittard was an immediate hit at Souths and formed a champion halfback partnership with Bob Grant in the years ahead.

Souths lost five first-round matches in 1968 and appeared to be struggling halfway through the season. When St George defeated Souths 28-19 at the SCG in June, the Rabbitohs weren't even in the top four. But the team came together in the second round, winning nine successive matches leading up to the semi-finals. In an even competition, Souths captured its first minor premiership in 14 years finishing on 32 points, ahead of Manly (31), St George and Easts (both 29). It took the last round, 24-22 win over Easts for Souths to secure the minor premiership, however. Simms' conversion of a Denis Pittard try right on full-time secured the top spot and gave the Rabbitohs a much-needed week off before the major semi-final.

Club Champions for the second successive year, Souths were sensationally beaten by archrivals Manly in the major semi-final, 23-15. Two tries by Pittard could not breach Manly's lead and the Sea Eagles charged into the grand final in search of a maiden premiership title. Souths' selectors made the necessary changes for the all-important preliminary final against sentimental favourites St George—dropping centre Arthur Branighan (who eventually held his position when Jim Lisle withdrew through injury); moving

Bobby Honan from winger to centre when Mike Cleary declared his fitness; dropping forward Paul Sait to accommodate the return of John O'Neill and promoting former Balmain halfback Bob Grant to first grade when Ivan Jones succumbed to injury.

Souths duly defeated Saints 20-8 and were installed firm favourites in the grand final. The club could not find a place for 1967 hero Bob McCarthy, who was returning from injury, and selected the same team that had beaten St George for the grand final. Clive Churchill told journalist Mike Gibson before the premiership decider; 'Since Manly defeated us in the semi-final two weeks ago, they've lost (captain) Ken Day and we've gained John O'Neill … I'm confident we'll be too strong in the forwards.'

Souths took on Manly in both first and reserve grades on grand final day, 21 September 1968. The Rabbitohs won the reserve grade grand final, 17-7, with the following team: Kevin Longbotttom, Alan Heiler, Ray Branighan, Ralph Grace, Russell Amatto, Greg Norgard, Ivan Jones, Gary Stevens, Paul Sait, Bob McCarthy, Dennis Lee (c), George Piggins, Chris Armstrong and Steve Kosta (reserve).

The first-grade grand final, which was shown live on ABC TV, drew a crowd of 54,255. Mike Cleary set up a winning 11-2 lead at half-time after scooping up a loose pass from Bob Batty to Les Hanigan and racing 80 yards to score under the posts untouched. It was the second intercept try in as many grand finals for Souths and the sight of Cleary steaming away sank the hearts of Manly fans. Simms landed his fifth goal soon after the break when Bob Fulton took a potshot at Ron Coote in front of the Manly goalposts. But the Sea Eagles came back with a try to John 'Pogo' Morgan in the Paddington corner, a goal to Batty and a towering field goal from Fulton. Souths held on for the final 14 minutes of the match, with Simms missing a field goal attempt and a sitter of a penalty goal minutes from full-time. The game threatened to get out of control at certain times—Coote and Bill Bradstreet clashed in the first half, 'Pogo' Morgan was penalised for retaliating against Coote, and Bob

Moses was set upon by the Manly pack after felling Fulton with a high shot inside the final 10 minutes. O'Neill and Honan both finished the match with broken noses, and a sporting rivalry that would last a generation was forged.

At the end of the year Souths travelled to New Zealand where they defeated champion Auckland club Mount Albert, 27-13, Ponsonby, 31-3, and a combined Maori team, 33-14. The players then took on Brisbane Brothers in a match promoted as the 'Australasian Club Championship' at Lang Park. The Souths team that scored 13 tries in the 55-15 thrashing of the Brisbane champions was: Eric Simms, Michael Cleary, Bob Honan, Ray Branighan, Alan Heiler, Denis Pittard, Bob Grant, Ron Coote, Bob Moses, Bob McCarthy, John Sattler (c), Elwyn Walters and John O'Neill. Paul Sait and Kevin Longbottom (reserves).

Rugby league was like a religion in the South Sydney district and the Rabbitohs played before more than half a million fans in 1968. For years the successful Souths Juniors club had provided jerseys, boots, socks and footballs for its district junior teams—which numbered almost 150, with more than 3300 registered players—and continued to go from strength to strength.

It was the high tide mark of Souths' last golden era, but the ensuing years would not be as kind.

JOHN SATTLER
(1967–72)

I am sitting in the Southport Leagues Club on Queensland's Gold Coast just after Boxing Day, talking to Souths' legend John Sattler as the early morning regulars start to come in. The newspapers are all over Australia's failure in the Fourth Ashes Test and the talking heads on the sports cable news are berating Ricky Ponting for arguing with the umpires over a failed appeal. 'Poor bugger, Ricky,' Sattler says, shaking his head. 'They wanted him to show some aggression and fight for the Ashes. As soon as he does, they're into him.'

John Sattler knew something about aggression and a lot about captaincy during his stellar ten-year career with South Sydney. Originally a firebrand lock forward from the Newcastle competition, Sattler was chosen to captain Souths by coach Clive Churchill in 1967 and led the club in five consecutive grand finals. When the Rabbitohs named its 'Dream Team' in 2004, celebrating almost 100 years of rugby league in the South Sydney district, Sattler was selected as captain of the team. The dramatic events that unfolded during the 1970 grand final against Manly, in which Sattler played almost the entire match with a broken jaw, have tended to overshadow his career as a leader. Sattler not only captained Souths for six seasons (1967-1972), but also NSW (1969), Australia (1969-70) and Queensland (1973).

Yes, he was tough, fearless and even reckless at times. But players wanted to play for him.

To meet 'Satts' in person and have the pleasure to sit and talk to him for a while opens a world of contradictions. Sattler is charming and well-spoken, nothing like his on-field persona, and is almost deferential in appraisal of his contribution to rugby league. As former teammate Bob Honan told me, 'Satts was always a thorough gentleman ... right up to the moment he put his mouthguard in.' The hair may be greyer, but at age 68, he is incredibly fit, even allowing for the fact he is about to have hip replacement surgery. 'Had both the knees done, the hip is next,' he says. 'I used to do a lot of road running during my career to keep fit. They used to tell me that would stuff my legs up—and they were right!'

John William Sattler was born in Maitland on 28 July 1942. Incredibly, the future Australian Test captain did not play a game of rugby league before the age of 16. Sattler preferred riding and tending to horses. Maitland had a strong trotting community at the time and a teenage Sattler started to drive the trotters in their training. He even drove a winner in his first race, the aptly named 'South Express'. He started playing rugby league for Kurri Kurri, west of Newcastle, and quickly developed a reputation as a talented, no-nonsense lock forward.

A snappy dresser who worked in the town's menswear store, Sattler was selected to represent Newcastle against the all-conquering Great Britain touring team in 1962. The bush lads beat the Lions 23-18 that day and a number of players, including fullback Les Johns and lock John Sattler, came to the attention of Sydney club scouts. Legendary St George secretary Frank Facer tried to sign Sattler to a contract but Sattler didn't want to move to the city. But all that was soon to change.

'On New Year's Day [1963] I was still in bed when a knock came at the front door,' Sattler recalls. South Sydney club treasurer George Hansen and club sponsor Joe Maloney arrived on the family doorstep unannounced and asked if they could speak to the young lad. 'Dad said, "Well, he's been out all night at a dance and he's in bed".'

The men said, 'Oh, that's good. We'll get him up.' And they walked straight in. Mum made us some breakfast and about two hours later I was in our car with Dad, bound for Sydney.'

Sattler only wanted to sign a one-year contract to begin with because he didn't know how he would go in Sydney. 'Souths talked me into a two-year contract because they said that it would take me a year to settle in. They paid a £650 signing on fee and £40 a win, £30 a draw and £20 a loss. I thought I was a millionaire.' Playing for Kurri, he had been happy to clear £50 a year.

The first season with Souths was a disaster. The Rabbitohs won only four games under coach Dennis Donoghue and finished second last in the competition. Playing in his distinctive white headgear, Satts was an easy target for opposing forwards—easy to rile, quick to anger and eager to retaliate. 'I got bashed in the first trial game against Manly,' he remembers. 'They really gave it to me. My eye was split open and my cheekbone got smashed.' Sattler stood up for himself, maybe even got in first, was sent off and earned a short 'holiday'.

'Dad said to me, "You've gotta back up on them or get in the car and come home with me now."' It was a philosophy that shaped Sattler's early career as a feared back row forward. It was the same philosophy that saw him stay on the field with a broken jaw in a grand final. Never give an inch, never let the bastards know you're hurt.

A teenager named Bob McCarthy also made his first grade debut for Souths in 1963, but under the coaching of Bernie Purcell the following year the team started to come together. 'Bernie was a great bloke, a real knockabout,' Sattler says. 'And there were some great juniors coming through. Ron Coote arrived on the scene that year, Gary Stevens came into grade the following year, and later Ray Branighan and Paul Sait.' It was Purcell who moved Sattler from lock to second row to accommodate a rangy-legged junior from Kingsford. 'Ronny Coote came up from Presidents Cup in 1964 and played the last game of the pre-season competition and scored a terrific try. At the next training session Bernie said I was in the second row. I stood my ground and didn't want to move. He said, "I've got good news and bad news. You're playing second row."'

The watermark of Purcell's ultimately brief time as coach was the 1965 grand final against St George in front of a record SCG crowd of 78,056. 'Well that's how many they counted,' Satts laughs. 'The fans kicked the gates in.' St George won 12-8 and kept their defensive line intact. Souths could have played Saints into the night and not broken their defensive line, Sattler says, 'That was the most frightening defence I've ever seen. Just so ... structured. Every time we played the ball they'd come up on us like a large white sheet and they just jarred us with their tackling. We were young and fit, but we grew up very quickly after that game. It was the best thing that could have happened to us.'

After the 1965 grand final, the Souths and St George players took over the Cauliflower Hotel in the heart of South Sydney. 'We'd just been bashed in front of 78,000 people and here we were drinking with our opponents. The St George team were a great mob of fellas. They were true sportsmen ... hard and tough when there was a job to be done but when it was all over, great mates. "Changa" Langlands, "Chook" Raper and Billy Smith were larrikins, and are still larrikins today.'

Sattler confesses that he wasn't a big drinker and would only go to after-training drinks a couple of times a year to keep the boys happy. He much preferred a quiet dinner with Bob McCarthy, Ron Coote and their wives at a local Chinese restaurant.

Despite the footballing education handed out by St George, Souths failed to make the finals in 1966. The nadir of the season was the 33-5 loss to St George. Souths were labelled 'lunatics' after attempting to bash their opponents out of the game. 'We had no chance of beating them the way we were playing so we just got stuck into them. It wasn't premeditated ... it was a frustration thing with us. Norm Provan wrote in the paper that we were going to kill someone. We narrowly missed the semis and they ended up sacking Bernie, sadly.

Clive Churchill, who put in for the coaching position, took over in 1967. We became a really good side together … a good team of blokes who played for one another.'

When Churchill told Sattler that he wanted him to take over from Jimmy Lisle as captain, Satts admits having mixed feelings about the move. 'I was really proud but I was also terrified. I don't know why Clive wanted me as captain. He just went to the Board and said "Satts is captain". All the other fellows told me not to not to worry about it. They were on my side.' Sattler's transformation from fiery forward to team leader was an integral part of Souths' success over the next five seasons.

Sattler was not a big fan of the four tackle rule which came in that year. 'Talk about frustration. You'd just go "one, two, and then three, and kick the ball". It was hard to get to a stage where you could build a play. We had to learn how to develop that skill quickly. Fellows like Kevin Ryan, big 'Sticks' Provan and Brian Hambly … that wasn't their type of play. They worked the ball and got into a position where their backs could take over. The six tackle rule [introduced in 1971] was much better.'

When Souths won the 1967 grand final, Sattler moved to front row. Jim Morgan was injured late in the 1967 season, Alan Scott was promoted to the back row and Sattler shifted to prop. Satts is not a big man. Looking at him now it's hard to believe he played prop forward in four of the five grand finals. At 5 feet 8 inches (about 173cm), and weighing 14 stone 8 lbs (about 92 kilograms) at the time, he may have been considered a lightweight prop but he was rock hard and mobile. Having progressed from lock to the front row in three short seasons, Sattler was quick learner in the art of scrummaging packing in against Canterbury captain-coach, dual international Kevin Ryan. 'I knew nothing about being a front forward,' Sattler admits. But Souths' forwards finished on top in a tense grand final, winning 12-10.

Sattler was one of three Souths players named on the 1967-68 Kangaroo Tour later that night. Having married in 1964, Sattler was living at Brighton-Le-Sands and his wife was expecting their first child. 'I was working as a rep for Garfield Gaskets, who were suppliers to the engineering industry. They were wonderful to work for. When I went to England and France it was the last of the long Kangaroo Tours and I was away for four months yet they paid me all my wages while I was away. My daughter Lisa was born while I was away and the company phoned every day to see if my family needed anything.'

Sattler made his Australian debut in the tour match against Yorkshire. Local lad David Hill, a blond-haired front row forward, decided to make a name for himself against the Kangaroos and riled Sattler in the first scrum by pressing his elbow into Sattler's neck as they struck for the ball. When Hill did the same thing in the next scrum, Sattler decided he had enough. At the third scrum of the match he laid Hill out with a short punch, which according to press reports of the time, travelled 'no more than 9 inches'. Sattler was sent off but Hill was carried off on a stretcher and required a month's dental work. Sattler found an unlikely ally in English League Secretary Bill Fallowfield who said the South Sydney captain had 'put up with more provocation than I personally could have taken'. Sattler was exonerated, and although a dislocated elbow prematurely ended his tour, he returned to Sydney a more polished and professional player.

South Sydney made it back-to-back premierships when they defeated Manly in the 1968 grand final. 'We'd go to the Leagues Club after the grand final but the Committee we had back then treated us like absolute dirt. They didn't want to know us. They acted like they'd won all those premierships and they didn't put the money they made back into the players.' One by one, the players drifted away from Souths.

'It hurt to see players like Bob Moses (Manly) and Jimmy Morgan (Easts) go because they couldn't get regular first grade spots. Gary Stevens and Paul Sait had to wait years to get a regular spot in the first grade side. Gary was a workhorse and "Saity" was a tough bastard … a real talent. There was a glut of really good players at the club but none of us were really on the "big money" other clubs were offering.'

However, it was a different story in the 1969 grand final, with Balmain's upset victory putting the brakes on any thoughts of celebration. 'We used be very quiet in the dressing sheds before a match with everyone relaxing, just doing their own thing,' Sattler recalls. 'That year there were blokes having a joke around and being far too blasé about things. There was a lot of talk, players asking about horse results and such, and I remember saying, "For Christ's sake settle down. This mob will be hard." I think everybody thought we just had to turn up and win. We lost focus.'

'He had no threshold of pain, John,' McCarthy says. 'I saw him signing autographs outside Cumberland Oval with his hand in plaster. He said he dropped a motor on it at work. I asked him how long he was out for and he said he wasn't out, he was playing that day. Satts cut the plaster off with a pair of scissors and then strapped his hand up and played. He then had it replastered after the match.'

Sattler refuses to use the fact that some Tigers players infamously stopped play by going down injured in the second half as an excuse for Souths' loss that day. 'I think everybody expected us to win but it just didn't happen. Balmain's tactics early were to get out there and tackle and tackle and tackle … to be there for one another. That's what we used to do. They did exactly that and put us out of business.' And the 'lay down' tactics? 'Once our side was put under that pressure, it was too late to fire up. Balmain shocked us with how well they played.'

The 1969 season gave Sattler a career high, and ultimately, a low point in the grand final. Earlier in the season Sattler was the preferred NSW captain over Graeme Langlands, and after leading the Blues to a 4-0 sweep of the series, he was selected to lead Australia on a short tour of New Zealand. As was often the case during that era, Australia returned from the Shakey Isles with mixed fortunes. 'We had seven Souths players in that team (also Coote, McCarthy, Walters, Cleary, Pittard and Honan) which made life a little easier for me as captain. We won one Test and lost the other one, but it was a good trip.'

The following year against Great Britain, Sattler captained Australia in the Second Test in Sydney after Langlands broke his hand in the opening Test of the Ashes series in Brisbane. 'The "Pommies" gave us a nice old tickle up in that one,' Sattler says, recalling the 28-7 loss. 'That was the last great Lions team ... Malcolm Reilly, Roger Millward, Cliffy Watson, Frank Myler ...'

Memories of 1970, however, are dwarfed by the 'broken jaw' incident in the grand final against Manly. Many stories and many different perspectives are raised in this book but Sattler is typically nonchalant about the whole incident. 'The broken jaw was just something that happened,' he explains. 'Everybody says I was silly playing on with the broken jaw. I knew it was broken and I just felt that I couldn't do any more damage to it. It wasn't as if I thought to myself, "Well, I'm not going to take the ball up." I'm not like that.'

Sattler doesn't recall too much of the commotion taking place in the Souths dressing at half-time because he went into the shower and locked the door so that he could get his jaw back into place. 'Clive didn't say anything when we came in because he didn't know about it. Bobby McCarthy told him my jaw was broken and Clive said, "Bullshit!" He came in and knocked on the door and when I came out my jaw was just hanging there.'

Other Souths players who stood with Sattler out on the field that day have differing theories about why their captain didn't come off the field, but it is testament to the innate toughness of the man that Satts never even considered it. 'Every other player lifted their game to protect me, especially the forwards. "Lurch" O'Neill, "Aubrey" Walters, "Macca", Gary Stevens and "Cootey" ... those blokes just bounced in front of me and took the ball up to Manly. I'd call for it and they'd push me out of the way.' Sattler remained on the field, took the ball up to the opposition and did his share of tackling. Incredibly, following his team's 23-12 victory, he somehow made a victory speech and then completed the lap of honour carrying the JJ Giltinan Shield.

Bob McCarthy remembers the chaotic scenes after fulltime as pressmen descended into Souths' dressing room to confirm the story. 'Satts immediately went into the baths and locked himself inside and tried to push his jaw back in place. The newspapers boys, Bill Mordey, Alan Clarkson and Ian Heads and co., came in and asked us if Satts broke his jaw. We were all squirting champagne and carrying on, saying "What are you on about?" so they went and asked Clive Churchill. He was holding the journos at bay and Satts called out that he would be out in a while. They had to file their stories by 6.00 pm so Clive went to John said you have to talk to them. We all thought, how's he going to handle this? We were waiting for the bathroom door to open and when Satts came out of the bath and tried to speak, his jaw fell apart. They all rushed outside to get to the phones and file their stories, "Sattler's Jaw Broken"'.

I first interviewed John for one of my first books on the history of rugby league grand finals more than twenty years ago. Even though it had then been twenty years since the 1970 grand final, I could still sense the bitterness and contempt for the man who broke his jaw, Manly's John 'Sleepy' Bucknell. I ask Satts, forty years after the event, if time has mellowed his attitude. 'I've never had a conversation with Bucknell about it,' he says. 'Look, it was all part of the game. I had my head in the wrong place at the wrong time. It was still a nice old king-hit, me being off the ball and everything, but that's all over with.'

Sattler spent grand final night in intensive care followed by three months rehabilitation with his jaw wired. The jaw bone was snapped in three places—on each side of his face and also directly down the middle of the chin. His entire bottom row of teeth had to be set back into place. Compounding the injury, if that was at all possible, Australian selectors had penciled in Sattler's name as alternative captain of the 1970 World Cup squad which left for England after the grand final win. '"Changa" Langlands had a broken hand and wasn't going to pass muster,' he recalls, 'and I was later told that I was the next in line. The beautiful thing about it all was that Ron Coote finished up getting the job. And what a great job he did!'

But there was trouble brewing at Souths. Coote sat out the beginning of the 1971 after requesting a contract upgrade from the club and Sattler could see, under the financial direction of the Club Committee, the Rabbitohs were going to struggle to keep their star players. 'All the young blokes who had come through the ranks were now seasoned internationals. The way the club was run we were never going to be able to keep all of them. The money in the 1960s and 70s wasn't great by today's standards—you couldn't really make a good living from it alone, you had to work, so you didn't begrudge the players who left for better money. And every one of our players who left made better clubs of the places they went to ... they taught the other clubs how to win.'

But they always came back and drank with the Souths boys after training at the Cauliflower Hotel, he says.

In 1971 Sattler made a tentative comeback from his broken jaw in the pre-season competition. In a match against Manly a long-haired, raw-boned centre named Terry Randall hit Sattler with an 'absolute ripsnorter' of a tackle in his first game back from his injury. As Sattler got to his feet, he instinctively felt for his jaw. 'I thought, "Oh shit!" but my jaw was still it one piece. I knew then that it was alright.'

Sattler was sent off in the opening match of the season and suspended for four weeks. He played only two club games and was carrying a niggling injury when called into the national squad for the short tour of New Zealand. Sattler was not seen at his best in the shock 24-3 loss to the Kiwis at Carlaw Park but he hit form when he returned to Sydney. Souths still had enough talent and self-belief to put aside the internal rumblings and win one more premiership. Sattler says he didn't want the season to end, but maybe he instinctively knew Souths were going to struggle in the years ahead.

'1971 was my personal favourite of all our grand final wins,' Satts says. 'It was also my last, so I have special memories of it. We beat a

St George team led by "Changa" Langlands but it went right down to the death. Billy Smith was just unbelievable that day.' Sattler was able to savour the celebratory champagne and the joy of that success has stayed with him for forty years. 'It was wonderful being the captain of a premiership winning team. It was a great honour. I was just so proud of being part of the crew we had at Souths ... being captain of that team was very special.'

Souths went into the 1972 season without Ron Coote (Easts), John O'Neill and Ray Branighan (Manly) and others soon followed. 'They might have stayed if the money was right,' Sattler says, 'but I think it was more to do with the way the Committee treated them. To my way of thinking, those men never really had the respect of the players. I think they enjoyed the ride more than we did.'

After losing the 1972 minor semi-final to St George, 14-10, Souths golden run ended and captain Sattler weighed up his future. Souths had an option on his services for 1973 but said they would consider releasing him if an offer came from Queensland, but not to another Sydney club. Sattler had been offered $13,000 a year as player-coach with Parramatta but admits that he couldn't have played against Souths. 'Senator Ron McAuliffe, the President of the QRL, phoned me out of the blue. I told him that I was at the end of my tether ... I could only play for another year or two. He said they wanted me up there. I signed with the QRL and they placed me with Brisbane Wests. They had a good mob of players up there.'

Sattler also captained Queensland during the 1973 interstate series. The maroons had not won a series since 1959 and were looking for any way they could stay in the interstate contest. While the results were not forthcoming in 1973, Ron McAuliffe was not a man to give up easily. 'McAuliffe came to the Queens Hotel at Southport, which is now the Courthouse Hotel, one afternoon and said, "Son, I want to have a talk to you. I have some great ideas. I'm going to follow Aussie Rules. They started this thing called 'State of Origin' but it wasn't a success. But I'm going to try it and I think it will be great for our game." The only thing was, it took several more years to get it off the ground because NSW didn't thnk of it first!'

After two years with Wests Brisbane, Sattler was thinking of retirement when Tommy Bishop and Bobby Bax came to see him and said they'd like him to have one final year with Norths in 1975. 'I was very hesitant but I knew the players they had there—a real good team of fellows—and we ended up getting beaten in the final. I was 33 years old, I had knee cartilage removed during the year and I still played on. But it was time to pull the pin.'

As part of his contract with QRL, Sattler was able to buy a hotel license at the end of his playing career. 'The first pub I had was the Young Australian in Gladstone. I was there for two years. After that we built a pub in partnership with a couple of other fellows on Bribie Island and it was a very good trading pub, particularly in holiday periods. I also ran a café bar down at Broadbeach for a mate of mine. I went there just for a Christmas period and I finished up staying for a couple of years. Now I'm at Southport Leagues Club ... they asked me to do a couple of days as bar manager and I'm now here five days a week.'

Along the way, he played a key role in establishing the Gold Coast 'Giants' in 1988. 'I was part of a consortium with Bob Hagan and Peter Gallagher that bid for the Broncos franchise. We ended up starting the Giants from scratch and it wasn't easy. We had some good players but not in the numbers needed to be successful. The NSWRL was always in our corner because they wanted a local rival to Brisbane. Ken Arthurson and Johnny Quayle were top class administrators and gave us every support. Bob McCarthy was always our first choice of coach. He'd had success in Brisbane and you knew he'd do the job for you. After the first year we sold the franchise to the Seagulls Leagues Club. We just couldn't afford to keep it going.'

As the locals start to come into the Southport Leagues Club our conversation is increasingly punctuated by hellos, friendly jibes and jokes. It's time for Satts to get busy managing the club, but I can't let him go before asking him about his son Scott who, in 2003, grabbed his own slice of grand final history with his desperate, try-saving tackle while playing for Penrith. 'I was watching the match in the drizzling rain on the other side of the ground and I didn't know if he was able to get to (Roosters winger) Todd Byrne in time. No doubt it turned the grand final for the Panthers. Scott was always superbly fit, as he is today. As a player you would have loved to have him in your team. I was just so glad that he got that sort of success for himself. Going to Penrith and playing under [coach] Johnny Lang was the best thing that could have happened to him. Throughout his career he always had a lot of people saying, "You're John Sattler's son." Now I say, "I'm Scott Sattler's father".'

We say goodbye at the bar where a large black and white photo of a teenage Steve Rogers, who started his career with the Southport Tigers in the early 1970s, looks down on the patrons. Sattler, who is also a member of the ARL's elite list of the Top 100 Players of the Century, then says without the slightest hint of irony, 'Not a bad player to have over the bar, eh? One of the greats ....'

He certainly is.

ERIC SIMMS
(1967–71)

In the early 1960s teenage aboriginal centre Eric Simms was playing for Raymond Terrace High School when his team won a weight division of the district inter-school competition. Handing out the trophies that day at Kurri Kurri was a polite, bald-headed man named Dave Brown. Known as the 'Bradman of League' in the 1930s Brown broke every record during his career with Easts and was the then NSWRL Schools Liaison Officer. Simms could not have possibly dreamed that at the end of that decade he would break Dave Brown's 33-year old record for scoring most points in a season. The two champions—one past, one future—did not say a word to each other, except 'thank you' and 'congratulations' but it was a moment when the future crossed paths with the past.

Eric John Simms was born on 2 August, 1945 in Newcastle, NSW. His family came from Karuah, north of Newcastle, on the Old Pacific Highway. His parents divorced when he was young and he spent a lot of his childhood at La Perouse in the South Sydney district. 'I went to La Perouse Primary School and then moved back to Karuah and went to Raymond Terrace High,' Eric Simms says when I catch up with him at his family home at Beverley Hills. 'I have a sister named Beverley, who is two years younger than me, but I also have a half-brother and five half-sisters because Mum and Dad remarried. My wife knows more about my family than I do—she knows all their children's names and everything. I am hopeless with names.'

Technically a South Sydney junior, 'I played all my junior football with Souths, starting in the 5 stone 8lbs division,' Eric says, Simms also played league for his high school and, at age 15, was a winger for Karuah A Grade on the weekend. 'And that's when I left school and came back to Sydney. I played seniors with La Perouse, and from there I kicked on to the Souths' Jersey Flegg team for a couple of years and then President's Cup. We had a lot of good players at Larpa but they just didn't want to go any further in the game—they just weren't dedicated enough.'

Another great Aboriginal goal-kicker, Kevin 'Lummy' Longbottom, had already made a name for himself in Souths' top grade. 'I had known him most of my life out at La Perouse because he was my stepmother's sister's boy,' Simms remembers. 'We got to know one another as teenagers and knocked about every weekend. We got to be great friends.' Simms can only think of one other player from that era who made it to first grade. 'His name was Ambrose Morgan. He and I were like blood brothers. He lived with my grandmother and we grew up together when I went back to La Perouse.' Morgan had played lower grades for Souths as far back as 1964 but did not make his first grade debut until 1975. Captain-coach of the Redfern All Blacks, Morgan was known as the 'King of Redfern'. He lost his life following a nightclub dispute on August 1 that year. 'Ambrose was a good footballer but unfortunately he got on the wrong side of things and was shot dead. He was a hard, big bugger—a bit like Bobby McCarthy—a big barrel-chested guy and a good ball player. And he could handle himself too. He was like a young Cassius Clay; no-one could see where the punches were coming from, he was that quick. But as I said, those things got him into trouble and eventually caught up with him.'

Of his own career, Simms says, 'I liked playing football and I just dedicated myself to it. I thought I had something, so I tried to develop it.' That 'something' was goal-kicking and Simms developed into the best goal-kicker of his generation. At high school, a teacher named Len Leggatt gave him some pointers but Simms was a natural. 'As a kid I was always kicking a ball around, but it wasn't until I went to high school that I started taking it seriously. Mr Leggatt taught me a lot of things about goal-kicking, but mostly how to allow for the wind. We'd practice by lining the ball about a yard out from the corner post and then kick it at an angle so the wind would swing it around and into the posts. Those little fundamental things he taught me I always remembered. As the years progressed, I just got better at it.'

After winning the grand final of the President's Cup competition in 1965, Simms was graded at Souths as a centre. After several third and second grade games, he was promoted into Souths' top grade on the eve of the semi-finals. Longbottom was going through one of his lean periods with the boot at the time and Souths selectors promoted the young Simms as a goal-kicking back-up. He kicked four goals on debut in the 17-8 win over eleven-time premiers St George in the SCG 'match of the day' and then appeared in another four consecutive matches at the SCG, culminating in the grand final against St George in front of 78,000 people. Incredibly, the following week, he went back to La Perouse and played in the local A Grade grand final.

'I have been lucky,' Simms says modestly. 'I played two years with Jersey Flegg and we won them both. I had two years at President's Cup, and we won them both. Then, to get called into first grade and play a grand final and to just miss against a great St George side, we were blessed. I had a few flutters before the 1965 grand final, running out onto the ground and seeing so many people. And of course you were lining up against the great Saints team of the era, but once you touched the football, you quickly got over those things.'

For the next few years, Souths carried two goal-kickers, with Simms playing centre or winger and Kevin Longbottom at fullback.

'Lummy was the long range goal kicker and I would take anything from 40 yards out or if it was in front. Lummy never had the confidence, I don't think, for kicking a goal from straight in front. Put it this way, he missed more than he kicked. But when he lined them up from the sidelines it was as good as a goal.'

Simms was selected as centre in Souths' 1967 grand final team and played an important role in the 12-10 victory over Canterbury. Longbottom landed three long-range beauties, but it was Simms' 40-yard toe-poke that secured Souths the premiership. Many of the players interviewed for this book have commented that Simms had ice water in his veins. 'They say you're ice cool, but you are never ice bloody cool,' he laughs. 'You always worry about it ... have I allowed enough for the wind, have I lined it up right? If only they knew. You just hoped and prayed that you struck it right and the ball was going to go through the posts.'

There was more to it than that, of course. Simms had a beautifully balanced kicking style—head over the ball, both arms outstretched with the grace of a ballet dancer and a faultless, right-foot follow through. He topped 200 points in four consecutive years from 1967 to 1970, including a premiership record 265 points in 1969, and only injury stopped him from topping the 200 mark in 1971. Out of Souths' total of 66 grand final points in five consecutive grand finals from 1967 to 1971, Simms contributed 39 points, or 59% of his team's points. In five seasons, Simms scored 1,137 points, at an average of 227 points a season. In those five seasons Souths scored 2,454 points with Simms contributing 46.3% of the points. But these are just statistics ... Eric Simms was an integral part of the Souths team, the South Sydney district and a great rugby league era.

In that time he averaged more than ten points a match and was often the difference between winning and losing. Simms, however, came with another attacking weapon in his armoury—the field goal.

Under the limited tackle rule, teams had fewer attacking options at their disposal but with field goals worth a valuable two points,

Souths' coach Clive Churchill opted to use Simms as often as possible. Originally Churchill preferred Simms at centre because he would be in the front line when a field goal was in the offing, but with further injuries limiting Kevin Longbottom's first grade appearances, Simms shifted to fullback. He had never played fullback before but he had a pretty good mentor. 'I might have filled in here and there but I had not played fullback a great deal. Clive thought I might be most useful there and he taught me a few things too.' Not a bad mentor to have, the greatest fullback—and the greatest player—the game produced.

Simms' field goal ability became an important part of Souths' winning culture in the late 1960s. 'Most of the time the boys would be looking for me around the third or fourth tackle. It was a five yard rule back then ... the defence had to be back five yards and you had to be five yards back in attack. I would be standing that extra couple of yards back and they would pass it back to me. You still had plenty of time to kick the ball over the crossbar.'

In his first two years with Souths, Simms did not kick a single field goal. In 1967, the first season of limited tackle football, he landed 12 field goals. The following year he kicked a premiership record 29 field goals. It was something he used to practice at every training session. 'Clive would get there early before the team started running around the ovals and we would start kicking. He was a great man. We used to have a kicking dual ... see how far out we could kick a goal from. He still had a good boot on him too for his age.'

Considered unlucky not to tour with the 1967–68 Kangaroos on his form in the open, Simms was the ideal candidate for World Cup selection in June 1968. After making his representative debut in City Seconds he was called into Australia's World Cup squad and played in all four Tests, including the final against France, and finished the competition's top scorer with 50 points—all from goals. 'Johnny Raper captained that team and Graeme Langlands was in the centres,' Simms recalls. 'Arthur Beetson, who was in the forwards, was one of the quickest blokes I've ever seen for a big man. We had all the fastest players in the game in that squad—Johnny Rhodes was bloody quick—but they couldn't get near Arthur over 25 yards. He'd be two or three strides in front of everyone. It was unbelievable how quick he was.'

When Johnny Raper threw him the ball in the opening Test of the series against Great Britain at the SCG, Simms was uncharacteristically nervous. Simms dared not lift his head and look at the kick but the roar of the 62,256-strong crowd told him that it was successful. At the Randwick end of the ground he aimed the ball at just outside the posts, knowing that the wind funnelled down between the grandstands and would carry the ball in a couple of yards. Simms kicked 8 goals in the 25–10 win against Great Britain; matched that with another 8 goals in the 31–12 win over New Zealand a week later, and contributed another nine goals in consecutive matches against France, including the 20–2 win in the World Cup Final.

Simms made his one and only appearance for NSW in a dead rubber after the World Cup competition and kicked six goals and a field goal in the 29–11 victory in Brisbane. In the 1968 grand final against Manly, he landed five great pressure goals to bring his tally to 141 goals, including 30 field goals, in all matches that year. In 2008 he was awarded the Clive Churchill Medal as 'man of the match' for the 1968 grand final when the awards were retrospectively handed out by the NRL as part of their centenary celebrations. Winning an award named after the man he admired most at Souths holds a special honour for Simms. He has the award mounted on his wall in his study alongside a framed Souths jersey of the era and other memorabilia.

Simms represented City Firsts in 1969 but was overlooked for further rep honours during the year. It was a disappointment after the highs of 1968. 'When you're successful at one thing, you tend to be known for one thing,' Simms says, but then he always knew he was much more than just a goal-kicker. Instead, he concentrated on breaking Dave Brown's season point-scoring record which had stood since 1935. 'It was played up a lot in the newspapers, saying I had a good chance of breaking the old record, and I knew if I scored so many points per game I would go close to it.'

In the match against Penrith in July, Souths hired an entire train to take 1500 supporters to the Western Sydney ground. Perhaps the club and its fans expected something magical that day.

Simms kicked six goals and a premiership record five field goals in Souths' 40-18 win. Press reports of the time stated that Simms 'received as big a reception as The Beatles' and the Souths fans among the crowd of 13,050 chaired him from the field that day. Simms kicked the final goal after full-time and his personal total of 22 points —the difference between the two teams that Sunday afternoon—put him over the 200 point mark in just 18 matches. 'It wasn't something we worked out before the match,' he recalls. 'It was just the way the game played out that day. I just took the opportunities when they came. If I had time to have a shot at field goal, I would have a go.'

Twenty-four year old Eric Simms ultimately broke Dave Brown's record of 245 points in the match against North Sydney the following month. Later that week, the 'Bradman of League' caught up with the unassuming South Sydney fullback and, for the second time in their respective lives, shook Simms' hand. Simms went on to set a new benchmark of 269 points which was not surpassed until 1978 by Parramatta's Mick Cronin. But in a record-breaking year, Souths missed out on the prize that mattered the most—a third successive grand final victory. Simms kicked Souths into the grand final when he landed a penalty goal against Balmain in the major semi-final, but it was a different story in the grand final. Balmain's tactics of slowing the game down were designed to stop Souths' momentum, but another motivation was to ensure Eric Simms did not get time to come into the front line and kick his deadly field goals. Balmain also played a mistake-free game and gave Simms only one shot at goal, which he duly converted.

Simms worked on the Balmain wharves and often ran into the

Tigers' premiership winning coach Leo Nosworthy who worked as a timber tally there. 'It took Leo ten years before he admitted to me that the Tigers' plan was to stop Souths by slowing the game down. Any time we looked like doing something, a Balmain player would go down injured in a tackle. The next minute the referee would blow the whistle and pull the game up. It just stopped us from getting into our natural rhythm.'

Souths lost the grand final, 11-2. 'It was not a good feeling. Losing any game is not a good feeling but losing a grand final was especially hard when we were odds on favourites to win it. After such a successful season, to come to that, it was very hard to take.'

Souths players were treated like superstars in the early 1970s. As a national sportsman Eric Simms was a significant role model, not only for young Aboriginal people but all Australian youth. 'I always thought I was a good enough role model for all kids ... I didn't drink a lot, I didn't smoke and I trained as hard as I could. You sacrificed a lot to try and achieve what you wanted to achieve in the game. Once I started playing rugby league and I made first grade, I just thought "Well, here I go—here's my chance now. Give it everything you've got," which is what I did.'

1970 was Simms' year. Injury robbed him of a place in Australia's Third Test team against Great Britain but after starring in the club's 23-12 grand final win—a match in which he kicked three goals and four field goals as the Rabbitohs toyed with Manly—Simms was the logical choice to replace injured fullback Graeme Langlands in Australia's World Cup team. 'It was a very big surprise, that one,' he says. 'Because I had to get a visa to travel overseas, they discovered I hadn't done any National Service training. Being Aboriginal, I didn't know if I had to register. It put the whole trip to England in jeopardy.' Did he have to do the three months compulsory training, I ask? 'No,' he says matter-of-factly. 'They failed me on my hearing.'

In England, Simms played in all four Tests, the second time in two years he had appeared in every match of a World Cup competition, and produced the game of his life in the final at Leeds. I recently watched a colour video of the match which I obtained from a keen collector and forty years after the match it remains one of the most vicious, yet exciting, games I've ever seen. Eric Simms at fullback was simply courageous that cold November afternoon—running the ball out from the line, kicking downfield in open play as fists and stiff-arms flew or landing three goals as in Australia's 12–7 win against all the odds. Simms was also involved in an incident that has passed into the annals of Anglo-Australian Test history.

Just before full-time, Australian halfback Billy Smith and centre Syd Hynes were involved in a punch-up which spilled over the sideline. As Simms came across to break up the fight, he was punched by Great Britain winger John Atkinson. Simms stood toe-to-toe with the lean Englishman but after Smith and Hynes were sent for an early shower, Great Britain launched one final attack to try and force a draw.

As Australia regained possession, Atkinson launched himself at Simms and struck him in the head. Full-time signalled an unlikely Australian victory and as Simms approached Atkinson to shake hands, the winger thought Simms was shaping up to him. Atkinson landed a straight right to Simms' chin, which the Australian fullback responded in kind. As others joined in, English 'bobbies' came onto the field to break up the fight. In fairness, Atkinson did seek Simms out among the crowd to apologise and shake hands properly, but by that time Simms' only interest was to take the victory dais with the Australia players and receive the World Cup trophy.

It would be the last time he would wear the green and gold.

The International Board of Rugby League changed the value of the field goal from two points to one in 1971, not least because Simms was such an expert proponent in the Sydney premiership. The result? Simms landed a solitary field goal that year and even then it was in the final match of the season. 'We didn't really worry about it after that,' he admits. 'The six tackle rule gave us more time to set up.' But when a scoreless first half was drawing to a close in the 1971 grand final against St George, Simms could not help himself. 'I thought we'll take the point and see what happens after.' The famed SCG scoreboard ticked over a soccer score, 1-0. When Saints came back into the match late into the second half and trailed 11-10, the value of that one-point field goal was self-evident.

After the 1971 grand final, Souths' star faded, champion players left the club and Simms' goal-kicking feats diminished. Simms provided a cameo performance of his 'ice cool' goal-kicking when he landed the winning goal against Easts in the final of the 1972 pre-season competition after the full-time siren. Souths made the semi-finals in 1972 and 1974 but there would be no more premierships. An interesting anomaly in his career stats is the fact that Simms scored more tries in his final year with the club—five tries in 1975 —than any other season. 'Does one try stand out in your memory, a special try or one you made yourself, I ask? 'No, probably the first one,' he says laughing. 'The problem was we had too many other blokes scoring tries.'

Simms scored 23 tries during his career, kicked 803 goals and 86 field goals—the most field goals in premiership history. 'It was a time when every club had a champion goal-kicker ... Graeme Langlands at Saints, Allan McKean at Easts, Bob Batty at Manly and Keith Barnes at Balmain.' But Simms was the best of his generation. As of 2010 he was still in the top ten of point-scorers of all-time having 1,841 career points.

By 1975, Simms' jet black hair was a little greyer and the easy smile topped by a black moustache which he still wears today. 'I was adamant that I wasn't going to another club and being a Souths junior, just stay with the club all the way through.' But at age 30, his body was giving out and once Clive Churchill left the club towards the end of the season, Simms decided enough was enough. In 1976 he left Sydney after a decade with the club, having become only the second clubman to appear in more than 200 games (behind Bob

McCarthy) and accepted a two year contract as captain-coach of Crookwell, in the NSW Southern Highlands.

'The money wasn't too bad,' Simms says, 'and they hit me with $10 for every goal I kicked. It didn't cost me anything for living and they supplied you with a house. The fridge was always full—there was always someone killing beef or sheep. It was bloody cold down there, of course. When I got down there they said to make sure you fill all your pots and pans with water the night before because you won't get any water in the morning. The taps never thawed out until 12 o'clock in the day.'

Crookwell was a young team in 1976. 'Typical bush blokes,' Simms says. 'They were hard little buggers. But when you were playing against the Donny Furner's Queanbeyan team you were up against it. One of our players used to always lock horns with a young centre from Hay. You could guarantee it every time they played each other there would be a fight, and it would be these two hard at it. They were both 18 then and my little bloke didn't give an inch. They would stand there toe-to-toe.' The Hay player's name was Gavin Miller.

Eric Simms worked in the local pub the first year he took his young family down to Crookwell and then transferred to the RSL the second year. When he returned to Sydney at the end of 1977 he returned to the wharves, but his first marriage floundered, and he started all over again. Simms has five children, three from his first wife and two from his second, ten grandchildren and a great-grandchild. After working for the P&O Company as a security guard he worked on the wharfs for many years. After retiring in 2008, he continues to work as a part-time courier. 'I like catching up with the Souths boys, having a chat about the old days,' he says. The boys still call him 'Ecca'.

He likes the game today but, 'It's not our game ... the game we played. It's very, very fast. You definitely have to be physically fit.'

The year before Simms left Sydney, Englishman John Gray introduced a new style of goal-kicking—'around the corner' style—

they called it, with players using the instep of their foot, rather than the toe, to get more control of the ball. 'I tried it, but I didn't like it. The balls they use today are different anyway. The players today wouldn't be able to kick the balls we used around the corner for too long otherwise they would end up with sore insteps. The leather balls we used were as heavy as lead in the wet. Today you've got Johnathan Thurston and blokes like Hazem El Masri,' Simms says. 'Hazem was just a freak, the way he kicked. I don't think we'll see another kicker the calibre of his accuracy.'

Simms' hair has now thinned out and turned white and gone are the Elvis Presley-style sideburns that were in vogue forty years ago. All this talk about goal-kicking has him instinctively rubbing his right knee. 'The old knee gets a bit sore,' he admits. 'I haven't had it checked yet, but it gives me a bit of hell every now and then.'

But Eric, I remind him, you kicked almost 1000 career goals and field goals bending that knee. 'That many?' he says with a smile of satisfaction.

BOB HONAN
(1968–71)

For a time, Bob Honan forgot that he had even played rugby league. After he returned to Queensland in 1976 with his wife, Barbara, and their young children after his football career ended and a major investment soured, he set about rebuilding his life and had very little attachment to the game. 'I wasn't hiding,' he says to me as we sit in his stylish home at Broadbeach on Queensland's Gold Coast. 'I just didn't stay in contact with many people from the game. In those days football was only part of your life. You worked, you raised your family and you played football on the weekends—but when it was all over, you put it aside and it stayed in the background. I also lived and worked overseas for several years and I'm sure some people thought I had died.'

Honan looks fit and relaxed when I catch up with him and could pass for a man decades younger. He says that with a lot of things in life you don't appreciate the good things until you're much older. Now that he has his first grandchild and is retired, he takes time to look back at his considerable achievements. 'It's a good time to take stock and celebrate Souths,' he says. 'The club was such an important part of our lives and I'm really glad they're doing well. I think Russell Crowe and his group has done a great job with Souths. He is a true

Rabbitoh supporter and I don't believe making a dollar out of it was a major motivation. If he does make a dollar out of it, then good luck to him but I'm sure he could put his money into a number of other investments which would have given him much better returns.'

Honan says that he has very little memorabilia of that era—his kids have his Test jerseys—and an acquaintance recently gave him DVDs of some old Souths games which he enjoys watching. He also has in his possession four lovingly assembled scrapbooks of his career that were presented to him by fan Shirley Langley when he retired. 'A beautiful lady, like a footballing mother, she said she wanted to thank me for all the games I played and all the enjoyment I'd given her over the years. She presented me with these scrapbooks one day and all I had to give her was an old pair of my footy socks. I just broke up.'

Robert Emmett Honan was born on 24 January 1944 in Brisbane. The middle son of three boys, he was a talented sprinter, cricketer and rugby union star with Marist Brothers College, Ashgrove—a strong rugby school that produced a long list of Wallabies over the years, including captain John Eales (1991–2001). After leaving school, he played for Brisbane Brothers and represented Queensland as a teenager in 1963. The following year he appeared in two rugby Tests as a centre on the Wallabies' tour of New Zealand. His goals were to gain selection on the 1966-67 European Tour and to play a Test with younger brother Barry, an equally talented centre who had made his State debut that year. Unfortunately, neither eventuated.

'I played a couple of Tests in New Zealand when I was still finding my feet. However, I had a great season in 1966 in preparation for the Wallabies Tour. The big European tours (where Australia plays five nations—England, Scotland, Wales, Ireland and France) only came around every eight years or so. I played in all the interstate games and was picked by all the experts, but I missed out.

South Sydney had great success with rugby converts Jimmy Lisle and Mike Cleary and they caught the young Honan already at the crossroads of his playing career. He admits he was disenchanted with the amateur code—not the players or his club—but the administrators who ran the game. 'I had just got engaged and had to start thinking about securing my future. Rugby back then was about playing for the love of the game and playing for your country but it was tough being a pure amateur. I had never thought about switching to rugby league. It was only when Souths approached me at the end of 1966 that I even considered a switch.'

Souths were looking to boost their backline and Souths' committeeman George Hansen signed the contracts of Honan and Dallas O'Neill. 'Dallas had a broken leg during the 1966 season. He was a lock who relied on his mobility, but unfortunately, he never fully regained his mobility and league never really saw the best of him. Souths were going to sign my brother Barry later on, but he was too honest. He suffered from a chronic knee injury from early in his career and didn't think it would stand up to the weekly grind of Sydney club football so he declined the offer.' Barry Honan played in nine Tests for Australia but his career was cut short by injury and he retired in 1970, at age 24.

Once he switched to rugby league, Honan learned the hard way about the defensive aspect of the game and the hurriedness of attack under the newly-instigated four tackle rule. Souths players called him 'Ra, Ra', which was short for 'The Road Runner'. Arthur Branighan, Honan's most consistent centre partner during Souths' golden era, told me, 'You didn't know which way Bob was going to go, but boy could he run.' Honan says he modelled his running style, with head held high, after the great Reg Gasnier ... not a bad role model for a rugby league career.

Honan admits he found his first season in Sydney pretty tough. 'I was living with Dallas O'Neill and a couple of other bachelors at Coogee and missing my fiancé, Barbara. We married in October 1967. We rented a flat at Ashfield and not long after bought a terrace home in Redfern, just down from the Cauliflower Hotel. Souths were a very sociable club and the players were very close. We played together, socialised together, even worked together. After training, most of the team liked to have a drink at the Ryans Hotel around the corner … Jimmy Lisle, John O'Neill, Bob McCarthy, Ivan Jones, Bob Moses, Gary Stevens, Eric Simms, Dennis 'Sluggo' Lee and Alan Scott were all regulars.'

Honan played in just four first grade games in 1967, scoring a try and kicking a field goal. A torn knee ligament late in the year saw him miss the reserve grade grand final. All the guys were saying 'next year, Bobby'. After marrying in the off season and training hard, he started to play well. 'Rugby was primarily a kicking game and tackling was fairly loose and more lateral,' Honan remembers. 'It took me a couple of seasons to adjust to the front-on defence in league,' he admits. 'I used to have a few people in the press remind me when I made a mistake but after a couple of seasons I could hold my own. I bulked up a little, training at City Tattersalls with the team in the off-season and started enjoying the defensive side of my game.'

Honan's breakthrough year was in 1968, even if Souths' selectors tended to treat his career like a yo-yo. After a good start to the season Honan was injured at the end of April and was then dropped to second grade for his return match against Penrith at Redfern Oval. Tom Craigie, the club's Chairman of selectors explained to the press that with Kevin Longbottom coming back into the team at fullback, Eric Simms needed to be in the centre of the field so that he could kick field goals. Souths were sacrificing their attack in the centres for the easy two points field goals had to offer in the era of the four tackle rule. Honan was quickly building up a crowd following at Souths and supporters on 'Baker's Hill' clapped him off the field when he was replaced so that he could sit on the bench for first grade. Souths' first grade lost to Penrith, 13–12, and Honan was reinstated the following week.

The major obstacle for Honan holding a regular first grade spot as a centre was that he was fast enough to play on the wing if Brian

James or Mike Cleary were injured. 'I was switched around a bit and just as I established myself in the centres someone would get hurt and the selectors would stick me on the wing,' he says. 'Another player would come into the centres and go all right and then I would get dropped.' When Balmain's former rugby international winger George Ruebner pulled out of the City Seconds team, Honan was given an early chance in rep football. Back at Souths he was dropped to reserve grade when World Cup winger Brian James returned to club football. When he came back into first grade in August, Honan was described as being 'by far Souths' most effective attacking unit.' He was selected on the wing for the major semi-final against Manly, and, following an upset 23-15 loss, returned to the centres for the final against St George.

Honan had 'ray treatment' for a knee injury to make the team for the final and potted a neat field goal to give Souths a 13-3 lead at the break. He then scored the winning try after Mike Cleary knocked over St George's Dennis Preston, loosening the ball from his grasp. Honan grubbered ahead and Cleary regathered the ball and sent Honan to the try-line. In the grand final against Manly a week later, a broken nose could not dampen the euphoria of a premiership title. 'It was a hard bloody game, a dirty game,' he recalls. 'I ran into [Manly's] John 'Pogo' Morgan some weeks ago at a function on the Gold Coast. I had a go at him about hitting the corner post when he scored his try.' Morgan's reply to his former opponent more than 40 years after the match was unequivocal. 'Bullshit! It was a dead-set try!'

It's clear Honan 'found' himself as a match-winner on the club's trip to New Zealand at the end of that year. He was the man of the match against Kiwi club champions Mount Albert, scoring two tries in the 27–13 win, and contributed another pair in the club's 13-try, 55–15 romp against Brisbane Brothers in Brisbane.

Honan worked in the accounts department with the insurance firm Legal and General when he lived in Brisbane. 'In Sydney they offered me an agency supervisor's position and I ended up having one of the most well-known sporting agencies in Sydney. I recruited Les Jones, Max Cole and Barry Phyllis from Canterbury, Grahame Williams from Manly and later Denis Pittard.' Honan also had a business renovating terraces with John O'Neill, Gary Stevens and Jimmy Lisle. 'I suggested that we do a couple of renovations at Paddington, as "Paddo" was just becoming trendy. We also did one in Redfern which we sold to Ivan Jones, who was working for John and Gary at the time. I was always entrepreneurial, so when I saw an opportunity like the renovations in Sydney, we went for it. We renovated a terrace in Balmain. Dallas O'Neill bought that one with another rugby mate of mine named Doug Ryan. I shudder when I think what they might be worth today.'

Honan signed a new four-year deal to stay with the Rabbitohs at the end of 1968 and continued the good form the following season when he set up the first two tries in the club's 17–10 win over Wests in the pre-season final. Honan's 'twinkle-toe stepping and running' were a feature of the win, wrote Bill Mordey in the *Daily Mirror*, while *The Sun*'s Ernie Christensen had no doubt that Honan was the 'fastest centre in the game.' His path into the Australia Test team that year was quite extraordinary. Selected in City Seconds, a team captained by John Raper, Honan also played half a game with City Firsts that day. Originally overlooked for State selection, he was flown to Brisbane before the first interstate match when Manly centre John McDonald was ruled out with injury. Instead of playing Honan in the centres, selectors shifted him to wing when teammate Mike Cleary succumbed to a throat infection. NSW won the match 26–0 and Honan played so well he retained his spot for the return match two days later.

Bob Honan joined the elite ranks of dual internationals when he was selected along with six Souths teammates for the mini tour of New Zealand in June-July. He made his Test debut in the First Test in Auckland as a winger when Cleary was ruled out with a pulled hamstring. Australia won the match, 20–10, and Honan retained his place in the Second Test six days later when Cleary failed a fitness test. The Kiwis won that match 18–14 to even the series. Honan played in five of the six matches on the tour, crossing for one try, but his brief Test career was over. Selectors at Souths and for NSW proved to have short memories.

Bob couldn't hide his disappointment when he was selected on the wing for the match against Balmain at the SCG on his return from New Zealand—not that he ever got too much encouragement from selectors. Souths defeated the Tigers 22–5 and NSW selectors missed his man of the match performance against Newtown the following week when they overlooked him for State duty in Queensland's tour of NSW. There was another late call-up to the team when NSW Country winger Don Pascoe withdrew, but Honan, the form centre of the competition, just couldn't get off the wing. He didn't get a chance back in the centres at Souths until Arthur Branighan was injured late in the season.

Honan formed a great on-field partnership with five-eighth Denis Pittard, whom he talked into selling insurance with him at Legal and General. 'In a match against St George at the SCG in August 1969, we did a runaround move twice in 10 minutes to swing the match our way. We'd been practicing it for weeks and it came off perfectly. I got the ball, Denis ran around me, I dummied to him and stepped past a few players, and then passed to Ron Coote coming through and he scored. About 10 minutes later, pretty much in the same spot, we put the move on again but this time I gave it to Denis. The Saints players went for me, and Denis scooted through like a rabbit and went straight to the try-line.'

Honan broke a couple of toes in this 36–15 victory over St George and did not make it back onto the field until the semi-final … but at least that was in the centres.

Of the loss to Balmain in the 1969 grand final, Honan says, 'People keep saying that we didn't play well and that the Tigers layed down. That's true, but they played a smart game and we didn't counter it.

In retrospect, we didn't kick enough. We could have kicked over the top a bit more. We just didn't play at our best. We'd beaten them a fortnight before, but only just.' Following Souths' 14–13 win in the semi-final, the press declared Souths hot favourites. With the extra week off, there was a noticeable lack of nerves amongst the players, he recalls. 'There wasn't that tense atmosphere before the match. I had one of my best defensive games and there was only one try scored in the game but you could tell they were very keen from the outset. Balmain won on their merits.'

What was the mood like back at the League Club? I ask. 'The Club Committee never made a big fuss after the grand final at the Leagues Club. Today they take the players back to their home ground and present them to the fans. I think that's a great idea. Souths rarely had any official functions … it was an ordinary managerial group. There was never enough money to pay the players what they were really worth and by 1971 we could see the writing on the wall. We lost a great team. We should have kept together until at least 1975.'

Honan had one of his best seasons in 1970, but incredibly, after representing City Seconds on the wing, he was dropped from first grade after pulling out of the match against Norths with the 'flu. He was then fined $50 for being late for training. After fighting his way back into the top grade, he was again dropped on the eve of the major semi-final. 'I had a late business meeting on the other side of town,' he remembers. 'I rang and left a message with the Leagues Club office that I would be late. It was raining and I got stuck on the Harbour Bridge … there were no mobile phones in those days,' he laughs. 'When I got to Redfern Oval training was almost over. One of the committeemen said I had to get out there and train and I said, "You're kidding … for ten minutes? The other players are coming off. What do you want me to do, run around by myself in the rain for 10 minutes? Throw the ball to myself?" I said I'd come and train the next night, but they dropped me from the team.'

Honan missed Souths' 22–15 win over Manly in the major semi-final but was selected as a reserve back for the grand final a fortnight later. He replaced Paul Sait inside the final 15 minutes after Sait suffered concussion but it was a token appearance. 'It was an entirely different atmosphere to the previous year's grand final,' he recalled. 'Before the match in 1970, everyone was quiet and moody, and snapping at each other. When Souths are in that mood before a game then you know they were unbeatable.' In a major shock, Paul Sait, who partnered Arthur Branighan in the centres that day, was selected in Australia's World Cup team. It was another lost opportunity for the enigmatic speedster and he was determined to make up for it in 1971.

In 1971 Honan formed an effective centre partnership with another rugby recruit, Phil Smith. With Paul Sait undergoing a knee cartilage operation and coming back into first grade as a back rower, press reports rated Honan the 'class centre of the competition.' That year he rejected an offer from Queensland Rugby League supremo Senator Ron McAuliffe, who was a personal friend of Clive Churchill, to return north and play for Brisbane Souths. Honan's considerable business interests were in Sydney and, at age 27 he felt he had several good seasons left in his career.

In the grand final against St George that year, Honan was heavily concussed but stayed on the field with Souths, content to play the game in the forwards. After declining a lucrative offer to go to Brisbane Souths, 1972 was shaping up as another great year for Honan and for the club. Despite losing Ron Coote to Easts, and John O'Neill and Ray Branighan to Manly, Souths captured the pre-season final against Easts, 11–10, and were competitive during the first half of the season before injuries took their toll.

Honan returned to the representative scene when he was selected as a winger in City Seconds and was then promoted to Firsts when Manly centre Bob Fulton withdrew with an injury. Although Souths selectors had six seasons to determine what everyone else in the game already knew—Honan was a class centre—he was consistently selected on the wing. He first felt his hamstring tear slightly in the match against St George at the SCG in May and says he, like the rest of the team, was struggling in the lead-up to the play-offs. 'They didn't have the injury management skills in those days,' he says. 'When I tore my hamstring, the club doctor shoved me in a hot bath. He meant well, but he was a gynecologist and knew very little about sports injuries. I told him that I'd read somewhere you should put ice on a tear. He said to sit in a hot bath because it relieves the pain, but the haematoma in my leg was enormous.'

Honan didn't know it, but his playing career was effectively over. He had been trying to negotiate a group contract for Bobby Grant, Bob McCarthy, Gary Stevens, Eric Simms and himself—an unheard of arrangement in the game at the time—but never made it back onto the field in 1973. 'I'd torn the [hamstring] tendon right off my tailbone and in those days they never operated on those injuries.' Things were really bad at Souths at a managerial level, so after turning down an offer from Manly, he signed with Easts. He never played for the Roosters. 'My hamstring still wasn't good enough but I was keen to give it another go. However, it never came good, so I gave it away.'

He kept fit in 1974 and when he thought the hamstring had mended sufficiently, he returned to Souths in 1975 because, he says candidly, 'I missed the game'. After one first grade game against North Sydney, he retired for good. He had proved something to himself in coming back, but for a player whose entire career had been built on speed, he was a metre or two slower than at his prime.

'I was going well in the insurance business at the time,' Honan explains. 'I was working with a syndicate of business and sporting people on a development called the "Cox River Country Club" in Little Hartley in the Blue Mountains, the first of its kind in Australia. It was a magnificent location—1300 acres on the Cox River—was going to be a sporting/health, training centre and country club. I had a lot of the top sporting people in Australia involved … John Newcombe and Tony Roche were going to run the tennis camps, Ron Barassi the Aussie Rules, Ken Catchpole the Union, Ralé Rasic and Johnny Warren the soccer, and Bob McCarthy and Denis Pittard were going to assist with the League camps. The concept was to develop a golf course, tennis courts, swimming pool and a full-size football field surrounded by rustic estates and condominiums, based on the American model. We had log cabins planned for the kids to stay in when they did the training camps. All the necessary local and state government approvals had been obtained and substantial works had already been completed, including the construction of a private airstrip.'

What happened? 'The Whitlam government happened … four years of planning and work went down the drain. The recession hit and venture capital investment dried up. With 19% interest rates and the Australian government placing deposit bonds on foreign investment, within 12 months the project was gone. It really shattered me. I put a lot of time, energy and money into it; mortgaged our home and let my insurance company go.'

'I felt I needed a needed a change, both businesswise and for my family's future, so I said to my wife, "Let's head back to Queensland".' On the Gold Coast, Honan focused on rebuilding his business career and cut ties with his football past. With friend and business partner from the Cox River project, Bob Page, he went into the commercial cleaning business. Within a few years he had the biggest independent cleaning business in Southeast Queensland, employing more than 300 people.

He also realised the importance of staying fit and healthy. He did a lot of research on nutrition, changing to a mostly vegetarian diet. He also started distance running. 'This type of training was pretty strange to me at first. My footy career consisted of sprint training and my muscles were mainly what they call fast twitch, so it took my body a while to adjust to the change in pace.' Honan helped to start up the 'Hash-house Harriers' on the Gold Coast—a mixed bunch of blokes from all walks of life who came together on Monday nights for 'a bit of a run'.

Honan went on to compete in eight marathons, a few City2Surfs and various triathlons. 'My hamstring was okay,' he says, 'but after almost 12 years of pounding the streets, my knee and lower back called it quits and I had to stop running.' He still remains fit by exercising most days, combining walking and swimming with some resistance training.'

After 10 years he sold the cleaning business and joined Page in developing a revolutionary new utility-pickup truck featuring a flatbed and tailgate which could be lowered to the ground for easy loading. Page, a backyard inventor, came up with the idea as a solution to pick up shopping trolleys but there was strong interest from the USA in developing an on-road truck with this unique 'drop-bed' feature.

The truck was christened the 'Kelpie Kargo'. A public company was floated to raise capital and a prototype was built and air freighted to the USA. Honan and his family moved to Los Angeles and his job as CEO of USA operation was to launch the project, continue to work with the Chrysler Corporation, establish a dealership network and source a manufacturing-assembly plant near the USA and Mexican border.

Honan and his team, which included his older brother John—a mechanical engineer and a 'whiz kid' with computer-assisted design who improved the vehicle's engineering capabilities—achieved all these goals during his three years in the States. As is often the case with public companies, however, disputes occurred with the Australian-based Board of Directors about the Board's direction in raising further investment capital and Honan was left with no other option than to resign. Consequently, the Board failed to raise the necessary capital, the company folded and another terrific idea and project was gone. Honan decided that he would never get involved in a business which involved large, corporate-type structures. A family-controlled operation was the only way he would function.

The Honans came back to Australia in 1991 and started again. 'We loved Mexico; we used to drive down there all the time and we saw a business opportunity. They produced a lot of home and garden housewares and handicrafts. The big rage back here was the

"Mediterranean" look and I said to Barb, "Why not import items from Mexico?" It was something different. I spent a couple of months in Mexico checking out product supplies and shipping. We did our homework and found that it was feasible.

'We started importing container loads of products. We wholesaled the goods throughout Southeast Queensland and the southern states through a Sydney-based company. Our son, Cameron, joined us and took charge of the Mexican operations, handling the buying and shipping. Our daughter Kelli started a chain of retail stores called "La Nichi" to market the products. A few years ago we scaled back, I retired and Kelli, with Barb's assistance, concentrated on the wholesale import of quality Mexican jewellery and built up a very successful business.'

Honan has been a generous and gregarious host but I have been dying to ask him a question all afternoon. He is barefooted and I see that most of the big toe on his right foot is missing. 'Oh that! I lost my big toe when I was ten years old. My brother and I were playing street cricket. The ball went down a drain and it was covered by a heavy concrete slab. We got it up OK but lost control when lowering it and it landed on my foot, crushing my big toe. Luckily there was a brilliant doctor at the Brisbane General Hospital who saved the lower joint of my toe and rebuilt it, without a toenail, into a broad pad of flesh.' Honan remembers what the doctor said to him at the time. '"You might have trouble running"'… not the sort of thing a ten year-old kid with lots of sporting dreams wants to hear. I had to learn to run all over again. It took me a couple of years to learn to balance my right foot through my second toe. I'd be leaning to one side in races. Running in bare feet was still very hard for me.'

Bobby Honan went on to become a beach sprint champion at Northcliff Surf Club and a dual international. An effective runner in shoes and spikes, he used to have a lot of trouble wearing football boots because his right foot was smaller than the left. Many times during his career Honan had to stop in the middle of a game and retie his right boot. Mike Cleary introduced him to shoemaker Bill Connelly in Bourke Street, Sydney, who handmade football boots from kangaroo hide and positioned a stud under his big toe for extra grip. Honan recalls, 'When Adidas agreed to supply footy boots for the club I said I couldn't wear them because of my condition. Souths said I had to because sponsorship was just coming into the game.'

In the end Honan and Souths came to a compromise. 'Adidas gave me the three stripes and I sewed them onto my handmade boots.' He has been bouncing on his feet ever since.

ELWYN WALTERS
(1967–70)

Elwyn Aubrey Walters has come full circle. Born in Murwillumbah on 25 June, 1943, his parents sold the dairy farm they ran at Terranora after World War II and moved to Tweed Heads on the NSW side of the Queensland-NSW border. Today Walters, the veteran of six grand finals, two Kangaroo Tours, two World Cup competitions and 12 Test appearances, lives in the centre of Tweed Heads with partner Denise, not far from where he started his playing career as a teenager with the Seagulls Club.

'We used to play on the field across the road there at recreation park,' he says when I catch up with him at his family home. 'That was the club's home ground back then and they had their clubhouse there. I started out as a back rower and ended up as a hooker. I hadn't had any real tuition about how to play as hooker, I just sort of learnt as I went along. You had to know how to win the ball back then but it's all changed now. The halfback puts it straight in the second row. How easy is that?'

Walters attended school in Tweed Heads and started his working life as a 16-year-old pastry cook with a local baker at Coolangatta. 'Tweed Heads has always been a good rugby league town … the same with Murwillumbah. There used to be some hard-fought games back then. A lot of the men were cane-cutters and they'd come straight from the cane fields straight onto the paddock and they'd give it to you. There wasn't much tackling but there was plenty of biff. There was blood flying everywhere.'

Walters spent three years in the local under-18s team, three years in A Grade and always thought rugby league could provide a pathway to success. He was a goal-kicking back-rower back then but started playing more and more as hooker. 'I just wanted to better myself. I didn't know how far I could go in the game but my goal all along was to play for Australia. I went to Norths Brisbane from here. No-one came down and had a word to me or anything. Dad actually made contact with Norths. There was a great coach up there named Bobby Bax and he said to come up and have a trial in 1964. Norths signed me when I was 21 years old. At the time Queensland didn't pay their players too much … all the money was in Sydney. Anyone with any talent went straight down there. It's a different story today.'

Norths played Brothers in the 1964 Brisbane grand final and Walters started the match at lock before shifting to five-eighth. The following year he played mainly hooker and the scouts from Sydney started looking at the nuggety, ball-playing forward. 'I don't know who told them about me,' Walters admits. 'They interviewed me and Brian Blowes, who went to Newtown, but Souths decided to bring me down to Sydney.' Souths paid Norths a £750 transfer fee for Walters.

'It was a big change going down to the city. I was only a young bloke but they were a great crowd at Souths. They looked after me while I was down there. I boarded at Coogee just up the hill from the old Oceanic Hotel. The lady running the boarding house was related to Tommy Green, the horse trainer. I knocked around with Jimmy Bonus and Mark Anderson, some mates I played with up here in Brisbane who were both playing for Balmain at the time. I lived with them at Coogee although three of us in one room was a bit crowded.'

Walters, who the Souths players called 'Aubrey' when they found out it was his middle name (it was actually his father's Christian name), proved to be a more than capable defender in the last year of unlimited tackle football. But Souths had an established ball-winner in Fred Anderson and Walters had to mark his time in second grade. He played the entire 1966 season there, culminating in Souths' 12–5 win over Balmain in the grand final where he was moved to second row to accommodate the good form of local junior George Piggins. Walters got his chance in the top grade early in the next season.

'Fred Anderson was a very good player but he was getting a bit slow around the ruck. I played a couple of games and then broke my arm at Redfern Oval. It was my own stupid bloody fault. I threw a coat-hanger at someone, but I can't remember the team. George played most of the season but he got sent off late in the year and I was recalled to first grade. I went on the Kangaroo Tour that year and held the top spot for the next five years.'

But Walters is rushing over the details in his casual, country manner. The stats show Walters played in just four first grade match in 1967 before gaining selection on the Kangaroo Tour. This is an extraordinary achievement in any era. 'I played a few games in reserves before George got sent off and I went straight back into first grade. I played the semi-final and grand final and was selected on the Kangaroo Tour. It was a bit of a shock. I was very surprised to hear my name called out in the Australian team. They only picked three Souths players—me, Satts and Ron Coote. Bobby McCarthy was the big talking point back at the club because he scored that great try in the grand final but it makes you wonder why they didn't pick John O'Neill or Brian James. They could have picked any of the Souths blokes.'

The 1967 grand final against Canterbury, co-incidentally, was won on a scrum penalty and Walters had a front row seat. 'In those days you could kick a goal from a scrum penalty,' Walters explains. 'Canterbury's Ross Kidd fed the ball into the second row and Eric Simms did the rest. It was so easy to lose a game by doing something wrong in the scrum in those days—not packing in straight, taking the loose head, having a loose arm in the scrum, having your feet across the tunnel or striking too early. I can remember being in your own territory in a lot of matches and you'd be frightened to strike for the ball because a penalty goal would lose you the match.'

To make Walters' achievement even more incredible, he had not played in any representative matches to that point. 'I couldn't believe my ears when my name got mentioned in the Kangaroos squad with all the great players … Graeme Langlands, John Raper, Les Johns and Reg Gasnier.' Walters roomed with Newcastle (and later Manly) forward Allan Thomson on that tour. 'A lovely fellow, I didn't know him at all before the tour. The managers just used to mix us up and throw us in together. I think some of the more experienced players may have done a bit of wheeling and dealing to bunk in together but it was my first tour overseas and I was just a rookie.'

Selectors opted for Peter Gallagher and Noel Kelly in the Tests, but also took away Queenslander Noel Gallagher as a hooker. Walters, who was used mainly as a hooker forward, appeared in eight minor tour games. When injuries hit the squad he was even selected at halfback for the match against Rochdale Hornets. 'It was absolutely amazing going to England in 1967. We stayed at the Ilkley Moor Hotel and it was terrible—an absolute shocker. The food was pretty ordinary and the maître'd who showed you to your room was like Lurch from the Addam's Family. He wore this old black coat and he had all these stains down the lapels and stuff. It was hilarious.'

After the highs of 1967, Walters started slowly the following year and missed the rep season. 'I didn't look after myself for a while after that tour. I put a bit of weight on and I left it too late to get myself back fit to play representative football. Clive Churchill loved to make us run at training but I realised I had to do a lot of my own training. A lot of the players—John Sattler, Gary Stevens, Ron Coote and Macca—used to do their own training. To be on top you had to do the work. If you didn't do the work, you missed out and I let myself down in 1968 because I didn't keep myself in good shape. I turned myself around and got myself back on track because I wanted play Test football.'

Walters formed a great front row partnership with John O'Neill and John Sattler. 'We used to practice scrummaging a lot in those days. It's probably not even heard of now at training. Ernie Hammerton [a premiership-winning hooker with Souths in the 1950s and a former Test player] helped me out a lot at training. Lurch O'Neill was the loose head prop—which was on the side the scrum the ball was fed into—and you had Satts on the other side. We were never even. Lurch was this big guy and Satts was only my size. We used to always lean in a scrum. You could strike for the ball, which was important in those days, and we had the second row and lock to keep the scrum nice and tight. Jimmy Morgan, who played in the 1968 grand final against Manly, was a great loose-head prop as well. He was also one of the good rakers of the ball.'

Walters was the first choice hooker at Souths over George Piggins for the next six seasons (Walters played 128 games for the Rabbitohs, from 1967 to 1973, to George's 56 appearances). 'I don't think George liked me too much,' he says with a smile. 'There was this competitive thing between us but he kept me on my toes. I knew I had to play well to keep him out of the side, so you could say he helped me along the way. We were different types of players, actually. I think that's why they picked me for so long. I always looked after the middle of the ruck pretty tightly. The hooker had to be dummy half, but we also went for a run if the opportunity was there, and, of course, you had to win the ball. I wouldn't say I was the greatest hooker ever but as long as you won your share of the ball, you were doing the best by your team.'

Walters bristles when I bring up the 1969 grand final. 'I don't like talking about that very much. Fair dinkum! What a way to play a bloody grand final. Their stop-start tactics were absolutely frustrating. They didn't give us a chance at all, to their credit, but we couldn't do anything about it at the time. Balmain tackled well and got away with it so good luck to them. As soon as we looked like getting to the try-line some Balmain player would go down injured. It threw our plans right out the window. The rule at the time was that once someone was injured, the referee had to pull the game up and they had to attend to him. They changed the rule after that and so they bloody should!'

In 1969, Walters broke back into the Australian Test team for the tour of New Zealand. Seven South Sydney players were named in that squad—Sattler (c), Walters, Coote, McCarthy, Pittard, Honan and Cleary—but the Kiwis proved hard to beat on home soil and the Test series finished one-all. 'The Pommies in 1970 were no easier,' Walters says. 'We played them in the 'Battle of Brisbane' in the First Test. Jimmy Morgan got his nose smashed all over his face. Fancy taking on Cliff Watson! He still scored two tries, Jimmy. He had plenty of heart.'

Walters was injured in the NSW–Great Britain match and missed the Second Test of the series but was recalled for the deciding Test in Sydney, which the Lions won. 'We beat them at the end of the year in the World Cup though,' he says with a smile. 'We rallied behind [captain] Ron Coote and surprised them in the final at Leeds. Australia was given no hope. Langlands was out. Sattler was out.'

After winning the 1970 grand final against Manly, the following season saw Walters set to make it six consecutive grand finals in six seasons when fate intervened. 'I broke my collarbone in the semi-final against Manly in 1971. (Bill) 'Herman' Hamilton was diving for the try-line and I ran in to tackle him and I heard it snap.' Having had the disappointment of missing selection in the Australian Tour of New Zealand (coach Harry Bath and selectors opted for Queenslander Brian Fitzsimmons), Walters was looking to finish the year on a high note. 'It gave George Piggins a crack at a premiership, and what a game he had, but it was hard playing the whole year and then missing the grand final. It was also our last one.'

Walters was a familiar figure in the Australian Test team during the next three years, often wearing tape around his forehead and fashionable sideburns of the era. He played against the Kiwis in 1972, toured overseas with Australia's World Cup team at the end of the year and in 1973 made a second Kangaroo Tour where he played four of the five Tests. But the golden era of grand final appearances had ended at Souths. 'Once Souths let all those players go ... Moses, Morgan, Coote, Branighan and O'Neill ... you could see the writing on the wall. Satts left in 1972 and when you start losing all your best forwards it's hard to be competitive.'

In 1973 Souths shifted Walters to prop and played George Piggins at hooker for the latter half of the season. The club also delayed contract negotiations until he came back from the Kangaroo Tour. 'I roomed with Bob McCarthy and John O'Neill on that tour. It was a bit hairy. We had a fairly long room with three single beds in it.' Walters played in 14 of the 19 tour matches, crossing for two tries, but also playing prop and second row. 'Lurch O'Neill was playing with Manly by then but there were no hard feelings. There was an understanding that you sometimes had to leave a club to do better for your family. If the club wasn't going to look after you, you had to look after yourself, especially in those days. The money wasn't that fantastic then but it wasn't such a big thing. Everybody just wanted to play footy at the top level.'

This is the situation Walters found himself in at Souths when he returned from England and France. 'I could sense I was on the outer at the club with George (Piggins) coming through. Souths didn't seem to care whether I played for them or not. I thought that was a bit odd seeing I was had just played all these Tests and had been there for eight seasons but I got to thinking that Souths didn't want me. I went over to talk to Arthur Beetson and he said I should have a chat to Jack Gibson, who had taken over as coach of Easts in 1974. I came back and saw Souths and they said that I would be better off going to Easts because they wouldn't be able to match what they were offering. I was 30 years old, but still felt I had a couple of good years left in me. I thought I might as well go to the Roosters.'

Walters found a different set-up at Eastern Suburbs. 'Jack Gibson was pretty strict but I got on well with him. I think as long as you did your work he was happy. You could probably get away with a few shortcuts with Clive Churchill but Jack wouldn't tolerate cutting corners or fooling around. Jack had new ideas. He'd brought back American training methods and we were doing a lot more technical work with him than we did at Souths. Video sessions were just coming in and we'd look at our games and our performances. We had great success in 1974 and 1975, but at the beginning of 1976 Jack brought in this bloody Nautilus machine and I reckon, to this day, that that's what stuffed us up. With Nautilus you had to improve on your last effort. Jack used to keep records on all of us to make sure that we were improving week to week. And if you weren't improving he'd want to know why. We just didn't have the energy in our games that year.'

Easts had a champion team in 1974 but they surpassed even that benchmark against St George in the 1975 grand final. Did Walters feel for the Saints players after the 38-nil onslaught? 'No, that's footy. I always admired Changa Langlands. We used to love playing against him because he was such a good player. Towards the end of his career, he'd try and step around you and we started to read him after a while. And when he had a crook leg in the grand final he couldn't do much at all. He just wouldn't stay off the field.' Easts' captain Arthur Beetson was masterful that day. 'Arthur was the best forward I played with,' he says, 'with his ability to turn the ball and get a pass away. You always backed up Arthur because you knew you were going to get the ball.'

Walters made his final Test appearance in the First Test of the 1974 Ashes series. Australia used three hookers in three Tests—Walters, 1973 Kangaroo John Lang and 1970 World Cup hooker Ron Turner—as selectors tinkered to get a winning combination.

Although Australia won the First Test in Brisbane, 12-6, Walters was part of a shake-up that saw even the great Changa Langlands sacked—and he was the Australian captain-coach. He contemplated retirement when Easts were bundled out of the semi-finals in 1976 but received a call from Manly-Warringah. 'Max Krilich broke his sternum during the pre-season competition and they needed a hooker to replace him. Manly wasn't my favourite team, being from the south side of the city, but I ended up signing for the season. I played eight first grade games that year and they wanted me to sign on for another year but I'd had enough. There were no real injuries to speak of, just the body telling me it was time to retire.'

Despite the signals, Walters received an opportunity to captain-coach in the bush. 'I got a phone call from Mullumbimby which is not far down the track from here and they wanted me to captain-coach their club so I came up and had a yarn to them,' he says. 'They seemed to be pretty keen about it all. I wasn't doing anything else so I thought I'd come up and give it a go. It was the hardest job I've ever had to do, especially after all the football I'd played in Brisbane and Sydney. All the young blokes wanted to get a hold of you and sort you out so they could say "I belted Elwyn Walters." Apart from that it was a good experience and I made some good friends there.'

Walters says that he has no regrets about his career because he played with two championship clubs and won six premiership titles (as well as a reserve grade title) at a time when there was great football being played and many friendships made. 'The thing that made Souths such a champion club was the combination of all those great players in the one place. We all knew what we could do and we just all did our work. I got on very well with Bobby Grant because you had to have a good relationship with your halfback. It used to get pretty rough in scrums in those days when you had your head down and blokes were belting you in the face and so forth. You had to have an understanding about how and where you wanted the ball put in the scrum. It was the same in rep games with Tommy Raudonikis.'

He can only remember being sent off once in his career. 'Laurie Bruyers sent me off for repeated infringements in a match for Souths —feet across the scrum too many times, I think—the bludger!' he laughs at the memory of it. 'I was a bit dirty about that. I didn't get into much trouble on the field. You had enough problems coming your way without looking for it. If you thumped somebody you knew there was going to be a square-up, so why go looking for it? You copped enough as it was.'

When he moved down to Sydney in the late 1960s, Walters went into bricklaying. 'The idea was that it would keep me fit but being a brickie's labourer was bloody tough. Later on down the track I worked for a sign-writer. I used to do a bit of carpentry work for him, making his signs. Then I left that and went back into the bricklaying. A mate of mine and I did a bit of work for John O'Neill and Gary Stevens with their building company … they liked to keep the work "in the club."'

Walters also met his first wife in Sydney and had a daughter, Kendall, born several weeks before he left for England for the 1970 World Cup. After opening a seafood restaurant in Brunswick Heads and operating it for seven years, he moved 'a stone's throw from where I grew up' he says. 'I felt I wanted to come back home. My mum and dad were here and I had two sisters, Loise and Jan, up here so I wanted to come home and live at Tweed. I'm retired now. I might do the odd job now and then, but not very often.'

Walters says he doesn't get recognised too much at Tweed as a former Souths great but he is on the committee in the Tweed District for the Men of League foundation. 'We recently had a race day at Murwillumbah—unfortunately they couldn't run the races because of the weather but we had a fan day and had about 250 members turn up. It's always nice to catch up with blokes you played with. There are quite a few who live up here … Satts is at Southport and Bobby Honan at Broadbeach … and a few of the St George boys are up here as well. I still enjoy the game today and like to keep in touch with it. At State of Origin time, I'm a NSW man. Although I played in Queensland for a couple of years and they all thought I was a Queenslander, I was actually born in NSW. I played for the Blues and I'll stick with them.'

ARTHUR BRANIGHAN
(1968, 1970)

The older of the famous Branighan brothers at South Sydney during the club's last golden era, Arthur Branighan was part of the changing culture at the Rabbitohs during the 1960s and 1970s. Known by a variety names during his career—Souths' teammates called him 'Tired' and his kid brother Ray 'So Tired', he explains, because they had reputations for not being the greatest trainers—Arthur started his grade career during the club's 'easybeat' days under coach Dennis Donoghue, played in the historic 1965 grand final against St George in front of a record SCG crowd, won two premiership during the Rabbitohs' run of five straight grand finals and watched his immensely talented younger brother represent his country and then walk away from the club. 'In fact, I told him to go,' Arthur says.

'I thought we trained pretty well,' Ray Branighan interrupts, deadpan. The brothers have a good laugh at their own expense.

We are sitting in Ray's house not far from Malabar Beach discussing their respective playing careers with Brad Ryder, Souths' erstwhile club historian. The four of us are sipping tea and eating cake and scones prepared by Ray's wife, and talking about the old days. Arthur is taller than I remember—a touch over 6 foot topped by a shock of wispy, grey hair and a grey moustache—but looks fit and trim for a man of almost 68. Ray's blonde locks that were often taped out of his eyes during his playing days are now gone and, at age 63, he prefers a low maintenance crew cut. During an afternoon of 'war stories' and playful banter between the pair Ray refers to his brother as 'Pasty'—a nickname attributed to Arthur's pale complexion as a teenager—and Arthur calls his brother 'Kraut'. It is clear their brotherly bond remains unbroken and their sense of humour is quite infectious.

Arthur James Branighan was born in Redfern on 28 February 1943. The oldest of three brothers (middle brother Alan, like Ray, was a Moore Park junior), the family moved to Revesby when he was 13 years old. 'Our dad Jim was the smallest guy in the family … he was a laborer who loved a beer,' Arthur says. 'We were always Souths fans. Friends would come over in their removal truck on Saturday afternoon and I would sit on the back and go to Redfern Oval.' Branighan did not play rugby league as a teenager—he gave the game away in high school and played rugby union, he says, because he was too slight. 'I was 5 foot 7, barely 8 stone and got battered from pillar to post.'

Playing tennis and basketball at nearby Coronation Playground, Branighan represented NSW Under 18s in basketball. In 1961, NSW came fourth in the Australian Championships and Branighan was the highest point-scoring forward in the tournament. 'I left school and was working for the Commonwealth Bank,' he recalls. 'We started to do circuit training and within two years I had put on six inches in height and 6 stone in weight. I was to able to hold my own so I decided to go back to rugby league and tried out with Redfern United and played B Grade (Under 21s) in 1962.'

Branighan was approached by legendary junior coach, former international Clem Kennedy, and was tagged for selection in Souths' President's Cup team. 'I wrote down my grandmother's address in Redfern but I was ruled residentially unqualified because I was still living in Revesby in the Canterbury district. Everyone did it at the time—even Johnny Raper—so I was told to try out for grade at Souths.' The club ran almost a dozen trials, one after the other, and graded prospective players in each of three grades. Arthur started at 10.30 am and scored the last try of the day in the 4.30 pm trial. He was graded in second grade as a centre.

Arthur didn't notice the jump from B Grade in club football to grade at Souths, he says, because everything happened so quickly. 'I only had one year in B Grade to compare it with. I played the first six games of the 1963 season in second grade and then got promoted to first grade. I found every grade hard. Second grade was just as hard as first grade, it was just that first grade was much faster. Souths' reserve grade, with players such as Paul Sait, Gary Stevens, Kevin Longbottom, and later Ray, was like a first grade team anyway.'

Souths had a very good team on paper in 1963 and Branighan believes the club should have done much better than the four wins, and a second-last placing on the premiership table, the records show. Fullback Darrell Chapman was a former Test player; Mike Cleary and Jim Lisle were dual internationals; centre Alan Skene was a South African international who played Test football that year; budding champions John Sattler and Bob McCarthy were in their first season with the club, as was Billy 'Baggs' Owen, a Test forward the previous year for Newcastle; former Queensland hooker Bill Gehrke toured New Zealand with the Australian team in 1961 while prop, Barry Harris, was a State representative. Add talented locals like goal-kicker Kevin Longbottom and ball-playing forward Richie Powell and how did it all go so wrong?

'We only trained on Tuesdays and Thursdays, about 20 minutes each night, then we went to the pub,' he says. 'There were no real tactics—our coach Dennis Donoghue used to say to just go out there and bash the opposition. You don't like to compare coaches but Bernie Purcell was the man who started Souths' success. He got all the young players onside … there were eight juniors in first grade in

1964 and he had a good rapport with everybody. He called a spade a spade and you respected him.'

Souths showed marked improvement under Purcell in 1964, winning 11 of 18 matches to just miss the semi-finals by a point. The following year the young Souths team took on St George in the grand final after qualifying for the play-offs in fourth place. Film of the match shows Branighan using a neat step and some resolute toughness. When a St George player strikes in the play the ball, his knee connects with Branighan's mouth and he continued the match dazed and bloodied.

I ask Ray Branighan if he was among the record crowd at the SCG to watch his brother play in the historic match. 'Me? I was at a little place called Captain's Flat near Wagga on a country trip for Moore Park playing Under 18s. On the way we stopped at a pub at Braidwood and the SP bookie was offering four and a half points start Souths so we pooled our money. Straight after our game a group went back and collected the money.'

Compared to the highs of the previous year, the 1966 season was a disappointment. Arthur broke his collarbone and only played five games that year. Having won barely half their matches, Souths approached the last game of the season needing to beat Manly at Brookvale to force a play-off for the semi-finals. Manly won a tryless match, 8-2, with referee Col Pearce recalling Branighan as he ran in the try and awarded a scrum feed to Souths after a minor infringement. With that failure coach Bernie Purcell was replaced.

'Bernie spoke his mind,' Arthur says. 'That didn't go down well with the club committee. He had faith in you as a player and he was outspoken as a coach and stood his dig against the selectors. He was still on contract when they sacked him. Clive Churchill inherited a side that was still very young, had already been beaten in a grand final and had a disappointing season where they didn't make the semis. The team was hungry for success. Souths already had a good team that ran itself through the captain.'

An interesting statistic is that Churchill used five different centre combinations in five consecutive grand finals—Moses and Simms in '67, Branighan and Honan in '68, Honan and Burke in '69, Branighan and Sait in '70, and finally, Honan and Sait in '71. Some of the pairings were necessitated by injury, some by form, but Arthur says there was never a lot of planning, or tact, when it came to team selections at Souths. And the selectors mainly tinkered with the centres.

'You'd come to training after you got beat and Clive would come out and announce the side and say "Right, let's get training." He wouldn't say you were dropped or anything, your name just wasn't called out.' He and Ray laugh at the memory. 'You'd walk off and train with the second graders (at Souths the three grades trained on the one oval, one after the other). There was never any discussion why you had been dropped. The centres were always very competitive … Greg Norgard, Jimmy Lisle and Kevin Longbottom also played in the centres, as did Ray when he was graded, and what did Souths do? They bought Kerry Burke from Parramatta and Phil Smith from rugby union. The selectors never dropped the forwards because they were such a stable pack.'

Working for the Commonwealth Bank at a time when banks were often open on a Saturday morning, Arthur would man one-teller operations at Enmore, Glebe, King Street, Martin Place, Coogee and Kingsford and then rush to the SCG for the match of day. 'The selectors at Souths never made life easy for you,' he says. 'You felt like a bit of a yo-yo at times but you became good mates with all the players. All three grades got on really well. Sometimes when you got dropped from first grade you'd find yourself in third grade because of 'personalities' at the club. When Les 'Chicka' Cowie was second grade coach I got dropped from first grade to third. I scored three tries and I got reinstated back into firsts. Chicka was a terrific bloke who had his own opinion.'

Arthur was not sure about brother Ray coming to Souths at first. 'Clem Kennedy was the third grade coach and he told me to tell

Ray to try out for grade in 1967. Jim Lisle and Greg Norgard had a mortgage on the five-eighth role at the time so I told him to go and play rugby union instead and if he didn't make it, he wouldn't be as disappointed.' Not for the first time during his career Ray Branighan did not listen to the advice from his older brother.

Arthur was later selected in the second grade grand final and partnered his brother in the centres. Balmain defeated Souths on this occasion, 11-7, and the pair would share first grade grand final success together in 1970. Arthur, however, got his opportunity for a first grade title in 1968 against Manly. But it almost didn't happen.

In 1968 Souths captured their first minor premiership since 1955 but were soundly beaten by Manly in the major semi-final, 23-15. Arthur had been in good form all season, playing 17 of 22 club games, but turned up to training before the all important preliminary final against St George to find that he'd been dropped. 'I'm usually pretty laid back but I did my block that night,' he laughs. 'I picked up my kit bag, walked out of training and went straight to the club and got drunk with the second graders who had already finished training. When I came back for Thursday night training, I turned up 45 minutes late to train with the second graders and the boys told me I was back in first grade—Jimmy Lisle didn't pass the fitness test.'

In the lead-up to the final, Branighan caught a bad dose of the flu but wasn't going to miss this chance. According to press reports of the time, he and Bobby Honan outplayed St George's 'international pairing' of Graeme Langlands and Billy Smith in the 20-8 win and the two centres were retained for the grand final. 'My brief, to a certain extent, was to keep [Manly centre and captain] Bobby Fulton quiet. I marked Reg Gasnier in the 1965 grand final so I was confident I could do the job. Fulton was a physical instructor in the army at the time and was supremely fit. He'd also played in the World Cup earlier that year so he was pretty cocky. He was in my ear all the time and he started early. "What are you doing here ... you're an old man ... you're grey ... you shouldn't even be out here ..." When we got near the final hooter he was still going strong so I said, "Bob, you're gone mate. Look at the scoreboard … 13-9.'"

Branighan continued his good form into 1969, and by midseason the Honan-Branighan partnership helped to propel Souths to another minor premiership. But another injury to Arthur gave former Parramatta centre Kerry Burke the inside running to a grand final which is memorable for all the wrong reasons. Sitting on the reserves bench as Balmain frustrated Souths out of a third straight title were the Branighan brothers. I asked Arthur if it was hard sitting on the sidelines while Souths was being beaten. 'We were both dying to get on. The frustrating thing was that some of the players took pain-killing needles into the match.' This was another contributing factor in the upset loss to the Tigers that was not widely canvassed at the time.

Arthur and Ray Branighan played their only first grade grand final together in the 23-12 win over Manly in 1970. Arthur was centre, with Ray on his outside on the wing. This time Arthur had to have a pain-killing needle to take his place on the field. 'I pulled my hamstring and I was a bit scratchy at the last training session. I told the selectors a furphy and said that I was just hungover.' There was no doctor assigned to the club at the time so on the morning of the grand final Arthur drove from the family home in Revesby to the surgery of a local GP, a former classmate. 'I got needled and took some painkillers and saw out the match. About 15 minutes to go I could feel the pain-killers wearing off. Although we had the game won, I didn't want to miss a tackle and draw attention to myself.'

This was a common practice with rugby league players at the time, Arthur and Ray admit, getting pain-killing needles to play the big matches. Sometimes the needles would work, sometimes they would wear off and sometimes they would go awry. 'Once I kicked off in a match, pulled my hamstring and walked straight off … replacements were allowed then, thank goodness.' Playing injured, playing needled, was just part of the game back then, but this pales in comparison to what John Sattler went through.

Arthur Branighan was standing in the line of defence when his captain was hit on the jaw by the forearm of Manly forward John Bucknell. 'When Satts broke his jaw, Bobby Grant tried to cut him out by passing the ball to the other forwards. Satts said that he wasn't coming off but the next Souths player who cut in front of him to take the ball up was going to get carried off on a stretcher. He was just so tough—I'm glad he was on my side. I remember we played Canterbury at Belmore one year. Kevin Ryan and Neville Horney belted Satts from daybreak to dark. Satts copped it sweet ... and then got square when the match was won.'

1970 saw Ray named in the Australian World Cup team. 'I'm very proud of Ray's career,' Arthur says. 'He played in four straight grand finals (1970-71 with Souths and 1972–73 with Manly), scored tries in three consecutive grand finals (1970–72) and represented Australia in six consecutive seasons (1970–75) including three World Cups (1970, 1972 and 1975).' They are impressive stats but Ray interjects again, breaking the room into laughter. 'In the 1970 grand final program it said you were 25 and I was 24 ... you were actually 27 and I was 22, so figure that out.'

Arthur was a strong defensive centre with a good step, but late in his career Souths tried him in the second row. 'That was a completely different education,' he smiles. 'You had to put weight in the scrums back then ... pushing hard, and if the ball was lost you had to break quickly and cover in defence. You'd get the ball back and before long you were attacking again. It was nonstop under the four tackle rule.'

Injuries restricted Arthur to just six first grade appearances in 1971, and after a long stint in second grade, the grand final against St George found him on the bench as a non-playing reserve. The following year he retired. 'A groin injury ended my career. There was no effective treatment for it then. I'd often play two games an afternoon ... a reserve grade game and then most of a first grade game. I was 28 years old, putting on weight and starting to slow down a bit. It was time.'

Arthur Branighan played exactly 100 first grade games during his eight-season career with Souths. He says Ray's decision to leave Souths for Manly after the 1971 grand final did not influence his decision to retire. 'I remember saying to Ray when he came into grade not to come to Souths because the club committee at the time didn't look after the juniors. Ray was a promising five-eighth in 1967 and the following year the club bought Denis Pittard from Wests. When Ray had enough at the end of 1971 and said he might leave I told him to go to a club that would be competitive and would look after him.'

'Arthur always gave me good advice, even when I didn't listen to it,' Ray laughs. A little known fact is that Arthur tried to make a comeback with Manly in 1973. 'I played six half trials but I kept breaking down,' he says, without a hint of regret.

After his career ended Arthur coached his sons Luke and Ryan, winning a Wayne Pearce Shield in one knockout, and watched with pride as son Luke played for St George-Illawarra (2000-2001) and Cronulla (2002). Is he a fan of the current game? 'It's a bit like gridiron and I don't like the "bomb"… lots of points are scored but is that all people want to see? Where's the defence? The average points in a Toyota Cup game was something like 70 points. What sort of preparation is that for a first grade career? In the 1960s, you received a real education in second grade. Players like Kevin 'Bilko' Roberts and Dennis 'Sluggo' Lee taught you where to stand and how to run off them… and they wouldn't let anyone belt you. Where's the second tier competition today that will educate players for first grade?'

Now semi-retired Arthur Branighan doesn't live far from brother Ray and catches up with Ivan Jones, Bob McCarthy and Ron Coote when he's in town. He often runs into Darrell Bampton, the Souths stalwart who was also a non-playing reserve in the 1971 grand final, but admits he doesn't get back to the club too much. 'It's not like it used to be,' he says frankly. 'The whole district is changing … Souths are struggling to attract enough C Grade teams to even have a competition. Last year seven teams competed in A Grade. Ten years ago it was 16.' But when Souths was excluded from the NRL competition and sought through the courts and through sheer people power to be readmitted to the League in 2002, he marched to Sydney Town Hall alongside George Piggins, his brother Ray and a galaxy of club greats from the past.

Arthur Branighan may have played the game in a bygone time when rugby league was truly in a golden era but his good humour, candid opinions and gentlemanly ways remain timeless.

THE CLASS OF '67
KEVIN LONGBOTTOM, JIM LISLE, IVAN JONES, ALAN SCOTT AND GREG NORGARD

Nine players made one appearance during Souths' run of five straight grand finals. Five of these players—fullback Kevin Longbottom, halves Jimmy Lisle and Ivan Jones, second rower Alan Scott and replacement back Greg Norgard—made their sole contribution in the 1967 grand final. In many respects Souths' win in '67 was the start of a golden era for the club but the end of an era for several of the club's established players.

Kevin 'Lummy' Longbottom was a particular crowd favourite at Redfern. Big, barrel-chested with thin, spindly legs, he was surprisingly fast for a big man and originally played centre for the Rabbitohs after being graded by the La Perouse club in 1959. A feature of Longbottom's game was his long-range goal-kicking which was to seen to good effect in the 1965 grand final against St George. Longbottom landed three massive goals to keep a young Souths outfit in the match. A teenage Eric Simms added a solitary goal in that match and was related to Longbottom through marriage.

Longbottom was a big man who wore his big heart on his sleeve. John Sattler tells the story of Longbottom walking out of training if Bernie Purcell criticised him for missing a tackle or dropping a ball.

'Bernie was a Redfern bloke who'd say what he thought. Lummy was a very temperamental guy, but not in a bad way. He was very sensitive but gee he was a good player. Lummy would come back to training with his tail between his legs and just get on with it.' Longbottom won a reserve grade premiership with the club in 1968 but retired as a player the following year. He later worked as a professional caddy for golfer Bruce Devlin but passed away in 1986 after a long illness.

Rugby Union international Jimmy Lisle had a meteoric rise to the Australian Test team after turning professional with Souths in 1962. Lisle was a champion schoolboy athlete at Grafton High School before joining Drummoyne Rugby Union in 1959. Forming a brilliant halfback partnership with the great Ken Catchpole, Lisle made his Test debut against Fiji in 1961 before touring South Africa with the Wallabies. After four Tests as a centre or five-eighth, Lisle turned professional with the struggling Rabbitohs along with his Wallabies teammate Mike Cleary. A press report of the time quotes Lisle, a young teacher, as being 'flat broke' after the Springboks tour.

Lisle suffered the first of several debilitating leg injuries on that tour of South Africa, delaying his start with Souths in 1962. After just one match for the Rabbitohs, he was selected for City Seconds and was then rushed into the NSW team for a 'double header' against Queensland—all in the same week (12-19 May). From there he represented Australia in the Third Test against Great Britain, which resulted in an 18-17 win to the home side in Sydney, and toured with the Ashes-winning Kangaroos the following year. A highlight of his career was partnering Reg Gasnier in the centres against France in 1964. The following year he led Souths into the grand final against St George, but when Clive Churchill became coach in 1967 he plumped for John Sattler as captain.

While Lisle retained his place in the team for the 1967 grand final, his playing career waned under the weight of injuries. Always a brilliant cover defender, Lisle shifted to the centres when Denis Pittard came to the club, but a recurring hamstring injury saw him pull out of the 1968 semi-final and the injury prematurely ended his career the following year. When the Souths' 'Dream Team' was announced in 2004, Lisle was named five-eighth ahead of premiership winning captain Alf Blair and two-time Rothmans Medalist Denis Pittard.

Lisle was physical education master at Bass Hill High, Randwick Boys High, Orara High School, Coffs Harbour and Wyong High School before his retirement to the NSW Central Coast. He met his future wife Jennie at one of the many barbecues Souths players organised in the mid 1960s and together they had two children, Adam and Rachel. When Lisle turned 60 in 1999, son Adam, a pharmacist at Avoca Beach, organised a busload of Souths teammates and their wives to come up from Sydney for his father's surprise birthday party. 'They came up in the Souths Juniors bus and parked right outside the restaurant,' Adam told me on the phone from the Central Coast. Three years later his father went into hospital with inflammation of the heart, the result of a virus, and suffered a massive heart attack. 'Dad had never been sick a day in his life,' Adam says. Jimmy Lisle, the master of the low flying tackle, was age 63.

Adam Lisle recalled the following anecdote at his father's funeral in February 2003. A Souths fan had printed the story in a Sydney newspaper the previous year when the club was readmitted into the NRL and Adam's father had contacted him to thank him for it. That's the sort of man Jimmy Lisle was. 'In the early 1960s Dad was captain of Souths in their final match of the season against Norths. It was 22-all and right on full-time Souths fullback Kevin Longbottom missed a penalty kick. But the referee awarded Longbottom another kick because a couple of the Norths players had moved when he went in to kick. But dad took the ball from Longbottom and kicked it out over the sideline and walked away.'

Not everyone in today's era of 'win-at-all-cost' rugby league would have appreciated Jimmy Lisle's sportsmanship. Souths and Norths were equal last on the premiership table and the final match of the 1962 had finished in a draw—a dead-heat on a merry-go-round—

and Lisle saw no honour in profiting from an opponent's misfortune. A popular member of the Terrigal Bowling Club, Lisle's memory was immortalised by the naming of the 'Jimmy Lisle Sports Lounge' where his prized 1964 Test jersey against France is on display.

Ivan Jones, Lisle's halfback partner in the 1965 and 1967 grand finals, was one of a number of former League greats who attended Lisle's funeral at Ourimbah. 'Jimmy was a great player,' he says. 'He was dedicated to his game but he had problems with his hamstrings. Coach Bernie Purcell used call him "Tin Legs" but he always gave 120 percent in a game. His cover defence was brilliant with his big diving tackles. We had a great combination. I could always find him from the scrum.'

Queensland-born in 1942, Ivan Jones came to Souths in the mid 1960s after several years in the Brisbane competition. A first grader in Dalby at the age of 16, Souths Brisbane secured his services in 1961. 'Brisbane was a tough competition,' Jones tells me. '[Australian Test captain] Barry Muir was the best halfback at the time.' In 1963 he represented Combined Brisbane against the Kiwis and was spotted by Sydney scouts. 'Souths tried to get me that year but I had already signed a one-year contract with Rockhampton.' The Rabbitohs finally got their man in 1965.

In an era of unlimited tackle, Jones stood in the front line of defence and tackled big men ... and there was no bigger team than nine-time premiers St George. 'The 1965 grand final was the biggest game of my career and the biggest game in a lot of player's careers,' Jones says. 'When you ran out onto the field it was just a sea of people. We were a team of young players and they were a team of seasoned internationals and the score ended up being only 12-8.'

Jones was not a fan of the four tackle rule, which was introduced in 1967. 'The new rule was virtually "rush" football ... boom, boom, boom, kick. You had a limited time to do anything, unlike unlimited tackle which I loved. We had a great side at Souths. Everyone had a touch of individual brilliance which they brought to the team.'

'Clive was a great player but as a coach he left us to do our own thing. It would have been pretty hard to impart his brilliance as a player on to us. You could get a joke out of him pretty easily and he kept everyone happy. Training was enjoyable in those days ... short and quick.'

The 1967 grand final was 'scary at the finish', Jones says. 'I was determined to put the ball in the middle of the scum because referees in those days would just penalise you and bang, the game was over.' This, of course, is what happened inside the final five minutes with the scores locked 10-all. '[Canterbury's] Rossie Kidd was penalised and Simms kicked the goal. I could feel for the guy ... when you were in your own half and feeding a scrum you'd never feed the second row. I used to lean more to the opposition side more than anything so the referee couldn't penalise me.'

Celebrations at Souths Leagues were muted somewhat when the Kangaroo squad was named later that night. 'Bob McCarthy, Brian James, Mike Cleary ... we all missed out on the tour,' Jones says, with a hint of disappointment still in his voice. 'Everyone had us packed and ready go.' Selectors plumped for Easts' halfback Kevin Junee instead.

In 1968 Jones fought off a challenge from Bobby Grant for the first grade halfback position, only to be injured in the semi-final loss to Manly. Clive Churchill retained Grant for the grand final after Souths defeated St George in the final. 'Bob McCarthy and me won a premiership with the reserve grade team that year but I was happy to take the win. A title is a title.' After a disappointing 1969 season in which he appeared in just six matches, Ivan signed with Wests. He captained reserve grade for most of the year but when politics reared its ugly head after the 1971 pre-season competition he hung up his boots. He says he enjoyed his time at Wests.

After starting out as an accountant in Brisbane, he worked in the building game with John O'Neill and Gary Stevens, loaded coal on the wharves at Balmain and ran a few hotels in the inner city. A life member of the Souths club, an honour he says he really appreciated, he recalls the mateship and camaraderie at the club. 'But then the

South Sydney district always stuck together. If someone was in trouble, they'd come to your aid. The Redfern crowd was behind you too, but you didn't want to be out of first grade too long. You know what they say, out of sight out of mind.'

'To pull on the No.7 for Souths was something else' he said.

Diagnosed with lung cancer in 2014, doctors told the tough halfback that he had only weeks to live, but nothing would stop him from watching Souths win the premiership that year. The Rabbitohs' 30–6 win over Canterbury, for Jones, was a reminder of the 1967 grand final in which he starred. The grand final that brought the Rabbitohs' their first premiership in 43 years, and spurred the 72-year-old on to perservere through the New Year and see the club win again before he succumbed to his illness in February 2015. Vale Ivan Jones.

Former second row forward Alan Scott was a South Sydney junior from Alexandria Rovers when he was graded as a teenager in 1959. 'I wasn't good enough to get into the rep teams,' Alan says modestly from his home in Peakhurst, in the heart of St George territory. 'I started off as a lock forward at school but was graded as a centre. I played a bit of first grade in the centres and finished up in the second row when I got too slow.' Scott quickly earned a reputation as a talented ball-player in the era of unlimited tackle. 'If you kicked the ball at Souths in the early 1960s they would have cut your leg off … possession was everything. I fancied myself at being able to move the ball a bit. It suited me better than 'bash and barge.'

In 1961 Scott accepted a contract to play for Manly. 'There was no money in the game at the time. I was getting £10 pound a game so I asked Manly for a go. Ken Arthurson was an excellent coach who would talk to you and explain what you were doing wrong.' Scott appeared in 24 games for Manly over the next four years but following an injury and a long stint in reserve grade he found himself without a club in 1965. 'I played in the Sydney Business Houses competition in the Domain and we won the premiership,' he says. '(St George's) Bruce Pollard was in the same team and he suggested

I have another crack at grade with St George. I turned up to a trial against Souths at Redfern Oval and (St George Secretary) Frank Facer wasn't keen. There was still the issue of a transfer fee from Manly and he said "no transfer, no trial".'

Scott was walking out of the ground when he ran into Souths' reserve grade coach Les 'Chicka' Cowie. 'When I told him I came to have a trial with St George he said not to worry about the transfer fee, he would sort it out, and to come and have a trial with Souths. That's how I started playing with the club again.'

After winning a second grade premiership with the club as a centre in 1966, Scott got his chance in first grade the following year. Jim Morgan was hurt in the last match of the season and Scott was selected for the semi-final against St George. 'Apparently I performed pretty well because they kept me there for the grand final.' Scott did better than that. Captain John Sattler says, 'Alan Scott was a bloody marvel. He came back to us from Manly and we put him up for the grand final. He had great hands. He was a loping, wobbly sort of a runner but he was a very good ball-player on the blind side. They don't play there much today but it's a great area to score tries.' The semi-final and grand final were the only two first grade matches Scott started in that year.

'Winning a premiership was an extra good feeling,' Scott remembers. 'It was the best thing that happened to me in my career. Not too many players get to play in a grand final, let alone win one. We did a lap of honour with the JJ Giltinan Shield and then got shunted off,' he laughs. 'It was all over so quickly. But it helped me get a job, the goodwill the club generated. Souths always got good publicity. Reporters were always at Redfern Oval, even at training, because you were so close to the city.'

Souths virtually had two first grade-strength teams in the late 1960s and Scott played in seven first grade games in 1968 and five the following year. 'We all got on well at Souths, all the players in all the grades,' he says. Scott worked on the wharves and later for

Sydney City Council and finally retired as a player in 1969. 'I started to get a bit of concussion and the doctor at Prince of Wales, a fair rugby union player in his day, told me to retire. He was looking at the damage to my spine and the potential problems I could have.'

Alan Scott has lived in Peakhurst for forty years where he and wife raised two daughters. He lives two doors away from Freddie Nelson, his former Souths and Manly teammate from the early 1960s, but has battled cancer in recent years and admits he doesn't see too many players from the past. 'Bob McCarthy and Ron Coote were standouts for me in my time at the club. I was a huge fan of Ivan Jones but Bobby Grant steered us around the paddock really well. I don't think Souths would have stayed on top for so long without his general play, his passes and ability to read the game.'

Greg Norgard was the reserve back in the 1967 grand final. Having played in Souths' 11-7 loss to Balmain in the reserve grade grand final, Norgard, a talented centre-five-eighth, was Clive Churchill's half-time choice to replace injured winger Mike Cleary. Churchill instructed Jimmy Lisle to go into the centres, moved Eric Simms to Cleary's wing and had Norgard play his favoured five-eighth role. He was just 20 years old and the youngest player in the Souths team. 'Clive had Alan Heiler as the reserve centre,' Greg tells me from his home in the Hunter Valley. 'I don't know why he chose me, but after losing a grand final in reserve grade I'm glad he did.'

The answer to that question is hinted at in my discussion with Alan Scott. 'Canterbury centre Johnny Greaves was starting to cut loose,' Scott recalls. 'Moving Jimmy Lisle to the centres was a masterstroke because his defence bottled up their attack.' Souths led 10-8 at the break and edged out Canterbury 12-10 win their first title in 12 years. Norgard says, 'I look back at 1967 now and realise I was part of something very special ... part of history.' He even has a framed 'Glory Days' Souths jersey of the era with his autograph on it to prove it.

Greg Norgard came to Souths in 1967 from the Newcastle competition. A Waratah-Mayfield junior, he represented Newcastle against Great Britain the previous year and followed the path of other locals—John Sattler, Bob Moses, Jim Morgan, Eric Simms (a Raymond Terrace junior) and of course, newly-appointed coach Clive Churchill (1947)—to the Rabbitohs. Souths players affectionately called him 'Greg Knee-guard' (his name actually means 'North' in Norwegian) and Norgard admits that he was slightly overawed when he came to the club. 'I met Jimmy Lisle at training and I told him he was my hero. Everyone had a good chuckle at that.' The two five-eighths got on famously despite the fact they were often vying for the same position.

Norgard appeared in five first grade matches in 1967 before the grand final against Canterbury. 'I played in the pre-season competition under the new four tackle rule and I remember saying to myself, "What have I got myself into here?" It was so fast. I expected it to be faster that the Newcastle competition, but this was unbelievable.' On grand final night he remembers it taking 45 minutes to get his then girlfriend, now his wife Jan of more than 40 years, through the sea of fans at Souths Leagues club. 'Souths were extremely popular in the late 1960s,' he says. 'It was so jam-packed that if there had been a fire it would have been an absolute tragedy ...'

Souths' committeemen, however, never went overboard in recognising their champion team. 'There certainly wasn't the hoopla that goes on with today's grand final winners,' he says. Norgard remembers the club handing out the 1967 premiership blazers to the players one night after training at Redfern Oval. One memory he cherishes, however, is visiting Clive and Joyce Churchill at Christmas that year when they were all back in Newcastle visiting family. 'They were great people, the Churchills. As a coach it was hard to get to the core of the man, but he was a funny little fella, Clive, who got along with everyone.'

Greg Norgard played a lot of football with Ivan Jones but also combined well with Bobby Grant. 'I could beat a man without too much trouble but I wasn't a speedster,' he says. 'But I was never a greedy player, put it that way.' With Denis Pittard injured at the beginning of 1969 Norgard established a regular first grade position as five-eighth but broke his ankle in the first tackle of the match against St George at the Sports Ground in May. 'Saints kicked off, Eric Simms kicked downfield, Langlands fumbled and Alan Scott picked up the ball and floated a pass out to me. If I had taken it on the fly I would have scored under the posts but Johnny King rushed in from the blind side and hit me in a tackle.'

He stayed with Souths until the end of 1972 before returning home and playing with Wests Newcastle under the coaching of Dennis Ward. 'I had two young sons at the time and my eldest was ready to start school so I wanted it to be in Newcastle. We played in three grand finals and lost the lot of them. I regret that I didn't see out my career with Souths,' Norgard says. 'They were such a great club and I had made some good friends there. Eric Simms was a great mate, as was Bobby Moses, being from Newcastle. We had some great trips away to Queensland, New Zealand and the Islands. When we went on the cruise to Fiji after the 1969 grand final the first grade players would sing the Balmain victory song when they got drunk ... some weird kind of group therapy thing, I suppose. I went back to Redfern Oval last year and watched the trial against Manly. There was a pretty good roll up of past players there.'

An apprentice carpenter in the 1960s, Souths got him as job as part of his contract and he saw out his time working at Sydney Showground. '(Secretary) Charlie Gibson tried to get me a start with John O'Neill and Gary Stevens, but it never worked out and I went to the Showground. I have no complaints and later started my own business. I've slowed up a bit ... I had a fall and did my shoulder, and a knee injury from football gives me a bit of trouble sometimes but I'm still going strong.'

Referee Keith 'Yappy' Holman waves his finger at Souths captain John Sattler, 'Do that again and you're off!'

TOP: A rare action shot of the 1967 grand final against Canterbury shows Alan Scott getting his pass away.
BOTTOM: Eric Simms kicks the winning goal minutes from fulltime in the 1967 grand final against Canterbury.

There was no more fearsome sight in rugby league in the 1960s-70s than John O'Neill on the rampage against Balmain.

Souths players enjoy their lap of honour around the SCG following the 1967 grand final.
From left: Ivan Jones, Eric Simms, Bob Moses, Mike Cleary, John Sattler and Brian James.

Eric Simms consoles Australian captain Graeme Langlands after taking his place in the 1970 World Cup squad following the champion fullback's controversial exclusion because of injury.

Elwyn Walters, chased by Manly's Peter Peters, in a club match at the SCG in the 1970s.

Souths' dual international Bobby Honan with his beautifully balanced running style.

PART 2: YOU CAN'T ALWAYS GET WHAT YOU WANT (1969)

You Can't Always Get What You Want (1969)

'Souths to Shine in '69' was the catch cry for Rabbitoh fans in 1969 and the premier club was confident of winning a swag of premierships at all levels of the game. Souths started the year in a positive fashion with a last-minute, 11-10 win over Wests in the final of the pre-season competition and won a clean sweep of the junior rugby league competitions that year—SG Ball, Jersey Flegg and President's Cup. Defending premiers in first grade, with a first grade-strength pack in reserve grade and a new generation of youngsters in third grade, Souths duly won the Club Championship that year, but the year would not go all their way.

There was a worrying undercurrent of apathy from some club officials. Ray Branighan and Brian James were dropped from Souths' pre-season training squad when they arrived late to training. Both players blamed work commitments, and rightfully so. This was before the era of full-time professionalism and all premiership players worked 'real' jobs to support their families. Pre-season match payments were cut from $50 to $40. With Bob Moses pursuing an offer to return to Newcastle as captain–coach, Souths' Secretary Charlie Gibson admitted that he had not spoken to a number of players about their playing intentions for the year. Souths' administrators seemed out of step with the times ... much was made of the club's 'generous gesture' of paying its Australian representative players $100 for being selected to tour New Zealand later that season. It was then pointed out that the players would miss three premierships matches and this would not cover them being out of pocket for lost match payments.

Souths fans were given a glimpse into the future in the opening match of the season against Balmain at the Sydney Sports Ground. The Tigers surprised the defending premiers, winning 16-7, and kept pace with Souths for much of the year. The Rabbitohs then won six consecutive matches and were on track for another minor premiership by the middle of the year. The champion club supplied seven players for the Australian tour of New Zealand in June—John Sattler (c), Elwyn Walters, Ron Coote, Bob McCarthy, Denis Pittard, Bob

Honan and Michael Cleary—and could have easily added several more. The rep players offered to defy an edict from the League to stand down from club duty before leaving for New Zealand, but Souths' officials over-ruled them and a second-string Souths team courageously beat close rivals Manly at the SCG, 16-4.

On the same day of the First Test in Auckland, a depleted Souths team lost to Norths, 21-12, proving that no club could lose so many star players and remain competitive—a lesson Souths would learn painfully in the coming years. The club lost only one second round match in 1969 and broke almost every league record in the process. Eric Simms surpassed the great Dave Brown's individual point-scoring record, setting a new bench mark of 269 points, and the club won $1500 offered by the WD and HO Wills Company for scoring the most premiership tries. Minor premiers in first and second grade, and semi-finalists in third grade, everything appeared to be going to plan for the champion club.

But the growing resentment of some players within the club was becoming increasingly tangible. On the eve of the major semi-final against Balmain, several prominent Souths players were reportedly 'hostile' with club officials when it was decided to use the $1500 try-scoring prize, and a further $500 won for securing the minor premiership, to pay for an end of season cruise to Noumea and Suva. The prize money had been promised to the first grade squad and the club's decision to use the prize money was made without any consultation to the player representatives John Sattler and Wayne Stevens. When told of the unrest, Souths Secretary Charlie Gibson, who organised the trip (and also worked for the travel company) was quoted as saying, 'I'm certainly not going to let it split the club, and as far as I'm concerned, the players can have the meager $1500 if it will make them happy …'

Several Souths players told champion Norths winger Ken Irvine, who was also a Sydney newspaper columnist, that morale at the club was at rock bottom. Sattler, Ron Coote, Elwyn Walters (who was getting married) Denis Pittard (who was travelling to England) and Bob Honan (whose wife was expecting their first child) ultimately did not go on the trip. They didn't see any of the prize money, either.

On Saturday 6 September 1969, Souths defeated a 12-man Balmain team in the major semi-final, 14-13. 'A magnificent pressure goal by nerveless Eric Simms two minutes from the finish gave Souths a dramatic 14-13 win and a place in the grand final,' the peerless Alan Clarkson wrote after the match in the Sun Herald. Balmain played the second half minus star forward Arthur Beetson after he was sent from the field two minutes from half-time. Beetson had been niggled by the Souths forwards after knocking out Bobby Honan in a heavy tackle, but then took on Ron Coote and was promptly dispatched to the sheds by referee Keith Page. The Tigers lost captain Peter Provan and hooker Norm Miller at half-time but held a 13-12 lead with seven minutes remaining. Simms landed the winning 45-yard penalty goal when replacement Balmain hooker Jack Crawford fell on the loose ball and was judged to be off-side.

Souths' narrow escape brought out the hollow bravado in some of the club's officials. Outspoken sports commentator Ron Casey wrote in his *Daily Mirror* column, 'South Sydney President Dennis Donoghue came in for criticism from members of his own first grade team after South Sydney's one point win over Balmain. Leading members of the team didn't mince words when they said Donoghue's off-field boasts and challenges were like a man picking a fight and then walking away leaving someone else to do the battling ... so let's get it straight once and for all—footballers win premierships and not those who get a slight glow from the reflected glory.'

The club was sensationally knocked out of contention in the reserve grade premiership after winning the minor premiership by a commanding seven-point margin. Boasting a first grade-strength team, including Paul Sait who had played for NSW earlier that year, Souths lost both its semi-final against Balmain and preliminary final against Manly. After seemingly holding a mortgage on the second grade premiership, Souths received some consolation when its unheralded third grade team knocked over hot favourites Canterbury in the grand final. But on grand final day, would Souths win the title that mattered most?

Balmain only qualified for the grand final with a 15–14 win following a late try to winger George Ruebner in the preliminary final against Manly. Illegal bookmakers posted Souths as strong, 3/1 on favourite in the week leading up to the 1969 grand final (the Rabbitohs eventually started 11/4 on), happy in the knowledge that no rugby league favourite had lost a grand final since Wests defeated Souths in highly questionable circumstances way back in 1952. Balmain, which finished second to Souths on the competition table, should never have been considered such despised outsiders because their form against the defending premiers—one win each in the premiership season and a one-point loss in the major semi-final—was very competitive. The press played up the fact that Souths had nine current internationals in their team (Simms, Cleary, James, Honan, Pittard, Coote, McCarthy, Walters and Sattler) while Balmain's best player, Test forward Arthur Beetson, was suspended. How could they lose?

Souths' subsequent defeat in the 1969 grand final has become an important part of rugby league folklore—the upset win by an underdog club against a champion team. Balmain's victory, much to the chagrin of the club's hardy players and diehard fans, was largely attributed to the 'lay down' tactics of the Balmain players who allegedly feigned injuries to stop the champion team's momentum. But their stunning 11–2 win was not because of an isolated tactic, but the end result of a series of escalating events that produced the 'perfect storm' for a grand final upset. Consider that:

- Souths trained poorly in the fortnight leading up to the grand final. Bob Honan was reprimanded for being an hour late to training on the Tuesday night before the match and Mike Cleary battled a bad cold. Poor weather hampered training, resulting in the club moving one session to nearby Redfern Park where the team trained among the palm trees in total darkness. The final training session, which included an impromptu cross-country run to Centennial Park, was described by the Sydney press as 'a bits and pieces effort wound up early on a slippery Redfern Oval.'

- The team went into the grand final with a number of injuries to key players—Bob Moses' ribs, Bob Grant's injured finger and Mike Cleary's troublesome hamstring chief amongst them.
- Rothmans medalist Denis Pittard was heavily concussed early in the match and played next to no attacking role in the grand final.
- Many Souths players, notably captain John Sattler, state that there was a noticeable 'lack of tension' among the team on grand final day. Whether it was complacency after winning two premierships, or just overconfidence on the day against a young Balmain team, the Rabbitohs may not have had the right mental attitude that day.
- Controversial referee Keith Page caned Souths 16–7 in the penalties (8–2 in the second half) and disallowed three possible tries to Souths—a fair one to Bob McCarthy off John O'Neill's pass; a 50–50 chance to McCarthy from Ron Coote's pass; and a seemingly fair try to Paul Sait when the game was almost over.
- Balmain's 'lay down' tactics slowed the pace of the game to a crawl in the second half, stopped Souths from controlling the match and playing at their absolute best, and provided the deadly Eric Simms with next to no opportunity to post points.
- Lastly, something Souths could not combat, the Balmain players produced the game of their lives and tackled the defending premiers out of the match. Souths did not vary their tactics in the second half, despite being behind 9–0, and were always behind the scoreboard. Souths refused to kick on the last tackle, thinking their international hooker Elwyn Walters could easily

beat Balmain rookie Peter Boulton for the ball, but this did not prove to be the case. Souths won the scrums 19–13, but Boulton did his job in only his third first grade appearance.

Colour footage that survives of the match commissioned by the cigarette company which sponsored the game shows the South Sydney players arriving at the SCG in garish red and green promotional hats and blazers. The players look happy and relaxed as they dress in the red and green, but the grand final would not unfold as planned. Balmain five-eighth Dave Bolton, the former Great Britain international, kicked an early field-goal and South African winger Len Killen added two penalty goals to send the Tigers to the break with a 6-nil lead. Souths were denied two first half tries—to winger Brian James when he was ruled to have hit the corner post and to Bob McCarthy when Page ruled that the pass from John O'Neill was forward. Balmain also lost a chance when forward Barry McTaggart was penalised for a double movement, but interestingly Eric Simms was afforded only a single shot at penalty goal, which he missed.

Souths were frustrated in the second half—referee Page continued to penalise them, disallowed a field goal to Eric Simms when he ruled it had been touched in flight, and allowed the Balmain players to receive treatment for injuries when not in possession, as was the rule at the time. John Sattler yelled at the referee to 'get the bastards up' but Page was powerless to intervene. The NSWRL subsequently changed the rule to state there would be no stoppage in play if either an attacking or defending player was injured in the ruck—the game would play on.

When replacement Balmain winger Syd Williams dived over in the Paddington corner, the Tigers all but had the match won at 9-0 with twenty-five minutes still to play. Souths could not play themselves back into the match and when Simms posted first points with a penalty goal, Bolton responded with a second field goal to take the score to 11-2. The Tigers tackled their opponents to a standstill. Full-time signaled celebrations for the Balmain players and their fans, but for Souths' players the 1969 grand final left a hollow feeling that has not been filled in the decades since.

Years later Leo Nosworthy and his senior players acknowledged Balmain's tactics against Souths on the day, 'to move up on them, knock them over and slow the game down ... to attack the blindside and keep [Bob] McCarthy under control.' Souths' Club historian Brad Ryder says, 'I always likened what happened in 1969 to the "Bodyline" tactics in cricket's 1932–33 Ashes series in the sense that the Tigers played within the rules at the time, but not in the spirit of the game.'

Rabbitohs' fans have carried the pain of that grand final loss for more than forty years and show no signs of either forgetting or forgiving. Tigers' fans know their club won the 1969 grand final on its merits, but also that the controversy somewhat makes up for the forfeit South Sydney allegedly re-neged on sixty years before in the 1909 final.

RON COOTE
(1967–71)

Ron Coote, OAM, has come a long way from the brewery truck he first operated the year after he captained Australia to World Cup victory in 1970. Originally a panel-beater, he was smart enough to realise that spending his working hours kneeling on a concrete factory floor was not good for his burgeoning rugby league career. The economics of it didn't weigh up either, he recalls, because he knew that rugby league was going to be his life. Souths got him a job as a sales rep with Garfield Gaskets, the same company John Sattler worked for, but after buying a brewery truck business he switched to the Roosters in the early 1970s. A broken arm in 1976 turned into a nightmare for Coote and he was unable to continue his business. After a short time with a sportswear company, he was attracted to the McDonalds franchise because of their 'clean, organised image'. After operating franchises in the inner city (Ray Branighan affectionately refers to his former teammates' chain as 'Ronald McCootes') the beautiful South Coast of NSW beckoned.

But Ron Coote's lasting legacy, if he needed one after being named in the ARL 'Team of the Century' in 2008, may well be the 'Men of League' Foundation. When I caught up with Ron at his home on Lake Conjola, the charity has just named Bob Bennett, the brother of seven-time premiership-winning coach Wayne Bennett, as its new CEO. 'You never know when you kick something like that off what might happen. Obviously there was a need for it,' he reflects. The idea of a charity organisation that brought ex-players back to the game to raise funds and support fellow colleagues was born when Coote visited his daughter in hospital and ran into former St George great Doug McRitchie. 'He was in the late stages of prostate cancer,' Coote recalls. 'Although he had his family there I thought "why aren't some of his teammates here? Do they even know he's sick?"' It went from there. We had a meeting at the NSW Leagues Club and it grew into the Men of League.'

Ron Coote gave something back to the game that it had lost—a sense of community, a heart.

'Our number one goal was to bring people back to the game and we've done that, which is so satisfying for me because you now go to functions all over the country where there are blokes you haven't seen for 30 years or so, smiling and laughing. The money raised goes to support those in need. Billy Smith, for example, needs his knee replaced. Dick Poole, Australia's 1957 World Cup winning captain, needed both knees done. He was 78 years old and on the hospital waiting list so we helped him out. He was in a wheelchair and now he's back playing golf. We also helped Diane Brown from the Lightning Ridge Redbacks who had a stroke. We've fixed up her house to make her life more comfortable. We help at all levels of rugby league. We help youngsters who sign with a club, get injured and whose careers are suddenly over with schooling and job skills assistance. We give them a scholarship of up to $10,000 and we try to find a position for them.' In ten years The Men of League has grown to over 16,000 members from all levels of the game. Graeme Langlands is the No.1 badge holder.

Ronald Joseph Coote was born on 25 October 1944 in Kingsford, NSW. His father Jack had been a prop forward in the great Eastern Suburbs teams of the 1930s and rugby league was in the family DNA.

'I came from a poor background but no-one had money in those days. My Dad would have a few beers and get around the dinner table at night and tell his "war stories". I knew all those blokes he played with ... Dave Brown, Max Nixon, Ray Stehr, Joe Pearce, Viv Thickness and Andy Norval. They were all local Eastern Suburbs blokes.' Coote's father was president of the Kensington United Junior Rugby League and the budding champion spent his formative years in the red and white of the district club. Ron's older brother John was a talented junior until a shoulder injury ended his promising career.

Residentially qualified as a Souths Junior, Ron Coote was selected in the club's Jersey Flegg team in 1961. Originally a winger or centre, he was now a rangy, lock forward. 'Bobby McCarthy was in the same team and I was captain. We went to New Zealand that year. My family would go on holidays to Coffs Harbour, where my mother's family came from, but we weren't that well off. I'd never been out of the state, let alone on a plane before. I just remember saying to myself, "How good is rugby league?"'

Being graded with Souths was his goal after that.

In 1962 Coote and Bob McCarthy both tried out for the lock position in the President's Cup team. Instead of shifting players to the second row, something Coote would later get used to in the Australian Test team, Souths chose McCarthy at lock and failed to select Coote at all. He made the club's successful President's Cup team the following year and was graded with the Rabbitohs in the later part of the season. In quick succession Coote played one third grade game and five second grade games culminating in Souths' 6-5 loss to St George on a SCG mud-heap the day the famous 'Provan-Summons' photo was snapped.

Bernie Purcell, who had coached Coote in second grade, took over from Dennis Donoghue as first grade coach in 1964. It was Purcell who nicknamed the gangly teenager 'Solid' ... 'as solid as a Sao biscuit,' Coote laughs. After playing well in the inaugural pre-season competition, Coote debuted at lock in the opening match of the season against Easts and scored a try in the 17–8 win. 'Mother Nature was very good to Souths in the 1960s,' Coote says. 'We had all these great juniors coming through ... Bobby McCarthy, Arthur and Ray Branighan, Gary Stevens, Paul Sait and George Piggins... a whole generation of champion players. Richie Powell was an unsung hero at that time. He was a great, ball-playing forward. Bobby and I would run off him all day and we scored a lot of tries off him over the years. It could have been a lot closer in the 1965 grand final if Richie had been fit and been in our side.'

Coote quickly established his reputation as an attacking player with brilliant cover defence in the closing years of the unlimited tackle rule. A strapping six-footer weighing 14 stone 4lbs, he made his debut for NSW in 1965, shifting to second row because the great Johnny Raper held a mortgage on the lock position, and challenged the might of St George in the grand final at season's end. 'The 1965 grand final was an unbelievable experience for a 21-year old,' he recalls. 'We watched the crowd jumping over the fence before the start of the match ... just amazing. The St. George team at that time was the benchmark for all other teams.'

While 1966 was disappointing for Souths and for Coote ('I chipped my kneecap and was out for a large part of the season. I came back later in the year but it was still pretty weak'), he signed a five-year contract with incentives if he made the representative teams. Married to wife Robyn, the daughter of Kensington junior league identity Alma May, Souths helped him purchase the former home of champion jockey Athol Mulley. There they raised two daughters, Donna and Natalie.

Souths won the first premiership under the new rule in 1967, the year Clive Churchill returned to the club as coach. 'Bernie Purcell put that team together,' he says. 'Clive was a jovial fellow – one of the boys – and he'd have a laugh and keep everyone happy. He was the best "people person" coach I've ever played under but we knew what we needed to do to win. We were all winners and everyone had the desire to win. He allowed Johnny Sattler to be a strong team leader. Clive would say, "OK boys. That'll do you" and Satts would say, "No Clive. I reckon we should do a little bit more. That's only an hour." That's all we used to train … Tuesday and Thursday nights for an hour. We needed more than that, obviously. We were reasonably conditioned because you played for 80 minutes and you were match fit, but all players trained on their own time as well.'

Ron Coote and Bob McCarthy—'Solid' and 'The Body'—formed a lethal partnership at Souths during the club's golden era. 'The four tackle rule actually helped our game,' Coote says. 'Bobby McCarthy and I were runners and we got the chance to get the ball in our hands more often. And that's what we liked to do – run with the ball.' McCarthy gives a good insight into Coote as a player. 'Ron would let players get around him and then use his speed to nail them … even players as fast as Ken Irvine and Reg Gasnier. He chopped 'Gaz' off at the knees in cover defence in the 1965 grand final. Ron was quick but his timing was brilliant. He wouldn't let a player get more than a yard past him because they'd be gone. In attack, I scored many of my tries off a Ron Coote break. With him, he created many of the tries he scored. He was that good.'

Coote played in nine grand finals during his career and apologises that he can't remember the finer details of each particular one. Of the loss to Balmain in 1969 he says, 'Leo Nosworthy was their coach and he just outsmarted us. Souths were a great team because we were good athletes … we could keep going when everyone else had run out of petrol. The stop-start nature of the game just didn't suit our style of play.' There is a poignant moment in the 1970 grand final after Bobby Grant's first try against Manly when Coote is seen talking to John Sattler and trying to ascertain the extent of his broken jaw injury. Coote later said that it was 'a privilege' to be on the field with his captain in that match.

Coote's selection in the Australian Test team, however, remains fresh in his memory. 'The 1967-68 Kangaroo Tour was an amazing experience. I played 19 of the 27 games in England and France and I enjoyed every one of them. I would have loved to have played more if I could. I played a lot of games in the second row, including five of the six Tests, to accommodate John "Chook" Raper.' Coote roomed with Raper on tour, along with Queenslander Noel Gallagher, and says that he learned a lot from the champion lock on tour.

A conscientious trainer (too conscientious to be much of a drinker) English conditions suited Coote, 'I had a pretty good motor and I could keep going. I was never the sprint champion at school but I won a lot of 880 yards races. I scored plenty of tries in the last five minutes of a game.' If ever a match heralded the arrival of a new champion it was the Second Test of the Ashes series in London. Without Gasnier or Raper in the team, Great Britain was favoured to win the match and the series after taking the First Test at Leeds, 16-11. Making his Test debut as a lock Coote saved a certain try when he tackled Englishman Ian Brooke in a brilliant piece of cover defence. Brooke had his winger unmarked outside him but did not expect Coote to have the speed to come across and tackle him. Coote scored the match-winning try with a swerving run and Australia went on to win the Ashes in Third Test with Coote adding another try to his tally.

The downside to the tour, however, was being away from his family for so long with the Kangaroo Tour lasting more than four months, covering both Christmas and New Year. 'It was tough being away from the family, but for them too,' he says. 'You got £13 a week and I left about £10 at home for them to live on. We got by somehow.'

Selection in the 1968 World Cup followed, again in the second row, but he had the distinction of scoring tries in all four Tests during Australia's unbeaten run in the competition. The tour of New Zealand in 1969 resulted in a drawn Test series and a broken hand. Coote played all three Tests against Great Britain in 1970, winning the Harry Sunderland Medal as the best Australian player in the Ashes series, before leading the World Cup team to England. He then stood down from rep duty for the next three years for personal and business reasons.

'One of the regrets I have is that I could've played a lot more Tests during my career,' he says candidly. 'I didn't realise it until later, but I was hungry to chase a quid – that's why I got into the brewery truck business. I knew where I'd come from and I didn't want to go back there. The desire to become reasonably well-off was very strong for me. I felt bad I didn't represent Australia (in 1971-73) and I didn't go away at the end of 1975 when there was a World Series tour overseas. The brewery said I couldn't leave the truck, and then they said I could, but (touring) was a real disruption to family life.'

Originally named vice-captain to Graeme Langlands in the 1970 World Cup, Coote was charged to lead an Australian squad which had been soundly beaten by Great Britain in the Ashes series earlier that year when 'Chang' was ruled out with a hand injury. He first captained Australia in the 47–11 win over New Zealand at Wigan but missed the next match, an 11–4 loss to Great Britain, after injuring his collarbone. He came back for the next match, leading an Australian team with seven Souths players in the starting line-up (Simms, Branighan, Pittard, Coote, McCarthy, Sait and Walters—O'Neill was selected by pulled out). France won the Test, 17-15, but Australia scraped into the final at Leeds on the score of 'for and against'.

In the tense lead up to the match Coote had to stand against coach Harry Bath in the selection room. 'Ronnie Turner was the hooker in the final but he was injured and mightn't see out the match. Harry wanted to drop Elwyn Walters from the bench because he wasn't winning the ball and replace him with Barry McTaggart. 'Arko' (Manager Ken Arthurson) and I said no, we couldn't take the risk.' To put it mildly, Harry wasn't happy.

Coote remembers Australia's backs-to the-wall, 12–7 victory with immense pride. 'The final at Leeds was unbelievably difficult. Great Britain threw everything at us. Billy Smith and Syd Hynes were sent off, Billy had a sickening cut in his leg where he'd been sprigged,

Lurch O'Neill had his eyebrow opened and Eric Simms got punched in the face after full time by winger John Atkinson when he went up to shake hands. It was such a proud moment for me to hold the World Cup trophy after leading blokes who stood up to everything.'

When Coote returned to Australia and tried to negotiate a new contract with Souths, financial issues came to a head. 'I had just captained my country and they offered $8,000 a season. I knew other blokes in the team were getting a lot more than that. I had my family and my kids' futures at stake. I wanted more money and they just said no.' Coote sat out the opening five games of the season, giving his body the rest it needed after the World Cup and keeping a keen interest in the court case involving Dennis Tutty and the Balmain club. The former Test lock had taken the Tigers to court for 'restraint of trade' after the club blocked his move to Penrith but Coote ultimately came back to the Rabbitohs because, he admits, he missed the game. 'I played in 1971 but I told Souths I wouldn't be going any further if they couldn't upgrade the contract. The club committee just thought I would play out the year and then sign up for another three or four seasons. They wanted to determine both the length of the contract and the amount they thought I was worth.'

Ron Coote finished the year with a fifth consecutive grand final with Souths—scoring one three-pointer and setting up the final try for Bob McCarthy. Then he was gone. 'I had to think that was going to be my last game for Souths. They had no money and the club was falling apart. John O'Neill and Ray Branighan were also coming up for contract and there was no money on the table.' They left Souths before he did. Coote's offer to join the Roosters came at the beginning of 1971, he says. '(Roosters coach) Don Furner lived around the corner from me. Every time I'd come home in the afternoon with the beer truck, he'd be sitting in my lounge-room waiting for me. Easts offered me $12,000, which was a third again on what I was getting at Souths.' But how did his Souths' teammates handle the news?

'I don't remember much being said about it. That was part of the deal. We never discussed money. We were a family.' Looking back on those dramatic times almost forty years ago, Coote says, 'The club could have handled their success better. Souths should have been winning more competitions with those players who went to other clubs. There's no two ways about it. It was just poor management that killed Souths. There was a lot of money coming through the gates during that time and the club was trading well and yet, within two years, the club was almost broke. The club didn't plan for the future. They just seemed to be trapped in the past.'

Coote also considered several other offers. 'Manly wanted me to go there,' he explains, 'and I had an unbelievable offer from Senator Ron McAuliffe to go to Queensland, something like $25,000 a year for four years. It was written on Parliament House stationery. I had a manager at the time named Jim Comans, who later headed up the NSWRL judiciary. He managed me for nothing and handled all the negotiations. The idea of taking the family to Queensland was tough, though. We'd just built a new house in Maroubra which was our family home for 40 years. In the end, going to Easts made sense. It was so close to home and they had a great side. Dad being a former Easts player didn't influence my decision. Arthur Beetson was already there with Mark Harris, Johnny Brass, Jimmy Porter, Billy Mullins ... great players. Jimmy Morgan went there from Souths the previous year and Elwyn Walters came over in 1974.'

Coote was also impressed with Don Furner as a coach. 'Look at our record. We made the grand final in 1972 and then Don left for Queanbeyan. Easts then missed the semis the following year and we won two premierships under Jack Gibson in 1974-75. The main difference between Easts and Souths was the training was much harder, even before Jack got there. Don Furner was a very good coach. He was a student of the game. You can see what he did at Canberra in the 1980s, how he pulled all that together.'

Furner selected Coote over Beetson to captain Easts into the 1972 grand final against Manly, a team that now fielded former Souths players John O'Neill and Ray Branighan. 'If ever there was a game we should have won that was it,' Coote says. '[Manly captain] Freddie Jones scored beside the posts from a knock-on and Ray Branighan scored off a forward pass. I wasn't even going to play in the match. I had a badly corked leg and I dropped the ball over the try-line when [Manly's] Malcolm Reilly came across the top of me.' Manly, which had raced to a 19-4 lead, held on to win 19-14.

Coote had a disappointing season by his own high standards in 1973. 'I'd had a groin injury which was debilitating. If I trained Tuesday I couldn't train on Thursday. No-one could treat it or tell me what it was. I played 20 of 22 games that year but I wasn't that good. I had an operation in the off-season, had a great year in 1974 and decided to make myself available for rep football again.' Coote played in all three Tests against Great Britain, including the Third Test at the SCG in which Graeme Langlands was recalled to the team and Australia retained the Ashes. '"Chang" scored from one of my passes. He blew up at me because he reckoned I passed him the ball too soon and he had to dive to score.'

Coote won his final two premierships in 1974-75 under the coaching of Jack Gibson. 'Jack did a lot of things that were out of the ordinary. He went to America and learned about video sessions, tackle counts, kicking coaches and defensive drills from Dick Nolan who was the coach of the San Francisco 49ers. Before Jack, everyone used to run up and down the field for an hour, practice passing the ball and some attacking moves and then go to the pub. He had a pretty good team with the Roosters, but putting all those things into place really gelled with us. Jack was also a life-skills coach … he'd tell you about life and how you should perform in life. He said he'd never put a mug on the field beside you. He'd weed them out. We were very tight as a group—we used to train and socialise with the lower grade guys and put on variety nights where we would all perform an item. It was a very happy club.'

In 1976 Coote was in good form but he broke his left arm in a match against Manly at Brookvale Oval. 'I hit Graham Eadie on the head,' Coote remembers. 'He just put his head down in a tackle. It was stupid—just one of those things.' Although he played only half a season that year, he was still named Easts' 'Player of the Year'. He then contracted a golden staph infection and almost died (Coote has a huge scar down the length of his inside forearm as a memento of that injury). He came back in 1977, playing nine games, but lasted only another nine games in 1978 before calling it quits. 'Kerry Packer was giving me a lot of money, [captain-coach] Arthur Beetson supported me and I was determined to make it back onto the field and not let it beat me. I was still training well but I just wasn't the same athlete. I had an offer to go to Balmain as captain-coach in 1977 but I couldn't do that to the Tigers. I thought I had a lot to offer as a coach but only if I was healthy.'

When Bob Fulton took over as Roosters captain-coach in 1979, Coote coached reserve grade. Two years later he was running his first McDonalds franchise at Newtown. 'I had done well out of the game and I met the people at McDonalds. I thought it was a great organisation ... they had a great image and I could see them going places. McDonalds only started in Australia in 1972 and there were still only a handful of restaurants in Sydney at the time. I've made many life-long friends among the people at McDonalds.'

And the future? 'I'm still a McDonalds franchisee. I had stores at Marrickville, Kings Cross and Maroubra but I still hold the licence at Ulladulla. What I'm doing now is putting my kids into them. I have my daughter Natalie and her husband at Nowra and I've just bought one at Bomaderry. Donna, who has lived down here since she got married, runs the store at Ulladulla.'

In the early 1980s, 40 hectares (100 acres) of bushland at Lake Conjola, just north of Ulladulla, came up for sale. Ron and his wife, who regularly went out to dinner with the O'Neills, the Stevenses and the Pigginses, bought the land in partnership with his former teammates. George Piggins and Claire O'Neill are neighbours, although Gary Stevens never built on his lot and has a holiday house on the other side of the lake. 'We've got a great unique part of the world here which we really enjoy,' says Ron, who now lives on his property full-time.

'I still see Bob McCarthy,' he says. 'He and his wife had Christmas down here with us. We've been mates for a long time – since we were kids together and toured New Zealand. I'm still close with George – I'm going for a horse ride with him tomorrow.'

And he keeps in contact with hundreds of ex-players through the Men of League organisation. 'The Men of League does important work to keep the reputation and profile of rugby league high in the community. I believe that in the future we can be a force that will help to combat Aussie Rules coming in and taking our juniors. I think the saviour of rugby league must be the new deal the game does with the television rights.'

Coote fires off numbers quickly, stating that League received $500 million for the last five-year deal yet Aussie Rules received $780 million—despite the fact that league consistently out-rates Rules and we have such a better product, with State of Origin and Test matches. 'And that's where they've got the money to go into the development of their code and can throw a million dollars at rugby league players like Israel Folau and Karmichael Hunt and just drive another nail into the coffin. It's just a silent killer, Aussie Rules. They're everywhere and although they say they're not going to impact on us their whole goal is to kill off rugby league in Sydney's West by getting the young kids on board.'

When Souths was excluded from the 2000 NRL competition, Coote marched to Town Hall with all the other ex-Rabbitohs. 'I was glad Souths got back in. Rugby league needs Souths. I'm a passionate rugby league man—I have been in the game all my life and it's been really good to me. Any success I've had, I've learnt through rugby league and the lessons the game taught me on and off the field.'

Coote has high hopes for the new Independent Commission that heads up the game, and the financial reward garnered from the last television deal, but with one proviso. 'I've had nothing to do with the new setup but the fans shouldn't be kept in the dark. The game is owned by the fans – the people who pay their money each week to go to the game or watch it on television. Without them you've got nothing.'

Ron Coote may have spent his life 'chasing a quid', but he's put a hell of a lot back into the game. 'We'll be hanging in there as long as we can for a few more years yet.'

MICHAEL CLEARY
(1967–70)

By any measure, The Honorable Michael Cleary, AO, parlayed a unique sporting career into an extraordinary public life. One of only a handful of Australian sportsmen to represent their country in three sports—rugby union, rugby league and athletics—Cleary played a pivotal role in saving the Souths club from bankruptcy in the mid 1970s and was the State Member for Coogee from 1974 to 1991 where he served as the Minister for Sport and Recreation in successive Labor governments. Not bad for a man who, by his own admission, never read a book at school, suffered from hyperactivity for years before the term Attention Deficit Disorder (ADD) was even coined and discovered he was dyslexic when he stood to read a speech on the floor of State Parliament.

Michael Arthur Cleary was born in Randwick on 30 April 1940. The son of well-known Bondi Junction businessman Arthur Cleary, who ran the family menswear shop for 48 years, Cleary says, 'My father used to always say I was born with a silver spoon in my mouth, but he shoved it up my arse. We got evicted from our house during the war because my eldest brother taught us how to do SOS signals out the window with our torches when the blackouts were on. Dad said to the local member, "What do they mean, get out of the house?

I've got five kids." We moved down the road and Mum filled the air-raid shelter with Milk Arrowroot biscuits. What do we do? We go down there and eat them. By the time the Japanese submarines came into Sydney Harbour and they're bombing the place, there's no biscuits left when she goes to the biscuit tin at 3 o'clock in the morning. We were buggers!'

A talented athlete at Christian Brothers Waverley, where he was a member of the school's champion rugby team, Cleary was offered a scholarship to study at the prestigious Stanford University in California but chose to stay in Australia to make the Olympic team in 1960.

Glandular fever ruined that dream, but Cleary made a name for himself playing rugby for Randwick that year. 'Cyril Towers and Wally Meagher invited me to trial for Randwick. I thought I'd get into fifth division but I made first grade. I still hold the record down there for scoring seven tries in a game against Eastwood at Coogee Oval. It was just hyperactivity—natural ability—I guess. Anything with a bat or a ball I could play ... except golf.'

Cleary represented Australia in six rugby union Tests in 1961 and toured South Africa with the Wallabies. He had a number of offers from rugby league. Canterbury's Peter Moore and Frank Facer from St George both tried to set up meetings with him. 'My father said, "Don't go to them. Let them come to you and sit in your lounge-room."' Souths' Joe Maloney, who had just signed Cleary's Wallaby teammate Jimmy Lisle, came to the family home and asked if he wanted to play rugby league. 'I'd never thought about it because I'd only ever seen one game before that – Souths playing St George in 1959 – and I didn't know too much about the game.'

Cleary told Maloney that he didn't want to turn professional because he wanted to represent Australia in the Empire Games (now called the Commonwealth Games) which were being held in Perth in 1962. It was suggested that Cleary could play rugby league as an amateur. 'Joe explained, "You don't get paid. I haven't promised you anything. I just told you what you could earn but I have not told you what you would get." The amateur rules were so strong that when I won a Seiko watch from Frank Hyde as man-of-the-match in 1962, I couldn't keep it. It was valued at £21/10p ($43) and the limit for an amateur was £18/10p ($19) for the year.'

Although Souths finished equal last in 1962, Cleary was a sensation in the professional game. He scored 11 tries in the opening five matches of the season, including four against Manly. Selected for NSW against Great Britain, he was among six players sent off in a fiery match played in front of 60,000 fans at the SCG. Selected in the First Test of the Ashes series, Cleary admits that he was given a 'torrid initiation' by his opposite number, Great Britain's Mick Sullivan, but he learned fast. At the end of the year he achieved his goal of representing his country at the Empire Games and won a bronze medal in the 100 yard sprint final with a personal best time of 9.3 seconds.

Although he wasn't paid in his first season of rugby league he quickly learned about professionalism and the respect that came with it. 'When I toured with the 1963–64 Kangaroos, Reg Gasnier and Peter Dimond were in the team. They didn't like each other on the field but they had a great deal of respect for each other off the field. I asked them one day, "How do you get on so well?" Peter, who became a great mate of mine, said, "We respect each other and what you've got to learn about league is respect for your opponent. If you're silly enough to put your hand on the ground and they don't walk on it then that's a sign of weakness on their side. You learn not to put your hand down on the ground because a professional League player doesn't do that."

Cleary came back for that Ashes-winning tour, where he scored 14 tries in 21 appearances, including a Test match against France, and Souths had a new coach, a new attitude and a new generation of juniors coming through. 'Bernie Purcell came to first grade and he took it seriously. He coached us. He introduced a special pay system that if you played for Australia you had a signing fee of £2000, if you played for NSW it was £1500, if you played for Sydney you had £1000. After that you could negotiate for whatever you could get. That put a system into place where no-one had to worry about what anyone else was getting.'

1964 was a stark improvement on Cleary's first two seasons with the club and the 1965 grand final against St George produced scenes 'never seen before and never seen again,' Cleary remembers. 'I remember Jimmy Lisle saying to me early in the game, "Come round me, come round me!" So foolishly enough I came round him, he gave me the ball and I looked up and there was Kevin Ryan in front of me. I finished up with my head coming out of my arse! I actually used that story in Parliament when we were talking about an amendment to the Chiropractic Act. You wouldn't believe it but five minutes later in that match, Jimmy said to me, "Come round me." And I said, "Get stuffed!" He had to pivot around himself and ran right into Ryan!'

Cleary says that he had an uncanny ability to 'do the impossible', but didn't have the reliability of top wingers like Eddie Lumsden, Johnny King, Ken Irvine and Peter Dimond. 'If I was playing well, I played very well. If I was playing badly, well ... My weakness was my unreliability. I could do things that that most players couldn't do. I went through the whole Manly team from a 25 yard restart and zigzagged my way to the corner—sidestepped right through the whole team from a kick-off—but 10 minutes later I would do something stupid. I wasn't a strong defender. I could do it when I had to but I was more an electrifying runner. I had that much nervous tension in my body because I was so hyperactive, I used to just swoop on loose balls and I could catch them from anywhere.'

Teammate Bob McCarthy rates Cleary as the fastest player he ever saw in football boots. 'I raced Kenny Irvine for £1000 one year and beat him,' Cleary says. 'We had great rivalry and we were great mates but I wasn't in his class. Both of us played on the right wing so Mike Gibson, the *Daily Telegraph* journo said to me one day, "Why don't you ask if you can mark Ken Irvine?" Not only did I give him the headline, "Cleary to Mark Irvine" but I gave him the headline for the next week as well ... 'Irvine Smashes Cleary.' I gave Gibbo a gobful the next time I saw him at the SCG. He still remembers the story.'

Grand final success wouldn't be far away for Souths. 'Bobby McCarthy got the big intercept against Canterbury in 1967 and ran the length of the field,' Cleary recalls. 'Macca said he was looking around for me and I was playing hopscotch in the corner. I actually came off at half time with massive swelling on the knee. [NSWRL President] Bill Buckley said, "Mate, don't you go back on with that. You're going to England." I didn't go back on the field and then I wasn't picked in the Kangaroo squad that night either. That's just the way things go.'

Coming back into the top grade after a bout of pneumonia in the winter of 1968, Cleary was the only try-scorer for Souths in the 13–9 win over Manly in the grand final. Midway through the first half, Manly winger Les Hanigan, (incidentally, a Kangaroo tourist the previous year) fumbled the pass from Bob Batty and Cleary picked up the ball on the fly and sprinted 60 yards to score untouched. 'After I tore my groin muscle on the tour of New Zealand in 1969 I was a casualty right through to the end of my career in 1971. Everyone thought it was a hamstring injury—it wasn't treated properly and I was never quite the same player.'

After fighting his way back into the NSW team in 1969, Cleary withdrew from the interstate match in Brisbane with a throat infection but was still in good enough form to join six Souths teammates on the mini tour of New Zealand. A torn groin muscle ruled him out of the First Test in Auckland and despite scoring four tries in a midweek match against Wellington, he succumbed to the injury in the lead-up to the Second Test. 'I blame [champion Canterbury fullback] Les Johns,' he smiles. 'We were finishing up training and Les said, "c'mon, one more sprint" and I tore it for good.'

The grand final was a sobering way to finish a record-breaking season for the defending premiers. Balmain led Souths 6-0 at the break and went on to win 11–2. '[Balmain halfback] Terry Parker, who finished up as manager of the Souths club, came out in the second half and hit the deck before the ball was even kicked. [Balmain captain] Peter Provan turned around to him and said, "Terry, not yet, not yet! Get up!" We found out later he'd had a rub before the game and they got balsam on his balls and they were on fire! So that was an indication of what they were doing. They played it perfectly. Every time our momentum got going they'd hit the deck and stop play and we just couldn't get going.'

Cleary sees 1970 as the start of the downward slide. It was also his last year with the club. The grand final against Manly, though, has taken on legendary status. 'John Sattler was tough as nails and he had this philosophy that you never showed the enemy that you were hurt. There were many times Satts would come over to you and say, "What's wrong?" You'd say your knee was hurt and he'd say, "Get up or else I'll smash you in the mouth!" And he'd make you get up. You would never show you were hurt.' That's why Satts stayed out on the field in the grand final against Manly, Cleary says. Never show the bastards you're hurt.

'Satts was out on the wing with me so I asked, "What are you doing out here?" He said, "Just hold me up." What do you mean —hold me up? He said, "Grab my shorts. Hold me up." I grabbed his trousers, held him up and asked what was wrong. He said, "I've broken my jaw." I said, "Oh shit! You better hold me up!" because when he looked at me his jaw just hung down and I nearly fainted.'

Sattler was in shock after making the victory speech and he was whisked to South Sydney Hospital. 'We all went to the Leagues Club and had cold pies and hot beer while the directors went to a restaurant in Woolahra. When they came back to the club later that night John O'Neill and me gave it to [President] Dennis Donoghue and [Secretary] Charlie Gibson. "There's Sattler in intensive care and you've been celebrating our victory at a restaurant in the city! Well, go and get nicked!"'

Cleary got a cold reply when he went to negotiate his contract before the start of the 1971 season. 'Instead of the $4000 ceiling that had been set by Bernie Purcell, I was on $3000 a year and $120 a win, when the basic rate for an international was $4000 sign on and $40 a win. The league at that stage put the winning bonus up to $80 so I said all I wanted was the $3000 signing on fee and instead of $120 a win, I wanted $160 to bring me into line with the League's increase. Souths said no. It was quite obvious they wanted me out of the place because I was a trouble-maker. I'd spoken up against them. I also realised a few other practices at the club weren't right ... things I fixed later on.'

A colleague of Cleary's at WR Miller was Ron Jones, the secretary at Eastern Suburbs. After talking to Jones, Cleary signed a two-year contract with the Roosters for $5000 a season. 'I lasted 12 months,' he says. Injuries limited him to 11 games in 1971, his tenth year in the game, and when he knew wasn't going to 'make the grade' he asked to be released from the final year of his contract. 'I just missed my mates so much at Souths,' he says. 'I couldn't perform at my best and I retired.' The worse thing about 1971, Cleary admits, was that Souths won the grand final without him. He should have been there.

Having let many of their star players sign with other clubs, Souths was effectively broke by 1973. Cleary formed a 'Save Souths' Committee with club stalwarts Johnny Riordan, his father Arthur Cleary, Don Davies, Don Walker, Jack Purcell, Bernie Purcell, Norm 'Nipper' Nilson and Jack Coyne and challenged the existing Board. 'We marched down to League headquarters for a formal meeting, only to find I was locked out because I wasn't a member of the football club. That was the worst thing that they could have done because it brought them all undone. We finished up getting control of the Board. I took on a management role because the club lost $260,000 that year. We made $160,000 profit in six months and the big question from everyone was—how did we do it? There was a very simple answer ... we banked the money!'

They were heady times at Souths with everyone helping out—not unlike the fight to bring Souths back into the NRL after its exclusion in 1999. 'Don Lane put on a concert and raised $13,000,' Cleary recalls,' everyone pitched in. Bernie Purcell and I were at the Redfern Town Hall taking debentures [a bond acknowledging a debt that allows you to borrow money as an unsecured loan] to keep the club open and I got a call from the Chief Secretary's Department telling us we were both going to finish up in jail. I asked, "How are we going to finish up in jail?" He said we were asking for debentures and hadn't issued a prospectus [a legal document that outlines a business's securities or assets]. So we changed the receipt from a debenture to a loan. We kept out of jail and kept the club open,' he laughs. 'We carried on there for a number of years and then George Piggins and his team took over.'

The management team went to Cronulla the following year and saved the Sharks Club from bankruptcy. 'My years at Souths were fantastic,' Cleaery says, even acknowledging his affluent background at a working class football club. 'I came over to League as an "elite" person—that's how I was regarded. "Lummy" Longbottom used to ask if I could get him a shirt (I was selling shirts at the time) and I said "I can get you anything you want". We were silver-tails I suppose. Although my father was financially comfortable, when I turned professional he said, "Son, you're on your own now. I can't do any more for you. You handle all your own negotiations."'

Mike says his father never followed a rugby league team, preferring to play pennant bowls on a Saturday afternoon, but he became a very proud supporter of his. There is a wonderful film clip of the 1965 grand final showing Arthur Cleary sitting among the record crowd with a miniature TV—very much state of the art in the mid 1960s —watching his other son Denis play in the rugby union grand final. 'I brought that TV back from Singapore on my way back from the 1963-64 Kangaroo Tour,' Mike says proudly.

'Everyone knew when to come and see Arthur Cleary and get an order for a new suit,' Mike says. 'It was after I'd had a good game. I wasn't that consistent so it wouldn't be every week!'

I remind Cleary that he was one of the first players to use his public image to his advantage and that he started the trend of footballers doing modeling. A generation of television viewers who have been subjected to footballers doing Lowes ads have him to thank, I say. 'People used to ask, "Why do you get off the plane first?" I'd say, "Because they're the ones they take the photograph of." I always had this marketing and merchandising mindset. I used to drive people mad. My brother Denis used to take me to Nielsen Park to the Butcher's Picnic and he'd get me into the picnic races. He promoted me. He pushed me. He was younger than me but I never even thought of those things. I never even wanted to go and play football. I never thought I'd play for Australia.'

The chance to model came from a friendship with Tony Madigan, the Commonwealth light-heavyweight boxing champion. 'I used to train with him in Centennial Park and went to Perth with him in 1962. He had come back from America and had modelled in New York. He said to me, "You're a professional now, son. You make sure that you make a quid." When I went into modelling I got branded "Michelle" but it was great pay. I'd do commercials for Ernest Hillier and I'd be getting 70 quid a day. I was doing modelling at Farmer's Young Man shop getting £50–70 for one and a half hours of parade work. When I was selected on the 1963–64 Kangaroo Tour I went down to Marks and Sparks and got modelling jobs for Kenny Irvine, Johnny Raper, Peter Dimond and myself.' When the basic wage was £10-12 a week, modelling would often bring £300-400 a year.

Cleary got over the 'Michelle' taunts but admits that it did affect his confidence early in his career. 'People used to say, "Lift up your skirt" and "hit him with your handbag." And I used to say, "Which handbag? The one I've got in the bank or the one I've got on my arm?" he laughs. When humour didn't work, Cleary went another route. 'I got into a fight one day at Pratten Park. I was injured that day and I was on the hill with my golden retriever. This bloke called out, "I thought you were a "cat" Cleary, not a dog man." He was doing it in jest but I didn't know. I asked someone to hold the dog and smashed him straight in the mouth.' Don Lane, the 'Lanky Yank', was with Cleary that day and came to his defence, as did several Souths players. 'John Sattler said that all he could see was Don's head sticking out above the fight,' Cleary laughs.

Mike Cleary was close friends with Don Lane, the American-born entertainer who came to this country in 1966 to star in his own variety show on Channel 9. In 2009, Cleary delivered the eulogy at Lane's funeral after he passed away, age 75, from the onset of dementia. 'I was running around town with Don during the 1960s … it was a fabulous time,' Cleary smiles. 'I introduced Don to Souths, but also (Irish comedian) Dave Allen and (Channel 9 musician) Geoff Harvey. The Souths players were like superstars at a time when rugby league wasn't on TV so much. We'd get 30,000–40,000 people at the match of the day at the SCG. I was living at Darling Point with mum and dad and I'd pick Don Lane up and we'd go to Sydney Stadium on a Friday night and watch the wrestling … Tex Mackenzie, Red Bastene and Killer Kawolski, and all the old-time wrestlers.'

Before each wrestling bout, celebrities were introduced to the crowd and Cleary, being a popular sportsman of the era, received a huge cheer. 'Jim Barnett, the American wrestling promoter at the time, said, "I didn't know you were so famous, my boy. I'm going to make you a referee." Cleary was skeptical of the effeminate American promoter motives but he did become a wrestling commentator on Channel 9 when his playing career ended. What did he make of the wrestlers? Were they athletes or entertainers? 'I used to describe it as ballroom dancing. One wrestler led and the other followed and if you didn't know how to dance you'd get hurt. As they explained it to me—if I take your hand, you give it to me. If you resist, you get hurt. That's the game that they played. If I put your arm up your back, you bend over. They didn't rehearse but they did 10 shows a week so they knew what they were doing.'

Cleary went into politics about the same time as the 'Save Souths' campaign. '[State Labor Opposition Leader] Pat Hills approached me and said, "Have you ever thought of going into politics?" I was member of the Labor Party because Pat was a patron at Souths and he put me in there, but I said I wasn't interested. Don Lane told me I was mad and to have a go.' Cleary was nominated for pre-selection as the Labor candidate for the seat of Coogee. When he rang his brother Denis, Cleary learned his brother was going for pre-selection as the Liberal candidate for the same seat.

'I rang up Pat Hills and said, "Mate, it's all off. I'm not going to stand against my brother. He said, "No, you can beat him." I said, "No, I won't beat him. He's captain of the Surf Club and the March Past leader. He plays rugby for Randwick and has represented NSW. He lives in Coogee—and not only that, he's the Amateur Boxing Champion of Australia and he can knock me out." But then the Liberal Party didn't pick him for the seat.' Cleary lost his first election by a narrow margin but contested the verdict and won a bi-election by 54 votes. He was a Member of Parliament for the next 17 years.

'I was Minister for Sport, Racing and Tourism for eight years until 1988. I think the highlight from that time might be the start of FootyTAB. Jack Gibson actually helped me do it. Jack sold all the fixture cards around the hotels and service stations in Sydney at the time and showed us how to do it. We then brought in PubTAB. I spoke to the SP bookies around Sydney. That was the thing about being an ex-footballer. I could go and talk to people who most politicians couldn't talk to. I said we would make PubTAB punting close 15 minutes before the jump of a race. That gave them a window to get their bets on. The deal was they were going to lay off their bets on the TAB so we weren't going to lose revenue. They didn't keep their part of the bargain so we closed off at five minutes before the jump, and later, at the jump of the race.' The government picked up $700 million a year in revenue.

'Fifteen percent of that money went back into consolidated

revenue and into the clubs and racecourse development funds,' Cleary says. 'FootyTAB initially brought in about $17 million, of which 10 percent was put into a special sports fund.' Brookvale Oval, Redfern Oval and WIN Stadium in Wollongong were upgraded and the stand at Campbelltown Stadium was built for $3.5 million. 'That's all gone now with the privatisation of the TAB. That fund doesn't exist anymore. The State Government went into partnership with the Federal Government and Parramatta Council and built Parramatta Stadium in 1986. The Sydney Football Stadium was built for the bargain price of $65 million. 'You couldn't do it today for under $200 million. The basis of all that gave us the nucleus to bid for the Olympic Games in 2000 because we had the existing infrastructure.'

It was during his parliamentary career that he realised he was dyslexic. 'If I had to deliver a speech I had to get briefed under headings and then ad lib. Being both dyslexic and hyperactive, I fluked may way through it,' he says modestly. The previous Liberal members for Coogee had been the Speaker of the House, who never asked a question on the floor for 12 years, and the representative whose legitimacy was successfully contested by Cleary in 1974. 'And he never asked a question in the six months he was there either,' Cleary recalls. The people of Coogee never had a better public servant to represent them.

When he left politics in 1991, Cleary worked for Sky Channel as advertising manager, did some work for the Australia Hotels Association and worked for the TAB. He had bought property, including the Oxford Tavern at Petersham, as far back as the early 1970s and invested wisely. Retired now to the inner city suburb of Birchgrove, he remains on the Board of the NSWRL and is a member of the Sydney Cricket Ground Trust.

Cleary feels Souths are now in a good position to go forward. 'George Piggins did a great job and fought hard for the club after the Super League war. He's a fine fellow with all his dedication and strong beliefs. I'm really happy that Souths are where they are now—a club with so much identity from the foundation of the game in 1908—to be still involved in rugby league today is absolutely fantastic. Russell Crowe and his team are to be congratulated. They've done a marvellous job marketing the club and have the largest membership of any rugby league club in the NRL. It's fantastic. Glory, glory to South Sydney!'

Cleary is also a huge fan of the work Men of League do in the rugby league community and is at forefront of the changes that are happening in the game today. 'In my capacity on the NSWRL Board it was John Chalk from Balmain who moved the motion that an Independent Commission be formed to run the game and I seconded it. I am a great supporter of the Independent Commission. It was inevitable; it had to come and I believe it's the only way to go. The only problem is that they have to handle (the transition) correctly. Nine of the clubs are now privately owned. It's not just about the clubs getting more the money. You've also got to think about junior rugby league and the development of the game.

'The future of the game rests with the Commission.'

BOB GRANT
(1968–71)

In the 1970 grand final against Manly, South Sydney halfback Bobby Grant produced the game of life. With captain John Sattler remaining on field after having his jaw smashed in a vicious, off-the-ball incident, Grant guided the team around the field, scored two tries and set up another in a 'man of the match' performance. Less than 24 hours later, when Australia's World Cup squad was selected, Grant's name was missing from the selectors' list despite eight other Souths players being chosen in the 19-man squad. 'I was supposed to be there,' Grant says, 40 years later, 'but I got lost in the politics.'

Blind Freddy could not have missed Grant's star turn in the 1970 grand final. Good enough to deputise for an injured Billy Smith in the Third Test against Great Britain earlier that year, he was not rated good enough to be the shadow halfback behind Smith after winning a bloody premiership. How could that have been? Sometimes, in pursuit of state politics, selectors could not see the wood for trees. In a season dominated by NSW stars, it appears the Queensland selectors were resigned to having a token representation in Australia's World Cup squad. Their first choice, forward Col Weiss, was to be the second choice lock behind Ron Coote but Weiss was injured in the Brisbane grand final and the Queenslanders looked set for an embarrassing shut-out.

Coach Harry Bath allegedly did the deal. He told the Queensland selectors that they could choose one player for the squad if they backed his choice of Gary Sullivan as back-up lock to Ron Coote. Bath was coaching Newtown in the Sydney premiership at the time and Sullivan, a fine player who represented Australia again in 1972, was Bath's club lock. The Queenslanders chose little-known Ipswich halfback Johnny Brown as their sole representative on the tour and Bobby Grant missed out. Billy Smith played in all four Tests in the World Cup while Brown was relegated to one minor tour match.

Robert John Grant was born on 5 June 1946. A Balmain junior, he played with the Glebe Youth Club and the famous Coddocks Club. As a teenager he represented Balmain's Jersey Flegg team in three consecutive seasons before being called up to President's Cup in 1964. Graded as a halfback in third grade the same year, he moved to second grade in 1965. 'You got a lot of stick in second grade,' Grant remembers. 'You had older blokes coming back from first grade and younger blokes coming up, trying to make a name for themselves.'

Bobby Grant played seven first grade matches in 1965 when the Tigers' regular halfback, Laurie Fagan, broke his leg. 'Balmain had a really good team in 1965 ... [former Great Britain international[Davey Bolton was in the centres, Peter Jones was the five-eighth and Keith Barnes was the fullback.' Under the limited tackle rule of the time, the 19-year-old was developing good field vision and instinctive organisational skills to be able to direct the forwards and backs. He also had good leg speed and a nice step in his wiry frame.

At the end of the year, Grant picked up the *Sydney Morning Herald* one day to find that Balmain had placed him on the open transfer list for the bargain basement price of £200. 'It's just how it was done in the 1960s ... if a club wanted to off-load players, they published the transfer fee in the papers. Des Bryan [the former Balmain halfback who played in losing grand finals with the Tigers in 1947 and Souths in 1949] was at Souths and he got in touch with me and took me over to the club and introduced me to Bernie Purcell. I had a trial with them and the next thing I knew I was a South Sydney player.'

Souths' second grade team in 1966 was full of future first grade stars—Gary Stevens, Elwyn Walters and George Piggins—as well as established clubmen such as Wayne Stevens, Colin Dunn, Denis Lee, Alan Scott and Mick Falla. Grant 'fell into a really good side', he says, but first grade halfback Ivan Jones proved to be a very hard nut to crack and the former Balmain junior did not play a single first grade match in 1966 or 1967. He did, however, win a reserve grade grand final against his old club Balmain in 1966, although the Tigers got one back on him the following year. Considering what happened in the 1969 grand final, it would prove hard for Grant to shrug off his former club's shadow.

Under the four-tackle rule a halfback had a limited number of attacking options before the ball was invariably kicked downfield. 'You just had to look more and see where the gaps were,' Grant says. 'It was up to me to know where the players were going to run—to send McCarthy up the blind side or get him running wide off the five-eighth. Then you would use Ron Coote the same way. I'd tell Elwyn [Walters, the hooker and dummy half] or George [Piggins], to take it in twice among the forwards and tell Macca or Ronnie that I'd pick him up on the third tackle coming down on the blind side. And when they ran, the wingers were there ready outside them if they made the break. Satts used to say a bit to get the forwards fired up early but then he'd quiet down and I would say my part. It was my job to run the backs and get the forwards going forward. I told a few of them to go and get … whatever … when they didn't do what I told them,' he smiles.

'At Souths, the forwards were nearly as fast as the backs. So you had to have them running one way and then make sure the backs picked them up on the next tackle.'

In 1968 Grant played several first grade games, but when Ivan Jones was injured in the club's semi-final loss to Manly, he was called into first grade for the preliminary final against St George. Souths defeated Saints 20–8 to qualify for the grand final and Grant held his position for the premiership decider. 'I thought we had the game shot to pieces at 13–2 when they awarded the try to Pogo Morgan in the corner. I'm sure me and a couple of other blokes took him out. In those days if you hit the corner post you were out but the ref ruled a try. We were in a bit of trouble there for a while.'

Bobby Grant remained coach Clive Churchill's choice as number one halfback at Souths for the next seven seasons. 'Clive was great. He was like one of the boys. You would have your arguments with him but then you would have a beer and it was all forgotten. I would say to him, "I'll try your way and if it doesn't work I'm going to do it my way".' The best part about being at Souths was that when we had a barbecue it wasn't just for the first grade, it was for all three grades. It was just like one big family. 'If one went to the pub, we all went to the pub. If one had a barbecue, we all went to the barbecue. It was a very close club.'

The following year, Grant had to have a painkiller injection to take his place in the 1969 grand final after he injured his finger in a jackhammer accident while working for the council. The tip of the finger had been severed and sewn back on, but his memories of that controversial grand final are short and to the point. 'I remember the Tigers got plenty of help. Every time we looked like making a break, referee Keith Page would pull it up. If we played them another 10 times we would have beat them 10 times. But on that day Balmain did play well,' he concedes. 'They used their tactics to slow the game down. They were up in your face all the time and they didn't give us any room. They tackled well and we just didn't adapt to what was going on.

'About 20 minutes to go I said to Satts that something's going wrong here. We always had a play ready on the third or fourth tackle but we never got to the third or fourth tackle. We would get to the second tackle and there would be another scrum or penalty.' Grant is still invited to Balmain player reunions. 'Yeah, the Tigers' boys still give it to me about that match. Every time they have a turnout they invite me.'

The following year Bobby Grant represented City Seconds and was called up for Test duty at a dire time in Ashes history. Great Britain had thrashed Australia in the Second Test in Sydney, 28-7, and selectors were desperately trying to choose a team to save the Ashes in Third Test. With Billy Smith nursing a broken thumb, the selectors chose Grant. 'We were having a barbecue out at [Club President] Dennis Donoghue's place. We were all there and we got a message that I was in the team along with Macca, Ronnie and Elwyn so it ended up a big night. I thought they might have called up [Manly's] Dennis Ward because he had played in a Test before. It was a shock, really.

'Australia had three different captains that year—Langlands in the First Test, Satts in the Second Test and Phil Hawthorne in the Third Test when the other two got injured.' Grant partnered the former rugby union Test five-eighth in the Ashes decider. 'Phil was a nice man but he was very nervous before the match. Poor bugger had the weight of the world on his shoulders. Arthur Summons was coach and we only had two training sessions out at Cronulla or somewhere. Eric Simms should have played in that Test but he was injured so [Easts'] Allan McKean played fullback. And he almost won it for us too. McKean kicked seven goals that day and Macca scored a freak try but Artie Beetson threw an intercept pass and that was it.'

Australia were beaten by a better team, 23–17, but would have the final say at Leeds in the World Cup final. The only thing was, Bobby Grant wouldn't be there.

The 1970 grand final was Grant's fifth straight grand final appearance for the Rabbitohs in either first or second grade. It proved to be the defining match of his career. Grant scored the first and last tries of the match and marshalled the team after captain John Sattler had his jaw broken and could not call out to his players, but Satts was always a steely presence on the field. 'You couldn't get him out of the way,' Grant says. 'Satts would call for the ball and I would pass it to someone else. Next minute he would bob up and he would have the ball in his hands. We were trying to protect him but he didn't want protecting. He yelled at me, "Stop cutting me out!" He actually pushed John O'Neill out of the way to get to the ball.'

Grant scored the first try when he backed up a Bob McCarthy charge at the Manly line. 'Macca threw the ball inside to me and I jinked and beat the defence.' He then set up the try for winger Ray Branighan which set up a 12–6 lead. Grant's second try, midway through the second half, was all his own doing. 'I said to Eric Simms at training, "I will run to you one time out there, and Manly will think it's going to be a field goal, and I am gonna take off. He said "yeah, yeah." So when the Manly players moved across to block Simms, I just took off and the gap just opened up. As I walked back with the ball I said to him, "I told you that was gonna happen."

In 2008, the NRL retrospectively awarded Clive Churchill Medals for the 'man of the match' in each of the grand finals from 1954 to 1985. Grant was a standout selection for 1970 but it was not enough to get him into Australia's World Cup team. 'I said they should have taken the entire Souths team in 1970 and added another six or seven to form the squad,' he laughs. There were many Souths fans who would agree.

The following year Grant played in all the major rep teams after St George halfback Billy Smith broke his arm in the match against Souths. After making his state debut in the second match of the series at Lang Park, Grant's selection in the Australian squad to tour New Zealand tended to make a mockery of his omission the previous September. But for the second, and last, time in his career, Grant was again on the losing side.

Grant certainly earned his fare to New Zealand. 'I played for Souths before we left; the three games on tour, including the Test on Saturday, and for Souths again on the Sunday.' Grant believes the Australian selectors got it wrong again. 'Changa Langlands and Satts shouldn't have played because they were injured. When they took the squad over there they knew the players weren't fit. The selectors thought they would get over their injuries in the week leading up to the Test but they never did. They picked the wrong team for the Test and the Kiwis just flogged us in the mud.'

Grant's understudy on the Kiwi tour was 21-year old Wests' halfback Tommy Raudonikis. 'We ended up good mates, me and Tommy. I played one game with him over there, against Auckland, with Tommy playing five-eighth. He wouldn't cop anything, Tommy, even in those days. He didn't give a shit. He'd kick and jump on them … whatever it took.'

The season finished with another grand final, but it was to be the club's last. 'We led 11–0 but we just kind of eased a bit and St George took full advantage of it. We played the game in the forwards. George [Piggins, the replacement hooker] wanted to run the ball all the time so I would go in to dummy half and we had six running forwards in the second half. When I wanted to get the ball to the backs I just stepped back out and George would go into the dummy half and we would work it from there.'

Quiet by nature, Grant never seemed to get on the wrong side of referees. 'You can't do anything about it once the whistle goes. I never abused them. Tommy Raudonikis would always abuse them. Whenever we played Wests I would say, "Keep abusing, Tom" and next minute we would get the penalty. I just shut my mouth …'

Grant formed a championship halfback combination with Denis Pittard at Souths and the pair appeared in the same four grand final together. 'We just kind of clicked. I would say we're going the blind side or something and he never argued with me. Early in the grand final, he made a long run and got tackled a yard from the line and almost scored. But then he used to always go as far as he could to get to the try line. Denis was a very good player and he used to back himself all the time.'

Grant took no interest in the contractual negotiations that

ultimately saw John O'Neill, Ray Branighan and Ron Coote leave the club at the end of 1971. 'I couldn't have cared less if I got paid or not,' he says. 'I just liked playing the game. That was it in a nutshell. I never had to go and ask for contract money. The club just gave it to me.'

Souths were still competitive through 1972 to 1974 but slowly the players left because the club hoped the new generation of juniors coming through would be able to take the place of their champions. They never did but Grant always gave his best. 'In 1972 we got beaten by St George in the minor semi-final, we missed the play-offs by a point in 1973 when we were beaten in the last game and we made the semis again in 1974.'

Grant broke his arm in a game against Parramatta in 1974 when he went into tackle lanky forward Denis Fitzgerald. 'I went to clock him and he put his head down and whack!' he laughs. 'Clive Churchill kept on asking, "When will you be right?" And I kept on taking the plaster off and coming back and it would break it in the first few minutes. I'd stay on and play and then they would put it back in plaster and three weeks later the same thing would happen. In the end the doctors put a plate and seven screws in it. It's still in there today. You can still feel the screws through my skin because they sit on the muscle but it doesn't give me any trouble.'

Grant had already made up his mind to retire. 'Partway through the '75 season I thought to myself, this is enough for me. I was happy to retire. I was 29 and I had a few broken bones. My time was up. I got a few offers to go up the bush but I was quite happy to call it a day. Souths had a one year option on my contract but they didn't want to take the option up anyway.' It was indicative of how Souths were running the club at the time. 'The committee wasn't managing things very well and I think the club just lost its spirit right through the committee, the players and even the old supporters.'

Still, he has no regrets. 'Some blokes play football all their lives and don't even get to a grand final. I played nearly all my life in grand finals.' Of all the great players he played with at Souths, Grant holds a special affinity with Paul Sait. 'Saity was very underrated at Souths, especially in the 1970s when many of the club's great players moved on. I had the pleasure with playing with some absolute champions, and Paul Sait was one of the best of them.'

Grant worked for Sydney City Council during his playing days, moonlighting for John O'Neill and Gary Stevens in their renovation business. It wasn't the only moonlighting he did. 'I used to play rugby league for the council in the Domain in the Business Houses competition, which, of course I wasn't allowed to do. It was a breach of contract but a lot of players played in that competition on Wednesday afternoons. We had a pretty good side ... Terry Reynolds and his brother Barry, and Jackie Spencer played for us. But South Sydney Council had just as good a team. I think we beat them in the grand final one year, 4–2.

'One day I looked up and there was Bernie Purcell, who was a selector at the time, standing behind the posts waving his finger at me. I got a kick in the head in one match and I went to training at Souths with about 12 stitches at the side of my head. Clive Churchill asked what happened and I told him I walked into the back of a truck and it had a big steel thing hanging out of it. Bernie was just standing there shaking his head.'

Grant was always naturally fit and there was not too much training needed in the off season. 'A couple of years ago Russell Crowe got us over to Erskineville and we met all the Souths players. They had all the latest gear. I played dumb and asked what the weights were for. I said, "The only weights we picked up in my day were schooners." Well, they all broke out laughing.'

Although he has had a few battles in recent years with illness, Grant looks slim and fit for a man of 65 and has a clean bill of health at the moment. 'I suppose it's scary when you look at someone like Lurch O'Neill who was taken far too early. Jimmy Lisle's death was out the blue. Jimmy Morgan is another one. You have got to look after yourself.' I ask him if he's looking after himself and he says 'not really' with a cheeky smile. 'I go out to the Rusty Shovel and have a beer with [former Souths forward] Darrell Bampton and a few mates.'

Grant and his wife, Elaine, remained in Balmain territory, living first at Pyrmont and after in Haberfield, and raised three children—Troy, Jacqueline and Danelle. They have four grandchildren … 'four little headaches' Bobby calls them. The kids have got his prized Test jerseys—maybe he'll get them framed one day, he says—and also his Souths hat and other pieces of memorabilia. 'The kids say, "That looks nice" and I don't see it again.'

Although he lives in the heart of Balmain territory, he remains a Souths man at heart. A life member of the Football Club, he holds strong views on what's happened to the game over the past decade. 'I think one of the great tragedies was that Balmain and Wests had to merge. Balmain should never have merged. If they had stood alone, they were safe. Wests needed the merge, the Tigers didn't. Souths should never have been put out of the NRL. That was a disgrace. Here was a club that had won the most competitions and produced the most representative players. We walked from Redfern down to Town Hall and people came out of the woodwork to support the club.

'There are just Souths supporters everywhere.'

BRIAN JAMES
(1967–69)

The career of Brian James offers a number of contradictions and ironies. At the end of 1961 the promising Rugby Union centre left St George to play rugby league for the reigning Sydney premiers for no signing fee. After four seasons with the Dragons, a period which brought three reserve grade premierships but, frustratingly, did not see him secure a regular first grade position, he moved to Souths and won the premiership in 1967. A shock omission from the 1967–68 Kangaroo Tour, he then played for Australia the following year after battling glandular fever. In the 1969 grand final, James was denied a try in the upset loss to Balmain and then promptly retired from the game at the height of his career. Lastly, after taking over his father's transport business, he developed a fascination for yachting and has surrounded himself with the water ever since.

I caught up with Brian James at the Superyacht Marina, the business he operates at Sydney's Rozelle Bay. Now aged 67, grey-haired but still fit, he measures his words carefully as we discuss his role in Souths' golden era surrounded by a fleet of 'super yachts' docked at the marina he runs. 'I retired at age 27 and I bought my first boat about a month later,' James says. 'I've been lucky enough to be surrounded by boats ever since then. Dad was a transport carrier and truck stop operator, but he always had a marine interest. The Souths boys used to come down to Dad's place on the waterfront at Blakehurst and have barbecues after the big matches. I still remember those times very fondly.'

Brian Knight James was born in Sydney on 9 April 1943. His father, Jack James, was a talented Country Rugby League player in the 1930s. 'Dad was an old Maher Cup player with Cootamundra. His family ran the Terminus Hotel next to the railway there and operated the Christmas Gift Goldmine at Calinga—which is between "Coota" and Harden—during the Depression Years.' Jack James attended Sydney's Newington College and sent his sons Graham and Brian there after moving the family to Blakehurst and starting the Sydney Haulage Terminal. Brian won an academic scholarship to attend Newington but quickly forged a reputation as a talented athlete, cricketer and rugby player.

'I was a good runner,' he says, 'but nowhere near as fast as Michael Cleary.' Interestingly Cleary, James' wing partner in three successive grand finals at Souths, today lives a stone's throw away in the same building complex in inner-city Birchgrove. James says he drifted into rugby union at school, but this undersells his achievements. 'We had a fantastic coach at Newington named Guthrie Wilson, a former New Zealander who later became headmaster at Scots College ... a remarkable man. He was the Latin Master at Newington and quite simply the best football coach I had in either code and that includes a lot of people.'

After making the Greater Public School (GPS) representative team and completing his leaving certificate in 1960, he tried out for St George rugby union as a five-eighth but was eventually graded as a centre. A first grader at age 17, James was in the St George team defeated by University in the first grade grand final, 11-6, with former Scots College opponent Stewart Boyce scoring the winning try. That summer he played grade cricket for the St George club.

But James quickly became disenchanted with the amateur game. 'St George Rugby Union Club might not have had the community profile its illustrious rugby league partners had but they were a very good club. But fundamentally, St George fielded a forward-orientated team and I found it boring being a backline player. The ball would go to the halfback or five-eighth and they would kick it. Then you'd spend the entire game chasing it. After a year of that I thought there had to be a better way of playing rugby. If I'd played for a club like Randwick which liked to run the ball I probably would have stayed in Union.'

There was a popular myth at the time that James switched codes because of a back-handed comment from a teammate after a trial game in early 1962. 'St George Rugby Union does not believe in centres making long runs with the ball,' a press report of the time noted. 'James scored a try in a trial match and was asked if "he wanted his name carved on the ball?"' Brian disputes the account.

'Many other rugby players moved to league at the same time, including Michael Cleary (Souths), Ian Scott (Parramatta), Graeme MacDougall (Wests) and Georgie Evans (St George). Dad was heavily involved at St George Rugby League as a sponsor, was respected at the Club and was friendly with all the directors so he took me straight down there.'

At a time when clubs posted huge 'transfer fees' on their players, Brian James was something of a bargain. 'I went from union to league for a world record low transfer fee of nothing,' he laughs. 'I just walked into the club one day and got a start.'

James was also working and studying at the time, defying the image of rugby league as being a working class sport. 'My first job was as an accountant with Price Waterhouse before I came to Souths and I then shifted to IBM. While I was playing for St George I completed a fulltime Bachelor Degree of Commerce (Accounting). When Dad got sick in the late 1960s I went into the family transport business as a manager. We started a shipping container storage and repair business, a full distributorship, an air freight container repair facility, a CHEP pallet agency and a plan to expand Sydney airports, international airfreight facilities onto land across Alexandria canal.

He played four seasons at the Norm Provan-led St George club, appearing in 18 first grade matches but playing in four consecutive reserve grade grand finals. At the time, internationals Reg Gasnier, Graeme Langlands and Johnny Riley were ahead of him in the centres, and champions John King and Eddie Lumsden on the flanks. 'My goal was to become a regular first grader at St George but I didn't quite achieve that,' James admits. He made his first grade debut on 23 June, 1962, in the 16-all draw with Balmain and finished the year by scoring three tries in St George's 19-0 win over Wests in the reserve grade grand final. James, who partnered Billy Smith in the centres (future Canterbury international Johnny Greaves was one of the St George wingers that day) scored a spectacular try from the initial kick-off when he regathered the ball on the 25 yard-line from a Wests' fumble and raced past the startled defence.

The following year St George qualified for the grand final in all three grades on an SCG mud heap. Third grade defeated Canterbury 12-2 and James played in reserve grade's 5-4 win over a Souths' team which included a young Ron Coote in its ranks. Saints made it a clean sweep of premierships when first grade defeated Wests 8-3 in a match remembered today for the wonderful photo of rival captain Norm Provan and Arthur Summons embracing in the mud, but by that time James was showered and changed. A year later he scored the only try in St George's 7-2 win over Souths in the reserve grade grand final, and though he partnered Reg Gasnier on several occasions and travelled with the first grade squad on their end of season tour of North Queensland, Billy Smith beat him for the first grade centre position.

'One day on the Cricket Ground, strangely enough against Souths as I remember, I won the 'Best and Fairest' award in a game we lost and I got dropped for the following week. I thought to myself, "Well, this is not working out".' Saints reshuffled the backline and there was no room for me and I thought this is just going to keep happening.' Balmain defeated St George in the reserve grade grand final, 9-7, while the first grade team, with Gasnier and Smith in the centres, defeated a young Souths outfit in front of a record grand final crowd. The following year James would be wearing the red and green of South Sydney.

'I ended up fluking it at Souths just as they were coming good,' James says. 'I had some misgivings when they approached me about leaving the St George district but it turned out really well. I had played against Ron Coote, Bob McCarthy and Gary Stevens in a couple of reserve grade grand finals and I knew they were going to have a great team. I considered Bernie Purcell a good coach. The club came last in 1962 and then made the grand final three years later under Bernie. He was one of the boys, different to Clive Churchill, and more of a thinker. Clive was a happy-go-lucky little bloke who was happy to make jokes and not throw his weight around too much. I'd place Harry Bath [City, NSW and Australian coach] slightly above the pair of them.'

The Rabbitohs had a young team on the way up after their experience in the 1965 grand final and James fitted into first grade as a centre. Although the 1966 season was disappointing in that the club did not make the play-offs, James, at age 23, was just hitting his stride. Shifting to winger the following year, he says, 'I found the change from unlimited tackle to the four-tackle rule remarkably easy because I was playing more and more on the wing.' He remains fairly realistic about his best attacking asset—his speed. 'I wasn't that fast,' he says. 'I never had to train too much to maintain my speed. I trained one night a week on my sprinting. I used to enjoy that. I was a professional runner and was reasonably successful in that I ran off a handicap. I'd head off with a bunch of mates to a country town and race in the local "gift" and then play up a bit afterwards. I ran for fun for four or five years. Cec King, Johnny's father, used to be one of my trainers. John and I became good mates—we were doing similar things at similar times in the game, although he enjoyed much more success than me—but Mike Cleary and Ken Irvine were a class above us for speed.'

James' arrival as a class player came in 1967. He appeared in all 24 matches that year and was the club's leading try-scorer with 14 tries. In the 10–4 win against semi-final contenders Easts at the SCG, James scored a double, including one try where he beat the entire Roosters' team with a long, diagonal run. 'We weren't favourites to win the premiership until we got to the business end of the season,' he recalls. We crept up on everyone. St George fell over, Canterbury were on the rise but we won the grand final.'

Minutes before half-time with Souths holding a 5-4 lead, James was standing inside Bob McCarthy as Canterbury swept the ball back inside. James and McCarthy were clearly outnumbered when Canterbury's Col Brown threw the intercept pass. 'I always like to tell everyone that I was right behind Bobby McCarthy in case he got caught but if you look at the film you can see that's bullshit. He was well and truly a runaway train. It was a hairy moment though. We weren't raging favourites to win the match and we had a real fight on our hands. Winning a first grade grand final with Souths was an amazing experience after all those reserve grade premierships with St George.'

James' contemporaries and various press reports state that he was among the top three wingers in the game in the latter half of the 1967 season alongside John King and Ken Irvine. With a Kangaroos squad selected on grand final night it was expected that the premiers would supply a core group of players. Instead, because of conflicting agendas between NSW, NSW Country and Queensland selectors, players such as Brian James, Bob McCarthy, Eric Simms, Mike Cleary and John O'Neill missed out on joining John Sattler, Ron Coote and Elwyn Walters on the tour. 'Frank Hyde interviewed me after the grand final and said I should hear my name called out later that night,' James recalls. 'It wasn't to be.'

Only years later did it emerge what happened in the ARL selection room. NSW Country selectors, mindful that it was in danger of having no representatives on the tour, did a deal with NSW selectors to push for Newcastle second row forward Allan Thomson and Nowra five-eighth Tony Branson. Two fine players with undeniable credentials, once they were locked, it affected the make-up of the remainder of the team. With Queenslander Johnny Gleeson the first choice as Test five-eighth, there was no place for boom Manly five-eighth Bob Fulton. Manly's Les Hanigan and Canterbury's Johnny Greaves were selected as the other two wingers (Queenslander John McDonald was also a Test winger) and there was no place for Brian James.

In the early months of 1968 James then came down with glandular fever. At the time he was organising a charity rugby league day in aid of the spastic centre and put together what is possibly the first touch football tournament held in Sydney. So new was the concept that James and several other organisers had to sit down and write the rules of the competition. The field was set at 70 yards by 40 yards, they determined, with teams numbering seven players with two reserves. Each half went for seven minutes with a one-minute interval. A player is tackled when he is touched with two hands by an opposition player, the rules stated. 'When tackled, the player brings the ball into play by touching it on the ground before passing. The opposition team must be back three yards. If the ball is dropped, the opposition retains the ball.' Players wore full football uniform, including boots, and the only points that could be scored were three points for a try.

Held on Friday, 9 February 1968 at Redfern Oval, the night consisted of a touch football knockout with 10 teams taking part (Wests and Canterbury were the only clubs missing). The Souths team comprised Sattler, Coote, McCarthy, Jones, Lisle, Honan, James and Gary Stevens (reserve). Although Souths were knocked out in the early rounds, the night was a huge success with notable footballers Dave Irvine, Ken Gentles, Bill Mullins, Reg Hatton and Arch Brown competing against James in the heats of the Park Drive Gift (first prize $600). There was also a 'One Mile Handicap' with first prize of $400. Following the event, however, James' illness was diagnosed and he was warned by a specialist to take eight weeks off to fully recover.

'I surprised myself and everyone else with the speed I got back to grade,' he says, 'but I wasn't the same player from the year before … I couldn't do what I did in 1967.' His form was still good enough for the rep selectors, though. James was chosen for City Firsts after only two first grade matches and then represented NSW before Australia's World Cup squad was selected. He was the only Souths player chosen in the State team. 'Harry Bath was the NSW coach at the time. He was a cranky bugger, and pretty strict, but he couldn't watch us 24 hours a day,' James says with a wry smile.

After making his debut for NSW in the 30–7 win over Queensland at the SCG on 18 May Reg Gasnier wrote in his newspaper column, 'Brian James can go and get measured for his World Cup blazer.' James recalls, 'It was a huge rap from Reg but after the events of the previous year, it was also a bit of a worry.' James was also battling a shoulder injury and faced a long spell from the game if he was injured again. When he was one of four wingers selected in Australia's 19-man World Cup squad alongside Johnny King, Queensland's Lionel Williamson and Canterbury's Johnny Rhodes, his former St George coach Norm Provan observed, 'For sheer determination, James gets first prize.'

James made his international debut in the third match of the competition, against France in Brisbane on 8 June. Australia won the match easily, 37-4, which took out all the expectation out of the final, also against France, which was played a week later. 'The actual jersey I wore in Brisbane didn't have the Australian insignia on it,' he remembers. 'The ARL presented us with another one—I still have it somewhere—but I don't know what happened to the original.'

James appeared for NSW in another match later that month but his brief representative career was over. 'I wasn't at my best after returning from glandular fever, but it was good fun. Lionel Williamson jumped out of the ground and partnered Johnny Rhodes in the final.' He remains philosophical, more than forty years later. 'I was lucky in 1968 after being unlucky the year before, so it balances out.'

The season ended with a second successive premiership title following a 13–9 win over Manly, but Souths' fans were shocked to read of James' retirement at the start of the following season. The club dropped James and Ray Branighan from its pre-season squad when they missed training. 'I was tied up at work and I couldn't get to Redfern Oval in time for the 5 pm run,' James said at the time. At age 25, he was managing director of his father's transport company and was finding it increasingly difficult to balance work commitments and rugby league. Peter Frilingos reported James's decision in the *Daily Mirror*, 'My decision to retire has nothing to do with South Sydney's action in dropping me from its first grade pre-season squad. I've been considering in calling it a day for some time now. My reasons for retiring are simple. I want to start a part-time law degree and concentrate more on my business interests.'

But James reconsidered his decision and came to an agreement with Souths for the 1969 season. At the peak of his form, the year did not bring any representative honours. The grand final against Balmain, his seventh in eight seasons in the game, would not go all Souths' way either. 'It was a crap week all round,' James remembers. 'It rained all week and we even trained on Redfern Park one night. I guess we thought we would win, but Balmain had some form on the board against us that year. We didn't consider the tactics of the game enough … we didn't change our tactics when Balmain were controlling the match in the second half.'

Early in the first half James had his chance to score a memorable grand final try denied him by the touch judge. John Sattler made the initial break and passed to Brian James on his outside. As James approached the tryline he took on Balmain winger George Ruebner. 'My old Newington coach used to say that if you got anywhere near the line to dive low with your arms extended out, aim for it and just go. George Ruebner hit me in the tackle and rolled me over the touch line but I thought I had got the ball down in time.'

Film of the incident shows Ruebner hitting the corner post with his back at the same time James grounds the ball, but the sideline official had no hesitation in ruling 'no try'. 'I got to my feet and jumped up in celebration because I thought I'd got there but the rugby league gods said no. Bobby McCarthy maintains that if Sattler had passed the ball inside to him he would have scored under the posts,' he smiles. James can't help but smile at the irony of it all. 'I had played against Georgie Ruebner at school, and in rugby, and it was probably the best bloody tackle he made all year,' he laughs. 'Anyway, George injured himself in tackling me and had to go off at half-time. His replacement, Syd Williams, scored the only try of the match and won them the grand final. Stuff me if it wasn't the same Syd Williams who scored the winning try four years earlier in the reserve grade grand final when Balmain beat St George.'

James didn't know it at the time but the 1969 grand final would be his final match.

'The family transport business was going so well it was being wooed by Maine Nickless Ltd, which meant that ultimately I would have had to move to Melbourne.' James had enrolled to do a law degree at Sydney University and was in two minds whether he would have the time to play rugby league in 1970. 'I asked Souths if I played would I be on the same terms and conditions as my previous contract.' The response from the club committee was fairly blunt—'When you tell us if you can play we'll tell you how much we'll pay you'.

With his accounting and business background, James was less than impressed with the way Souths officials were running the club but he declines to go into details. 'I wasn't prepared to argue with

Souths about a new contract,' he says. He did not discuss his decision with any of the other Souths players. 'I was training with them in the early part of the season and then I left. I married in May that year and all my Souths mates were there.'

There were no regrets, he says. 'It was a different era with different ideas, which was reflected in that upset loss to Balmain. The Tigers did their homework and had a plan. We didn't change ours. In many ways 1969 was the end of an era. (Easts coach) Jack Gibson came back from America the following year with all his ideas and people started getting serious about coaching. I played in an era before tackle counts and no-one cared how many times you carted the ball up. I played before the era of weight training. Now, it's the first thing sprinters do ... go and do weights.'

'That era was just like rugby league today—professional ... and yet so unprofessional in many ways. Some of the players drank schooners the night before a rep match in those days. We'd train at the SCG No.2 oval, go to the Bat and Ball Hotel for a few beers and then go straight back and train with Souths. It was crazy by today's standards but I have no doubt that if we trained like they do now we would still have won premierships today. However, I don't see how you can say the current crop of players training under such scientific conditions aren't better players than we were. They must be. They have a different training methods and a different mindset.'

James is still remembered today as a Souths' legend. 'The Souths tradition still hangs around you and gives you a special feeling. I also played in that great era with St George. It was a fluke I just happened to play for both clubs at a great time in their history. We all clicked at Souths, but everyone in the district cared about you, not just your teammates. I've still got two handmade boomerangs the guys from 'Larpa' [La Perouse] made me. Playing at Redfern Oval, the fans on Baker's Hill were a turnout in itself. They were fanatics, but that was part of the fun. Following Souths was almost 'tribal'. After a match you'd meet people in the club who had never been north of the Harbour Bridge. They'd spent their whole lives in the district and they loved the Rabbitohs.'

James watched with some interest as Souths won two more premierships in 1970–71 but after buying his first yacht he was already out on the water learning how to race. 'I joined the CYC—Cruising Yacht club—and got into sailing. I did not have any major injuries during my career so my body held up very well over the years. I've had a very interesting business career. It hasn't been without some difficulties, but I've enjoyed what I achieved. It was a privilege to play for Australia and I was lucky to play three grand finals with Souths. We all kept in contact over the years and we still catch up.'

In 1970 Brian married Elizabeth Allen, the daughter of the future NSW Deputy Police Commissioner, Bill Allen, and together they raised three boys. 'Our son Julian plays rugby for Sydney University. He's a good clubman, a breakaway turned winger, and I enjoy watching him play. He went to Newington, as did my other two boys—twin Justin, a good tennis player, and Dominic, a good rower in his youth who later became a pilot. They've continued the family's GPS tradition.' Brian was recently inducted in Newington College's Sporting Hall of Fame, but he understates the honour, just as he does with most of his achievements. 'It was great recognition but there are a lot more famous people than me who have not been inducted yet.'

Brian James acknowledges the achievements of younger brother Graeme, an Honours Graduate in Economics at the University of NSW. 'Graeme played rugby league for the University in the South Sydney junior rugby league competition and was a first grade cricketer with St George in the 1960s at a time when they had players such as Norm O'Neill, Brian Booth and Warren Saunders, and like Saints in rugby league, were the best club in their competition.' Graeme James was granted a Commonwealth Gold Scholarship but tragically, died relatively young after a long illness.

James is proud of his association with the Men of League organisation. 'When Ron Coote started the charity I quickly came on board. I didn't have the vision for it that Ron had but I helped him with it because he asked me to. As a charity you have special duties and responsibilities regarding accounting etcetera, and with my background in business I was happy to help. Jim Hall [Former Souths forward and Chairman of the NRL Judiciary] and I were the first two shareholders of a shelf company, which was to save the time needed to creating a new corporation, and my solicitor registered the company. It's been amazingly successful and helped a lot of people. It's also bringing lot of ex-players back to the game. Strangely enough, many of the Men of League fundraisers we attend at various country towns remind me of the trips I used to have with my mates as a professional runner. I often say to myself, "I think I ran here in the 1960s".'

Together, with Tony Ellis, James operated one the biggest major boat refit businesses in Australia but he sold his interest in that business in 2009 and bought into the Superyacht Marina at Sydney's Rozelle Bay. The company offers berthing and a major concierge service for prestige 'super yachts' owned by prominent businessmen. 'The Marina area is undergoing a $25 million major redevelopment with shopping and plenty of parking. The big yachts attract big crowds and the owners don't mind people having a look at them as long as they can't get on them (there is s a private wharf). The business is a great challenge and I enjoy every bit of it. I get to come to work every day and stare at some really nice boats and think how lucky I am!'

BOB MOSES
(1967–69)

In September 1956, 16-year old Bobby Moses ventured down to Sydney from his family home in Belmont, a suburb of Newcastle, to watch his older brother, Ron 'Jake' Moses, play for Balmain against St George in the grand final. It was the start of St George's world-record 11-season reign as premiers and despite playing most of the match with 12 men, the Dragons defeated the Tigers 18-12. The youngest of four brothers, and a talented centre at the Lakes United club, Bob could not have dreamed that he too would one day play a part in St George's historic premiership run, bring it to an end in 1967 and then start another championship era with Souths.

I caught up with Bobby Moses at the curiously named Blue Cattle Dog Hotel in Sydney's West, not far from where I live. Now 70 years old, Moses has been the publican there for 20 years. We sit and chat in the public bar one morning before the regular customers come in, surrounded by rugby league memorabilia on the walls and ceiling. 'The guy who owns the pub loves rugby league,' Bob says as we sit down. 'I made sure there was plenty of Souths memorabilia on display.' Even though we are in the heart of Penrith's junior rugby league area, everyone loves Souths, he says. Many of the pub's patrons grew up during Souths' run of grand finals in the 1960s and 1970s and have fond, even idealised, memories of a simpler time when the

Rabbitohs set the benchmark for rugby league success.

'And they just love Satts,' Bob says, pointing to a picture of his former captain, blood streaming from his mouth, at the end of the 1970 grand final.

Robert Lindsay Moses was born on 26 July 1940 in Newcastle, NSW. He was to become part of the important 'Newcastle' connection at Souths which dated back to Clive Churchill—the greatest player of them all—who came to the club just after World War Two. 'A lot of players from Newcastle came to Sydney and made a success of it,' he says, citing John Sattler and Les Johns as two players who 'made it' in Sydney in the early 1960s. A first grade centre at age 18, he represented NSW Colts against France in 1964 in a team that contained future Souths teammates Ron Coote, Bob McCarthy and John O'Neill. The catalyst for his move to Sydney, however, was Newcastle's success in the 1964 State Cup knockout. After defeating North Coast, Southern Division and Western Division to take the country title, Newcastle—captain-coached by former St George premiership-winning centre Dave Brown—defeated Souths, 29-14, North Sydney in the quarter-final, 6-0, and a star-studded St George team 5-3 in the semi-final.

In the final against Parramatta in front of more than 20,000 fans at Newcastle's number one sports ground, the home team won 14–7. Of the players in the Newcastle team that day Terry Pannowitz, Allan Thomson, Allan Buman and Jim Morgan later played for Australia. 'I actually captained Newcastle in the win against Souths because Dave Brown was out injured,' Moses says. After the State Cup success, Moses was approached to join Souths in 1965. 'I hadn't had too many offers before,' he says. Already married, with two young children, he saw the move to Sydney as a great opportunity to better himself. A boilermaker by trade, there was more work in Sydney. Playing professional football with Souths had its rewards as well. The fact that his good mate Jimmy Morgan was also coming to Sydney made the move easier.

'I was almost 25—an older player in many ways—but not so much established in the game, so it was a case of do it now or never. It was a great opportunity. Our family moved to Chifley, near Botany, and Jimmy and I met all the guys at Souths. We fell in together so well; it was just so easy to play with them. There were a lot of young blokes in the team but you could tell they were going to be an exciting team. You could see it coming.'

Souths took on the might of St George in the 1965 grand final. 'Bernie Purcell was an excellent coach and a great man who got us ready for the match of our lives. I'd been part of a team that had beaten St George in the State Cup the previous year, so I knew they were beatable. It was a big occasion, playing in front of 78,000 people, and we were a little bit overawed by it all but we played well considering everything. We rose to the occasion and gave a lot more in the match than what we actually had.'

Moses partnered Arthur Branighan in the centres and the pair marked Reg Gasnier and Billy Smith. How do you mark someone as good as Reg Gasnier, I ask? 'Well, you have to be lucky,' he laughs. 'We ended up pretty good mates all of us, the Saints and Souths boys, so a lot of good came out of that game.'

The Souths players nicknamed Moses 'Ikey', which was traditionally a slang term for someone who was Jewish (from the Jewish name 'Isaac') but was more generally used to describe someone who was tight with a dollar. Bob Moses was neither Jewish nor tight with a dollar, but his last name certainly sounded biblical to his teammates and the nickname stuck.

The 1966 season was a disappointment, Moses admits. 'We had a lot of injuries that year and it just put us all out of whack.' Moses appeared in only 13 matches that season after suffering a knee injury, but was on the verge of representative duty before injury struck. He spent the latter part of the year on the sidelines as Souths stumbled in the run-up to the semi-finals and missed the play-offs altogether. It was an unhappy time at the club.

'I didn't know anything about the politics going on with Bernie and the Club Committee and I got a huge surprise when he was sacked as coach at the end of the year. He'd just taken us to the grand final the previous year—it was exactly what happened to Parramatta [in 2010]—so it goes to show nothing changes in rugby league. It was a huge downer but we more than made up for the following year.'

Clive Churchill was the new coach in 1967 and the season saw Souths return to the play-offs under the four tackle rule. 'Every coach had their different ways and it wasn't a case of one being better than the other. I enjoyed my football education under both Clive and Bernie. Clive talked really well to the players … he'd just get you on the side, talk to you calmly and get into your ear. He was behind my move to the forwards the following year.'

In 1967, the Sydney rugby league axis was slowly shifting from 'glamour club' St George to the working class Souths team. 'You could see St George slipping back to the field a little bit,' Bob says. 'It got to the stage where it was a really tight competition. We weren't minor premiers in 1967, but we'd beaten St George three times that year and were really confident in the grand final against Canterbury. Most of us had played in the 1965 grand final—Longbottom, Simms, Moses, Cleary, Lisle, Jones, Coote, Sattler, McCarthy and O'Neill—and the whole team knew what we had to do to win.'

Bob Moses partnered Eric Simms in the centres in that match. 'I wasn't the quickest centre around by any means. I was aggressive at times, which helped a bit, but I was a good defensive centre.' Of Souths 12–10 win in the grand final he says, 'It was a very close match except for Bobby McCarthy's great try—he just took off—and Ecca Simms came good with that penalty at the end, as he always did.' It was his final year in the Souths' backline, however. At age 28, and with young speedsters Bobby Honan, Paul Sait and Ray Branighan forcing their way into first grade, his future lay in the forwards.

'I always wanted to play in the forwards,' he says. 'I sometimes played in the forwards back in Newcastle. I was getting a bit slow so the club selectors gave me a run in the second row.' Playing in the front line suited Moses' aggressive, mobile style but he could still show the ball a bit when the opportunity presented itself. 'I held the centre with John O'Neill,' he says. 'He was left prop and I was the left second row forward so we stood together on the field. We often worked in tandem and could attack as well as defend, although Bobby McCarthy and Ronny Coote were the main thrust of the attack.'

South Sydney, circa 1968, was an improved model on their premiership-winning team with the inclusion of halves Denis Pittard and Bobby Grant, the shifting of Moses to the forwards and the selection of Bobby Honan in the centres. Although the club captured the minor premiership that year, they lost the major semi-final to Manly and had to beat St George in the final to earn a rematch with the Sea Eagles in the grand final. 'We didn't particularly like Manly, even back then we considered them silver-tails,' he says with a laugh, considering he would end up there two years later. 'Manly were very competitive back then—they made the grand final twice [1968 and 1970] and the final twice [1969 and 1971] in the years before they finally won the premiership, but Souths always had the wood on them.'

And so it was in the 1968 grand final, with Souths defeating Manly 13–9. Late in the second half, with Manly desperately searching for a converted try, Moses was involved in an ugly incident when he ran in and hit Sea Eagles' captain Bob Fulton in a high tackle. Fulton got to his feet and threw a punch at Moses and as referee Col Pearce signalled a penalty, a Manly player king hit Moses as he faced the opposite way. Moses never flinched, stood his ground and smiled at his attackers. He had succeeded in shutting down their attack and wasting precious minutes while maintaining his innocence of any wrong-doing.

The following year Moses broke his ribs in a club match and missed several matches, including the major semi-final against Balmain. When Souths defeated the Tigers, 14–13, it gave the minor premiers a fortnight's break before the grand final. 'I thought I was fine to play but Balmain found me out pretty quick and I only lasted half a game,' he says. It shows the importance Clive Churchill placed on Moses' position in Souths' 'international' pack that the experienced coach would chance Moses' fitness in such an important match. But when Moses was replaced by Paul Sait at half-time, Balmain were leading 6-0 and on their way to an upset victory.

'Watching the second half of the grand final from the sideline I could see we were doing it tough. Two tries were pulled back by the referee in the first half and we needed to produce something special to win it but we never got that special moment. Souths always played with momentum—once we got on a roll we were hard to beat—but Balmain tackled us out of it and slowed the game down to their pace. They did what they had to do to win.'

After contemplating a return to Newcastle in a captain-coaching capacity with Lakes United the previous year, Moses stayed with Souths but found it difficult to get back into first grade in 1970. Pushing 30, and a notoriously slow starter to each season, he left the door open for several younger players in the club. 'Pauly Sait was a great footballer. He could play in the centres or the back row. Gary Stevens came into first grade and stayed there, and rightly so.' Moses made just four first grade appearance in 1970 and missed selection in Souths' grand final team. During the off-season he was working on a building site on the north side of the harbour when the foreman said there was a man in a suit asking for him at the front gate.

'It was Manly chief executive Ken Arthurson,' Moses says. 'We had a chat, then another chat, and he offered me a three-year contract and a little bit more money.' Moses recalls thinking that Jimmy Morgan had joined Easts the previous year for pretty much the same reason and he had represented Australia, so maybe a change would be good. 'There was a bit of frustration on my part, playing reserve grade so much that year, and when another club wants you to come and play first grade for them, well you take it. I thought I only had a couple of good seasons left in me but I decided to give it a go.'

'Manly ...' he contemplates. 'It's funny how life works out.'

Bob Moses might have played for Manly but he still drank with the South Sydney players. 'The Manly boys didn't drink much—I thought they must have been in bed by 8.30—so I called into the Cauliflower Hotel on the way home from training one night. I was still living at Maroubra and all the Souths boys were there. Ivan Jones even offered to buy me a drink ... he bought me a saucer of milk!' Moses laughs at the memory. 'We still socialised together and there were no hard feelings about leaving.' In twelve months, he was joined at the Sea Eagles by Ray Branighan and John O'Neill.

I remind Bob that there didn't seem to be any love lost between his former teammates and him when Souths took on Manly in two 'match of the day' clashes at the SCG in 1971. 'I wasn't a good enough player to be spotted by Souths,' he says modestly, but the records show that he came in for some 'special treatment' from the Souths forwards. Maybe the idea was to put Bob off his game—perhaps it was their way of showing Moses respect—but Souths won both matches, 15-7 and 13-12.

'Manly had bought very well,' he says, 'and Ron Willey was a very good coach. [Englishman] Malcolm Reilly was a bit over the top in my book, though. He made me look like a choir boy.' Moses played in 12 matches in 1971 but by semi-final time he was back in reserve grade. While Manly were beaten by St George in the preliminary final, Souths won the premiership for a fourth time in five seasons. The following year Manly won its maiden premiership, but Moses made only one appearance in the top grade. When he got hurt again in 1973, he called it a day.

'When I first came down to Sydney I stuck with being a boiler-maker for about 12 months then started working with John O'Neill and Gary Stevens in their building business. It was a tight little

Souths unit, working with Ivan Jones and Bobby Grant, and Jimmy Morgan got rid of our rubbish.' Moses was especially close to O'Neill, a long-time drinking buddy and card partner.

Bob's eldest son, James, was apprenticed to John O'Neill and worked with Lurch right up until the big man's death in 1999. 'Ivan Jones rang me, actually, and told me that John had cancer. I couldn't believe it ... he was always larger than life. They gave him twelve months to live and he crammed another five years in. What a tough man ...' After O'Neill's death, James Moses took over many of O'Neill's building projects and has made a success of his career, much to his father's pride.

When his rugby league career ended, Bob Moses moved his family to Baulkham Hills when it was a young suburb on the northwest outskirts of the city. 'When I got too old to do building work I moved into the pub game,' he says. Bob was coaching the Baulkham Hills Bulls when he got a call from former South Sydney Secretary Charlie Gibson. A controversial appointment as manager of the battling Penrith Club by Kevin Humphreys, the chief executive of the NSWRL, Gibson asked Moses to take on the reserve grade coaching duties with the Panthers in 1981. The club was a still a decade away from winning its maiden first grade premiership and although success was elusive, Moses maintains he enjoyed all his years in rugby league.

'I look back and I have a lot of good memories,' he says. A hard man on the field, he is quietly spoken and reserved in person. 'I'm a very easy going bloke,' he smiles. 'I didn't get into too much trouble during my career.' Some former opponents may disagree.

The Blue Cattle Dog it is a long way from the Cauliflower Hotel in the heart of Redfern and living 'way out west' doesn't allow Bob the luxury of seeing his former teammates too often. [Former Penrith, Canterbury and Queensland State of Origin forward] Daryl Brohman pops in occasionally but usually I have to go into Sydney and see the Souths boys. Last year we went back to Redfern Oval for the first trial match of the season and we had a beer or two together. It was great to catch up with everybody.'

Bob says that he will get out of the pub game sometime soon, but at age 70, it's a hard lifestyle to get out of the blood. 'I have a daughter at Mermaid Beach (on the Gold Coast), so maybe we'll head up there when I retire.' Sons James and Matthew, and daughter Simone, have seven kids between them so he would find plenty to keep him busy in retirement.

As I say goodbye and thank him for his time this busy holiday morning we stop and look at the wall of memorabilia behind us. Our trip into the past has stirred many memories and some emotions, although Bob Moses gives little away on both counts. We stand in front of a framed Souths jumper with his signature on it and he smiles to me in acknowledgement of this modest nod to his rugby league career. The last thing he says to me is, 'Maybe I'll turn this into a South Sydney wall,' as he shakes his head and walks away to deal with the bustling throng of customers.

DENIS PITTARD
(1968–71)

Denis Pittard has rarely given an interview since he retired from rugby league 35 years ago. Invariably known as 'The Sneak', 'The Phantom' and 'The Scarlet Pimpernel' ('they seek him here, they seek him there') by his former Souths teammates, Pittard has rejected life membership at Souths on three occasions and shuns any contact with the game. Today, he works in radiology and spends the majority of the year pursuing business interests in France and Dubai. In researching this book the former Test five-eighth proved to be as difficult to corner off the field as when he played in the red and green for Souths. No amount of digging could lure Pittard from his rabbit hole and all attempts to contact him or his family over the past summer drew a dead end.

Perhaps some stories should remain untold, I told myself, rationalising somehow that not getting Pittard's story was the story. Then, one week before this book went to print, I received a phone call. 'Alan, Denis Pittard here. How are you? I've just received your letter but I have to leave for Paris tonight. Can we catch up?'

Denis J. Pittard was born in Victoria on 8 December 1945. His father moved the family to Sydney when he started work as a radiologist at Prince Henry Hospital in the 1950s. The Pittard family settled in the inner western suburb of Enfield and Denis attended Enfield Public School where he was introduced to rugby league.

'Dad never wanted me to play football at school because he wanted me to concentrate on my studies. I appreciated that wisdom later in life but not at the time. I was selected in the third grade team while I was at high school and my father told the coach if he didn't need to put me on that would be okay. I came on after ten minutes and scored two tries. I was always a halfback of five-eighth, where I could get the ball in my hands and control the game.'

'Dad died when I was quite young and I had two brothers—one five years younger and the other ten years younger—so it was important to earn a quid. In my first year at Wests I earned £506 for the year which helped a lot. It was a start, and to this day I have no regrets. It was a young boy's dream, really, and the start of 13 great years in the game.'

Pittard played for the Enfield Federals club in the Western Suburbs Junior League where a teammate was future Wests, Canterbury and Easts clubman John Armstrong. The promising five-eighth represented Jersey Flegg in 1963 but was called into grade the following year before he could be picked in President's Cup. 'I made my first grade debut in 1965 when captain-coach Arthur Summons promoted me after Roger Buttenshaw ran into the goalposts at training. Wests had a great team that year—Noel Kelly, Peter Dimond, Don Parish, Denis Meaney and Jim Cody and Gil Macdougall. They were very competitive and hungry after the loss to St George in the 1963 grand final.'

Former champion Test halfback Keith Holman had a lot to do with Wests before becoming a leading referee. 'Keith was a wonderful character. He was always at me to become a referee but I never pursued it. He said it was always handy to be able to cheat because you knew the rules. He stressed to me that you had to have something "on" at every scrum. "There were five ways of scoring a try," he'd say, '… the blindside, the open, the kick, the run-around or to run yourself. When you run across in front of another player in a scissors move, always show them the ball, pass it on the "up" and pop it in the air so they can see the ball. Lots of players drop the ball because the halfback throws it hard into their bread basket." He also taught me how to work the blindside—playmakers today don't even go down the blindside. At Souths Bobby McCarthy would attack that side of the ruck and have a winger outside him on either side of the field who could run 100 yards in 10 seconds.'

A year before Dennis Tutty took Balmain to court over the transfer system Pittard had his own battle with Wests officials over the same issue. 'Wests never signed me to a contract,' he says, 'because they said they had more important players to look after. Peter Dimond was off contract that year—I respected that because he was 'Wests" at the time and he was also an idol of mine and my role model—but as a matter of principle after four seasons there I wanted to move but they refused to put me on the transfer list. (Future NSWRL Judiciary Chairman) Jim Comans was my solicitor at the time and he told me to go overseas. I told Wests I was off to England to play for Halifax in the 1967-68 season. They didn't know what to do. Wests backed down—thanks totally to J.Comans—and the club released me. Souths said they were interested in me joining the team before the official contract deadline at the end of June.'

Pittard signed a three-year contract valued at a premium $8,000 a season, more than any Souths player was receiving at the time. The Rabbitohs didn't play over the long weekend in June so Pittard went down the NSW South Coast with some friends. Walking on some rocks at low tide he gashed his foot and played his first match with his foot heavily plastered. He scored a try on debut in the 33-8 win against Newtown and never looked back. Souths' attack galvanised with Pittard at five-eighth and the club lost only one game in the second round of competition.

'Souths had so many attacking options,' Pittard says. '"Evil" Bobby Grant ("Those eyes of his," Pittard laughs, "pure evil"), Ron Coote and 'Bobby Mac" ... two players would be working and one would be resting. If someone was injured they'd say "cover me for a while" and they'd back off a bit, and Cootey would come up the front and defend. Every player had a talent, that's why we had such a great team. I built a great rapport with Bobby Grant. We'd just call out the numbers or signal with our hands. We had great respect, friendship and confidence in each other's ability. We were the "dynamic duo" and the "odd couple". We never had an argument, just constructive conversations—and all in pursuit of perfection—and never in anger.'

After losing the semi-final to Manly, Souths put the cleaners through St George in the preliminary final. Pittard's form in that match was outstanding, creating runaround moves with Bobby Honan. At one point he scooted under the swinging arm of St George champion Graeme Langlands and off he ran. The Souths' players christened him 'The Sneak'. 'Rival forwards couldn't get down to my level. They'd swing their arm and I would sneak under it. Even "Lurch" O'Neill at training use to complain that he couldn't hit me.'

'The preliminary final against St George in 1968 was one of those milestones you remember in your career,' Pittard says. It proved that he could mix it with the best. Clive Churchill went as far as saying Souths would not have even made the grand final that year if Pittard had not joined the club. 'Grand finals are great to play in, that's why you play the game and that's what you're remembered for,' he tells me. 'Souths were the "people's team". We used to go and do presentations out west at Blacktown because it built our powerbase, our following. It doesn't matter where you go, to Gulargambone or Guyra, you'll find someone wearing a pair of red and green socks.'

Pittard's breakthrough year in representative rugby league was in 1967. 'I played for Australia, won the Rothmans Medal and got knocked senseless in the grand final,' he laughs. The Rothmans Medal was inaugurated the previous year by the cigarette company WD & HO Wills Company which sponsored the game. At the time it was voted on by the referees who awarded three, two and one points each match. 'On the night I never gave it a thought ... I wasn't even prepared. Clive Churchill leaned over to me and said, "You'll win this".' It wasn't the only time he would take the prestigious reward either.

Pittard is an unabashed fan of Churchill and rates him as the best coach he played under during his career. 'Clive made so many players at Souths. He was totally 'on' as a coach. He used to say to me, "DP, you gotta stay on your feet. You're getting knocked over too many times ... you have to cover, so stay on your feet." He'd ask me why I wasn't kicking in a game. "You haven't kicked in five games," he'd say. Clive would analyse these things ... "you're not going to the blind, you're not kicking enough" ... all in his head, not on a clipboard or on video. He was a great thinker; analytical, methodical and he never raised his voice. He was the court jester and a good man, our Clive. He was truly a legend of the game and as a human being.'

In June 1969 Pittard was selected in the Australian Tour of New Zealand and played in both Tests on tour. 'It's not the same as playing for your club,' he says. 'The camaraderie was very different. It was great touring with so many Souths players, but there were cliques among the older Test players from the other clubs. It was wonderful to represent your country, but it's the grand finals you remember. The grand finals are like the Olympics of rugby league.'

Pittard had no inkling of the upset that was to unfold against Balmain in the 1969 grand final. 'I don't remember much about the game. I got ambushed by Peter Provan and Dave Bolton early in the match when they upended me on my head. When I came 'round, I asked "Ecca" Simms what was happening. He said we're behind on the scoreboard and there's eight minutes to go. We never mentioned it (his concussion) because you can't make that your excuse, but I was an integral part of the attack and I wasn't sighted in the match.'

With one of their main playmakers out of game, Souths could not come back against a Balmain team that employed 'unique' tactics to win the grand final. 'Souths weren't off their game,' Pittard says, 'we were hot in 1969. The rules beat us. There is no question as far as I'm concerned that Balmain "sat down" to win that grand final.

We were a very fast team and Elwyn Walters and Bobby Grant were always in at dummy half throwing out long passes. We used to get the ball out quicker than another other team, but by the time it got out to our superstars in the 1969 grand final, a Balmain player would go down injured and the game would stop. Then we'd have to start all over again. We lost that snowball effect of getting on top of the opposition.'

The laws of the game at the time demanded that play be stopped for injuries. 'You have to hand it to Balmain,' he says. 'They picked up on the tactic. They changed the rules next year, that's the great joke of it all.'

Like all good playmakers, Pittard had a healthy opinion of his own ability and was able to back it up on the playing field. 'An opposition coach would come out in the paper and say his five-eighth was a good player and would get over the top of me. I'd wish them luck and say they'd have to be bloody good. In those days there were a lot of one-on-one contests in a game. You had to do your homework – prepare and focus – and you had to have a battle plan with a Plan B to fall back on.'

Souths took on Manly in the 1970 grand final. 'We hated Manly and we had to beat them no matter what. There was a lot of animosity between the two teams but we had them worked out by then. All I had to do was nullify Bob Fulton. He was the pea in the Manly team. "Bozo" Fulton would chase me all day and it was easy to get him off his game in the early days.' But the breaking of Sattler's jaw started the war. 'The forwards started all that stuff against Manly. Satts, "Aubrey" Walters and "Lurch" O'Neill caused a lot of trouble for us in the backs,' he laughs. 'Freddy Jones and Elwyn Walters were the best two hookers going around at the time, no question about it. As soon as we got out on the field Elwyn would turn into a psychopath. Satts, though, didn't have to change!'

I remark that Pittard that would have seen some broken jaws in his time in radiology. Could he believe Sattler would stay on the field with one? 'All of us would have,' he says quick as a flash, 'That's how much the grand final meant to us.' But he still marvels at John Sattler's competitive instincts. 'If someone was giving me trouble in a game I'd say, 'Satts the second rower is always at me. "Don't worry DP," he'd say, "I'll walk the scrum over him …"'

At the end of the season Pittard again represented Australia, in the 1970 World Cup in England. Pittard was the first choice five-eighth in all three matches of competition, with Manly pivot Bob Fulton selected in the centres, but he injured his collarbone in the 17-15 loss to France at Bradford in the last match before the Final in Leeds and lost his place for the decider. 'I was bit of a misfit on that tour as far as selections went,' he says. 'Harry Bath was a great coach, second only to Clive Churchill in my time as a player, but (Manly Secretary) Ken Arthurson was the manager of the team so realistically, I was never going to be the first choice five-eighth ahead of "Bozo" Fulton in the final.'

There was some talk that Pittard might be moved to the centres but Bath chose Souths teammate Paul Sait and Pittard remains philosophical about missing the Final. 'The first thing in life is that you have to be realistic and honest with yourself so you can sleep at night. You have to make the best of things along the way, which is what I did in England.' Two days later Pittard took his place in the Australian team that was beaten by St Helens, 37-10. He then started the international match against France in Perpignan, but his collarbone finally gave out and he was replaced by champion winger Ken Irvine. The irony of this selection is that Irvine was not a member of the Australian team, but a journalist travelling with the Australian team, but such was the dire nature of injuries in the squad.

His brief foray into international rugby league had ended but in 1971 Pittard won his second Rothmans Medal – the first players to win the award twice. In the grand final against St George he made a long break towards the scoreboard corner of the SCG in the first half but was pulled down a yard short of the tryline. 'Bob McCarthy said

I should have scored that try, but he called out to me and I turned to look for support instead of backing myself and heading straight for the tryline.' Leading 11-0 midway through the second half, Pittard could see that centre Bob Honan was concussed and was content to turn the ball back into the forwards. 'Bob was well and truly out of it in that grand final and we had all these moves worked out. The injury took him out of the game and then Saints came back at us, of course.' Souths rallied to win the grand final, 16-10, but it was the last grand final appearance for Pittard and for the club. 'That team was like a machine,' he says. 'We had so much talent in the club we were like a finely-tuned Ferrari.'

Forty years later Denis Pittard has nothing but the utmost respect for all the club's grand final players. He rattles off names like characters from a Quentin Tarantino movie; 'Paul Sait, "Mr Tough"; Bobby Honan, "Mr Quick" … you had the superstars but you also had some good, no-nonsense players who looked after each other on the field. That's why we were such a different club. We had so many players who blossomed in that team – Pauly Sait, Gary Stevens and Ray Branighan all became internationals – but guys like Arthur Branighan and Keith Edwards played their part in the club's success too. Arthur never got the accolades his brother received because Ray was faster and Arthur was more solid. He was the "Harry Wells" of our team – a big hard bugger in our backline. There was a lot of affection for a guy like Keith Edwards in the team. He was the untold success story of 1971. Every one of those grand final players put in, played to their best and never shirked their responsibilities.'

Pittard says that he never had any issues with the club regarding contract money and had no inkling of the problems other players were having at the end of 1971. 'I never had a beef with (Secretary) Charlie Gibson, (President) Dennis Donoghue and (selector) 'Chicka' Cowie, and I always got paid. I found Souths to be very professional and generous.' He observes that a club couldn't have so many good players under one roof in today's game. 'That's the tragedy of rugby league today. Melbourne did it—illegally, as it turned out under the existing rules – and got stripped of their premierships. It's ridiculous. Why would you want to break up a team like Melbourne when they were such a good side and the players wanted to play together? It makes no sense. There's no loyalty to the players any more because clubs will get rid of them if they can't afford them under the salary cap. If clubs want to pay a lot of money for their players, then so be it. It's a restraint of trade to deny players that right.'

'It's like the Premier League in English Club soccer where the top four clubs always remain at the top. The clubs with the star players know they'll attract fans through their gates. It's the same principle as when Tiger Woods came to Melbourne in 2009. It wasn't about whether he won or lost, people will go to see quality players and quality teams. People appreciate quality … the rich will get richer but the poor will also get richer.' He laughs at the last statement. 'Here I am a Labor supporter but I'm a staunch capitalist.'

In 1972 Souths lost the brilliance of Ron Coote, the muscle of John O'Neill and the finishing power of Ray Branighan. Souths came back to the pack of teams which had been challenging them for premiership honours during the previous five seasons and lost the minor semi-final to St George. At the end of the 1973 Souths missed the semi-finals altogether and Pittard joined the exodus of stars who left the club. 'At the time I would go out to Parramatta for work and I would have lunch with commentator Ray Warren. Ray was a mad Eels fan back then and a couple of directors stopped by our table and asked if I would like to play for Parramatta in 1974. I told them they didn't have enough money … it was sheer arrogance on my part. They asked how much I wanted. I told them and they said, "Done!" When I got home I thought to myself, "Do I really want to go?" My solicitor Jim Comans said I was mad if I didn't take the offer.'

Pittard played under coach Dave Bolton, his grand final nemesis from Balmain, in 1974 and former premiership-winning St George captain-coach Norm Provan the following year. He regularly captained

Parramatta during his two years with the club and even took on the goal-kicking duties towards the end of 1975 – a skill he had no need to develop at Souths. At the end of the season Parramatta qualified in equal fifth position with Wests and Balmain and had to survive two sudden-death qualifying matches to qualify for the minor semi-final. After defeating Norths on the final Sunday of the regular season, 28-13, the Eels accounted for Wests 18-13 on Tuesday and Balmain 19-8 on Thursday before upsetting Canterbury on Saturday, 6-5. This is where Pittard's 'big match' experience came to the fore.

'In those midweek games we had to keep lifting the young guys to get them "up" for the next sudden death match,' he recalls. '"We're not in the grand final yet," I'd tell them. After defeating Canterbury in the minor semi-final the biggest problem we faced was the week off before we took on Manly. Our coach Norm Provan had been there many times before, as had I, and we knew the week off in sudden death matches often leads to disaster. We ran out of puff against the Sea Eagles, losing 22-12. The campaign was historic and the effort the boys put in was remarkable. I was proud of the effort but disappointed with the result. We were ready physically, but not mentally.'

Pittard was tempted to play one more year under Terry Fearnley in 1976 (the Eels made the grand final that year) but retired after receiving an opportunity to study overseas. Starting out in radiology, he worked with Bob Honan in the insurance game during his playing career. 'Bobby Honan was before his time with a lot of the ideas he had. The sports resort in the Blue Mountains was a wonderful concept but he just didn't have the investment needed to get it going.' Both players lost heavily in the concept and the next decade was not all smooth sailing for Pittard. 'That's life,' he says, 'and that's rugby league. There are ups and downs, but you never give in and you just keep on going.'

Pittard declines to go into the finer details but says he has 'no qualms about anyone' from the past. It's just that he likes his anonymity and he says he no longer has an ego to feed. 'It's a case of out of sight, out of mind,' he says, explaining his absence from the limelight. 'I just roll along and mind my own business and I don't tell people what I do except that I'm still in the x-ray business. I haven't been to a game or a rugby league reunion for years. Don't get me wrong, I'm not a snob. It's a new chapter in my life – a new direction and a new comfort zone – and you don't tolerate fools or show-offs. You change your modality as you get older and yes, you become a little more conservative.'

Returning from overseas in the late 1980s he used to catch up with former teammates while working at Prince of Wales Hospital. 'I used to run into Bob McCarthy, Paul Sait and the late Gil Macdougall because they were patients there getting one thing or the other x-rayed,' he laughs. In the late 1990s, as a favour to Ray Warren, Pittard made a rare appearance on the Sunday Footy Show in the popular 'Legends of League' segment. 'The show was very light-hearted so I bought a red bowtie to wear on television. When I got back to work at Prince of Wales everyone from the doctors to the duty nurses were wearing red cardboard bowties. The camaraderie there was great, just like at Souths.'

Pittard and a group of past players used to catch up at Souths Leagues Club on Fridays but those days are gone and the game has moved on. Although he has taken only a passing interest in rugby league since Souths were excluded from the NRL competition and then readmitted, he says: 'I'm a huge Russell Crowe fan. To get a guy like that who is totally committed to the club and willing to put his own money into it was great for Souths. His commitment and loyalty is typical of Souths' supporters – on-going and a never-wavering believer in the club.'

In the past decade Pittard has been busy overseas setting up his x-ray business. Several partners and work commitments have kept him away from home and Glenda, his second wife of 37 years, for long periods of time. 'Life hasn't been a bowl of cherries; it's been a pretty hard slog, actually. When Souths last offered me Life Membership I was working hard and then I got sick. I wasn't even home to enjoy the honour, let alone go to the club and receive it. It can be lonely overseas—and there's never any NRL matches on TV on a Friday night!'

And yet, with only three days in Sydney before he had to return to Paris, why was it so important for him to have his story told in this book? 'Because I was part of that great Souths team,' he says simply, 'and that's important to me.' As one of only two members of Souths' golden era to decline Life Membership (Keith Edwards is the other) is there any circumstance, I ask, where he would accept the honour. 'I'm appreciative and I'm humbled to be asked, and my wife and kids would like me to have it, but it has been taken 33 years for Souths to get to me and therefore, if I was viewed as one of the major players of that era, then maybe I should not have been in the first lot of players to be recognised, such as juniors like Cooty, Macca and Saity, but then the second or the third intake. Yet it's taken all this period of time. It couldn't have been a fallout with George (Piggins) because I haven't spoken more than a handful of words to him in forty years and there was never an angry shot fired between any of the Souths player while I was there. George's job at the club was far more important than worrying who was on the honour list. He's "done good", our George.'

The issue is moot as far as Pittard is concerned. 'In saying that, I haven't been invited to a Parramatta game or given Life Membership there either. Both clubs have been negligent in that regard, I suppose, while Wests have always acknowledged my contribution. I wish Souths, Parramatta and Wests well, but I still hate Manly!' he laughs at the old competitive streak bubbling out of him.

Denis Pittard has worked hard to reconcile his past and has no grievances with Souths, any of the players or the game of rugby league. At age 65, he is content to work for another five years before retiring to some quiet spot on the planet—but once again, it will be out of the limelight. Maybe then there'll be time for some overdue recognition and club honours.

PART 3: LET IT BLEED (1970–71)

As rugby league entered a new decade, South Sydney was planning 'big'. At the beginning of 1970, Souths announced a $1.5 million dollar extensions to its leagues club in Chalmers Street, across the road from Redfern Oval. 'A three-storey addition, which should be completed next year, will double existing club facilities and entertainment areas,' the club trumpeted, '… 12 drinking bars and three separate dining rooms. The club will also have two sauna baths, one each for men and women, and a gymnasium. A new auditorium with its own mezzanine floor will increase the club's facilities for its top-line entertainment.'

Grand plans for a great club, but within three years, the premises would close and Souths would face bankruptcy.

At the same time as the leagues club was expanding, there were huge issues with the running of the Rabbitohs' football club. Jim Morgan left for Easts, Brian James announced his retirement before the start of the season when he couldn't agree to terms with the club and Arthur Branighan was in dispute with Souths until he was signed to a new contract. The club's football committee, which numbered 10 members with five forming a 'retention committee', faced the prospect of keeping all its star players under one roof. And Souths hoped to strike gold again with another rugby convert, Wallaby centre Phil Smith, who formed a good partnership with Bob Honan in the early part of the season but whose career was ultimately cut short by injury.

Souths started the road back to becoming the premier club with an easy 38–5 win over Penrith in the opening match of the season on Easter Saturday. There was still complacency in the South Sydney camp, however. After a not so convincing, 26–20 win over Newtown at Henson Park, Bob McCarthy was quoted in the press as saying: 'A spell seems to come over us every time we set foot on that ground … I knew before the game we would be flat to the boards winning. We were joking and kidding about and not in the right frame of mind.'

The Rabbitohs were back on the job against Easts at the SCG, winning 18–7, in one of four consecutive 'match of the day' fixtures at the SCG. 'They are a great side; whoever beats them this year will win the premiership,' Roosters coach Don Furner lamented. 'Souths owned the SCG during that era,' Bobby McCarthy told me without a hint of bravado. The 1970 season bears that out, with the club making nine 'match of the day' appearances in 22 rounds of football.

On 2 May, Souths defeated Balmain in a grand final replay at the SCG in the presence of Her Majesty Queen Elizabeth II. With the Tigers floundering in the early part of the season, Manly emerged as Souths' main rival for premiership honours in 1970. Manly won a tryless match at the SCG, 10–6, beating Souths at their own game by landing four field goals. In the domestic Test series against Great Britain—the only Ashes series played under the four tackle rule in this country—Ron Coote, Elwyn Walters, John Sattler, Bob McCarthy and Bob Grant represented Australia in different Test teams, but the selectors failed to find a winning combination and the Ashes were lost.

Souths, on the other hand, kept the nucleus of its champion team on the field during that winter with three juniors—Ray Branighan, the younger brother of veteran clubman Arthur Branighan; forward-turned-centre Paul Sait, and hard-tackling forward Gary Stevens—fighting their way into the team. Ray Branighan filled in at centre, five-eighth and fullback, and proved to be a more than capable back-up goal-kicker before finding a regular place on the wing. Bob Honan had a mixed season, with selectors once again displaying perfect timing in dropping him from first grade on the eve of the semi-finals after he arrived late for training due to work commitments.

A worrying sign for the club was reserve grade's failure to make the semi-finals that year (third grade were beaten 6-5 by Easts in their grand final). Souths still had a champion first grade team but the days of being Club Champions were now behind them.

In an anomaly of programming, Souths defeated Manly in the final three games of 1970, all at the SCG—24–20 in the final round of competition, 22–15 in the major semi-final and 23–12 in the grand final. After two straight losses, Manly's tactics were to strong-arm Souths in the opening exchanges in the grand final. But the move backfired when Sea Eagles' prop John Bucknell hit John Sattler in the jaw in a vicious, off-the-ball incident in the fourth minute of the match. Seeing Sattler injured so badly and then stay on the field actually lifted Souths. Two first half tries, to Bobby Grant and Ray Branighan, set up a 12–6, half-time lead but Souths punished Manly in the second half. The Sea Eagles could not breach Souths defence and resorted to kicking field goals to stay in the match. A record six field goals were kicked in the 1970 grand final—four by Simms and two from Manly's Bob Fulton—but when Grant strolled over for his second try with six minutes remaining, the grand final was well and truly won.

And still Sattler refused to leave the field. After full-time he made a short victory speech and completed the lap of honour with his players but hardened pressmen knew something was wrong. There were chaotic scenes in the South Sydney dressing after the grand final when news of Satts' broken jaw was revealed.

There were 'fisticuffs' back at Souths' leagues club and a lack of recognition and planning left the players high and dry. Contracts were torn up when players confronted officials over their decision to celebrate the premiership at an inner-city restaurant and failure to visit Sattler in hospital.

The ill-feeling towards certain club officials was put on hold when eight Souths players were named in Australia's World Cup team, and Ron Coote was named captain. When the tourists defeated Great Britain in an unlikely Cup final, 12-7 at Leeds, it was arguably the gutsiest win by a national team in Australian Rugby League history. And Souths players were right in the thick of it.

1971 saw the adoption of the six-tackle rule and the reduction of the field goal from two to one point. The field goal had become a blight on the game but neither rule change fazed South Sydney. Clive

Churchill was quoted at the time, 'Souths will show the spectators how six-tackle football can be exploited ... six tackles enables us to combine the backs and forwards in moves and gives us more scope to attack. We still have the best pack in Sydney and they'll give our fast backline plenty of opportunity. Our pack revelled in the four tackle rule as our three premierships in four years proves. This rule suits them better ...'

Before the start of the season, Mike Cleary was placed on $5000 transfer, reduced to $4000 on appeal, and joined Jim Morgan at Easts. Bobby Moses joined Manly and John Sattler and Ron Coote were involved in protracted contract negotiations during January. Sattler agreed to a three-year deal but Coote, Australia's victorious World Cup captain, held out for a contract upgrade. Feeling Souths were taking him for granted, Coote's request to be placed on open transfer was rejected and he opted to sit out the opening rounds of the season before coming back to the game disenchanted with his club's stance.

How could this have happened? Simple economics, mismanagement and a lack of planning.

At the beginning of 1967, Souths had only two international players in their ranks—rugby converts Jim Lisle and Mike Cleary (Jim Morgan was a non-playing reserve for Australia in 1966). By 1971 the club had eleven internationals—Ray Branighan, Bob Honan, Ron Coote, Bob Grant, Bob McCarthy, John O'Neill, Denis Pittard, Paul Sait, John Sattler, Eric Simms and Elwyn Walters. Conservative estimates indicate total contract payments had inflated ten-fold in four years. In five consecutive seasons (1967–71) Souths played in front of more than 500,000 people, but gate receipts alone could not cover increased match payments and upgraded contracts.

There is an old saying ... those who do not prepare for the future do not have one. Souths officials were on borrowed time, and the era of easy money and reflected glory from rugby league premierships was coming to an end.

Souths won the opening six rounds of competition, with the

prodigal Ron Coote returning to the fold in the 36–19 win over Canterbury. John O'Neill was sent off in the match against Parramatta and captain John Sattler lasted one minute against Canterbury before he too was given 'an early shower'. With two Test props rubbed out of the game, Bob McCarthy moved to the front row and Paul Sait shifted back to the second row when Souths suffered their only loss in the first round, to Manly, at the SCG. The club's lack of depth was exposed in the 15–7 loss to the Sea Eagles and Souths suffered a mid-season loss of form which saw them lose three consecutive matches and surrendered top of the table to Manly.

With seven top-line players carrying injuries following Australia's mini-tour of New Zealand, Souths considered resting key players and potentially sacrificing a top-two place in the play-offs. The idea was rejected and Souths thrashed Norths 40–7 to reignite their premiership campaign. The form of Denis Pittard was central to Souths resurgence in the latter part of the season. Later that year Pittard became the first player to win the Rothmans Medal for 'Best and Fairest Player' in the Sydney premiership for a second time (Pittard won his first award in 1969).

The Rabbitohs secured second place in the minor premiership ahead of St George and Parramatta and then shocked Manly in the major semi-final, 19–13. Bob McCarthy piloted Souths into the 1971 grand final with a masterly display in front of a crowd of more than 50,000. Manly led 7–6 at half-time, but McCarthy's try, and his setting up of two more, dented the Sea Eagles' hopes of a maiden premiership title. The following week the Sea Eagles suffered a 15–12 loss to St George in the preliminary final and Souths were installed as short-priced premiership favourites.

It was only fitting that Souths took on St George in the last of its five consecutive grand finals. The only remnants of the great Saints team that had defeated Souths in the 1965 grand final were Graeme Langlands and Billy Smith, the two champions who had combined to defeat Manly the week before. This was a new look St George team, however; coached by Jack Gibson with a lighter, more mobile forward pack. 62,838 fans crowded the SCG for the grand final—the biggest grand final crowd since the heady days of 1965—but Souths would have the final say in the 1971 premiership.

The only score of the first half was a field goal to Eric Simms, his first of the year. There were other missed chances—Denis Pittard was pulled down a yard short of the line after a long run to the Paddington corner of the field abd Bob McCarthy was called back after scoring a try from a forward pass—but the teams went to the break with the unfamiliar score 1-0 posted on the historic SCG scoreboard. Quick tries to Ray Branighan and Ron Coote, and two goals to Eric Simms, gave Souths and 11-0 lead midway through the second half. Souths tended to go into their shell and play the game in thee forwards. St George were not done with yet, and Billy Smith sent Barry Beath barrelling over the line in the 66th minute to start the comeback. Lock Ted Walton scored minutes later and Langlands' conversion reduced Souths' lead to a solitary point. It was left to Souths' 'old firm' of Coote and McCarthy to produce the winning try which sealed the 16-10 win in the final minutes of a classic match.

1971 produced a different grand final feeling for John Sattler to 12 months earlier, although he was just as inspirational in setting up the try for Coote and marshalling his forwards late in the match. Replacement hooker George Piggins, called into the grand final team when Test hooker Elwyn Walters broke his collarbone in the semi-final against Manly, won the scrums 15–12, made the initial break that led to Ray Branighan's try and changed the flow of the match on several crucial occasions when he raked the ball back in the play-the-ball. Ron Coote was judged 'man of the match' (he received the Clive Churchill Medal in 2008 when the award was handed out retrospectively) but this was to be his final game in the red and green of South Sydney.

On 13 December 1971, the High Court of Australia upheld the NSW Equity Court's decision that the transfer system clubs operated at the time was a restraint of trade. Instigated by Balmain player Dennis Tutty after he was denied a transfer to join Penrith in 1968 (Tutty sat out the 1969 and 1970 seasons, missing out on a premiership with the Tigers) the ruling freed up players to move from club to club without clubs posting huge transfer fees for their services. On Christmas Eve, 1971, Ray Branighan signed with Manly, John O'Neill followed him days later and Ron Coote agreed to terms with Easts before the start of the 1972 season.

Souths' last golden era had come to an end.

BOB MCCARTHY
(1967, 1969–71)

Bob McCarthy is sitting in his apartment overlooking picturesque Coogee Oval, contemplating the irony of his rugby league career. After scoring one of the iconic tries in grand final history, the free-running second row forward was controversially overlooked for selection on the 1967–68 Kangaroo Tour. Today he is chairman of selectors for the Australian Test team and looks back at that disappointment with a matter-of-fact, business-like attitude. '[Queensland] selector Duncan Thompson told Clive Churchill I was in the team,' McCarthy says. 'It's funny how things turn out.'

McCarthy—known as 'The Body' by his teammates because of his commanding physique—so revolutionised the role of the second row forward in the limited tackle era that selectors were slow to recognise the immense change that was happening in the game. Consider these statistics: McCarthy scored 12 tries in four years under the unlimited tackle rule and did not even cross the try-line in 1965 when Souths made the grand final that year. In 1967 he scored 13 tries, was often the leading try-scorer in the club and ultimately scored a century of tries for the Rabbitohs. Several excuses were trotted out as to why McCarthy was overlooked for the Kangaroo Tour—he stood too wide, he didn't pass the ball enough, his speed was not suited to the soft English grounds—all of them discredited over time—but it wasn't until 1969 that he broke into the Australian Test team.

McCarthy still looks incredibly fit and trains four days a week at a nearby gym. 'Ron Coote, Gary Stevens and myself were all fitness fanatics. When the forwards used to do sprints Ron would come first ahead of Gary and me but the others—John O'Neill, Elwyn Walters and John Sattler—weren't that far behind us. We were a very mobile pack. We'd go on road runs, which they now say is suicidal and we're paying for it now. I've had two hip replacements and a knee cleanout. Ron and Gary used to do a bit more stretching at training so they're not too bad. I'd go straight to the pub.'

Robert John McCarthy was born in Redfern on 5 August 1944. The middle son of a working class family in Chelsea Street, older brother Bill (1962–64) and younger brother Rick (1978) also played for Souths. 'I was a good player at school, a chunky five-eighth,' Bob recalls, 'but as I got older, I got faster. One year I went down to the beach and played beach football … I couldn't believe how fast I was, going from the beach to the grass.' Bob was selected as a second row forward in Souths' Jersey Flegg team in 1961 and toured New Zealand with Ron Coote, who became a lifelong friend.

'I grew up in Redfern surrounded by terrace houses,' he says. 'I was only 16 and had never been out of Sydney before, and Christchurch was like a picture from a book with a beautiful mountain with snow on it.' Coote, as captain, was billeted at the ground where the team trained but Bob stayed on a farm 15 miles outside the city. 'On the first morning the lady cooked a mixed grill for breakfast … I could smell bacon, eggs, sausages, chops, lamb's fry, steak … and I said, "Who's this for?" She said it was for me. I asked where her husband was and she said he was at work. "How am I supposed to get to training?" I asked. "It's 15 miles away." She said there was a bike outside or I could ride a horse.' Bob took the bike.

McCarthy represented President's Cup the following year and

was graded with Souths in 1963. His older brother, Bill, was already playing first grade for the Rabbitohs. 'Billy was a fiery, red-headed, wild bugger. He might have even been a better player than me, but he didn't like training. He'd get to the ground to play reserve grade and Bernie Purcell would find him with a pie and a coke in his hand, but he'd still be the best player on the field. He could fight like a threshing machine. He fought two heavyweights at the Showground at Jim Sharman's boxing troupe as a 15-year-old and knocked the pair of them out. You were supposed to get £10 if you lasted three rounds. Sharman gave him 30 bob to piss off.'

At Souths, McCarthy was supposed to serve an apprenticeship in reserve grade. 'I had a big future in the game, they told my Dad, but they had bought a new lock from Newcastle called John Sattler. The club said, "We'll nurture Bob for the year and we'll give him £500 for four seasons," which I thought was as good as gold. We played Manly in a trial match and Satts got sent off. When I went to training, the players were all shaking my hand and saying well done. I'd scored three tries in reserve grade and I thought they were talking about that but they said I was in first grade. I played almost every game that year as lock, and when Ron Coote came to grade the following year I moved to second row.'

1965 was a breakthrough year for the young Souths team. 'We beat Saints three times that year and each time we beat them, Richie Powell played. We could have won the grand final that year had Richie played. He had the best hands you'd ever seen … as good as Bob O'Reilly.'

After the disappointment of missing the play-offs in 1966, the following year brought a new coach at Souths and a new era in rugby league. 'Clive Churchill realised that under the four tackle rule I wouldn't get the ball if I didn't stand out wider. Clive remembered that I'd played a couple of games in the centres and had scored a couple of tries against Canterbury when he was coaching them in 1964. He just said to stay out wide and work your way back into the centre for defence. We won a lot of premierships under that rule so it obviously suited our style of play.'

Of that famous moment in the 1967 grand final when McCarthy intercepted a pass and ran almost the length of the field he says, 'I was on the blind side and I could see the Canterbury players coming across after a switch of play. I said to Brian James to move up with me, and as we moved up Les Johns was chiming into their backline. Canterbury had the overlap but their hooker Col Brown turned and passed without seeing me there. I just went "wooshka." If he had seen me, I would have had to have tackled him and Canterbury would have scored the try.'

As McCarthy streaked away from the Canterbury chasers his hamstring went on him at the 25 yard line. 'I went in to Churchill at halftime and said I was gone, but he said I had to stay out there. You were allowed one replacement up to halftime and Mike Cleary had to come off. He had a crook groin muscle and it was easier to hide me in the forwards. I went to dummy half with my leg strapped up and Elwyn Walters played second row. There were a few other tries on offer in the second half that I could have scored had I been fit but it was my job to get the ball out to the other players.'

He is philosophical about his omission from the Kangaroo Tour, read out on grand final night. 'I may not even have been able to pass the medical,' he says. 'Dave Watson, one of the selectors, was a Souths man but never spoke a word to me. I wasn't even the shadow second row forward for that tour. I later found out that Queenslander Geoff Connell was on standby if anyone pulled out. And they didn't take Arthur Beetson or Bob Fulton. In those days there were three Queensland selectors, two City selectors and one Country selector, so the Country mob must have done a deal with Queensland.'

Such was the public outcry over McCarthy's omission, food chain Flemings gave him an all expenses paid trip to watch the Kangaroos play every match in England. 'Flemings were opening a food store in Mascot and I think they wanted to appeal to all the Souths fans,'

McCarthy says. 'I stayed in a little unit near the Ikley Hotel where the Kangaroos were staying. John 'Pogo' Morgan was leading a tour to England and he came and stayed with me as well. We used to mix with the players all the time. Reg Gasnier said there were 28 players on that tour—not just the 26 that were selected—it was just that Pogo and I couldn't play.'

McCarthy was injured for most of 1968 and made his comeback in reserve grade late in the season. Not that any of the clubs had access to state of the art treatment. 'We didn't even ice an injury back then … the only ice you saw back then was in a scotch glass at the leagues club,' McCarthy says. 'I kept pulling the quadriceps in both my legs and the doctors didn't know how to treat them. I came back for the semis but Clive said he couldn't trust me not to break down again. He got me, John O'Neill, Mike Cleary and Ivan Jones to play reserve grade and we thrashed minor premiers Balmain. I scored a couple of tries and thought I'd be picked for the grand final but on the Tuesday night Clive said he wasn't going to pick me. I wasn't happy but I did have the habit of coming back from injury too quickly and he just wasn't going to chance it. In the reserve grade final against Manly, Ivan Jones made a break and I ran 50 yards to score under the posts to wrap up the win. So much for breaking down.'

In 1969, McCarthy was selected in the Australian team to tour New Zealand with six Souths teammates. The Rabbitohs had usurped St George as the glamour Sydney club. "We had a brilliant team in 1969. Mike Cleary and Brian James killed them and Bobby Honan was no slouch. Mike Cleary was our movie star, our 'ET'. When we used to come to training we would park on the street. Mike was allowed to park inside the ground. Freddie West was the Australian masseuse and he only worked with superstars. When I first went to Souths he said for me to hop up on a table and he'd give me a massage. I felt really privileged. I'd never had a massage before. Cleary walked through the door and Fred said, 'Want a massage Mike?' and told me to get off the table because it wouldn't do me any good anyway.'

The grand final loss to Balmain remains a sore point, as it does for many of the Souths players. 'I never conceded defeat until a minute to go but (referee) Keith Page kept on taking tries off us. Brian James was disallowed a try in the corner ... if he'd passed inside to me, I was under the posts and it's 5-nil. Minutes before half-time John O'Neill took the ball, turned his back on the opposition and passed it to me on the blindside. I took off and cut inside [Balmain fullback] Bob Smithies and Page called us back. He ruled I was offside. How could I be offside when I came from behind O'Neill? Ron Coote put me under the posts, the pass was marginal, but the try was disallowed again. Every time I questioned him, Page would just yell at me to get away.'

And Balmain's tactics? 'Dave Bolton was a pale pommie and he had a suntan by the end of the match,' McCarthy laughs. 'Satts yelled at Keith Page to get them up but under the rules of the time, play had to stop. Balmain were a good side and they were good tactics but the penalty count that day (16–7 to Balmain) made it a carve up. Put it this way, we won the next two competitions and they didn't even make the play-offs. We were angry about 1969 and we were determined not to lose another one.'

McCarthy propelled Souths into the 1970 grand final with a masterful, two-try effort in the 22–15 win over Manly in the major semi-final. The Sydney press heralded him as the most dynamic second row forward in the game. But the grand final started in the worst possible way. 'I was standing beside Satts when he had his jaw broken. Satts went up to smack John Bucknell in the tackle but [Manly hooker] Freddy Jones darted back inside after a runaround. As they came back onside, Bucknell punched Satts in a downward motion. If he'd hit him from underneath, Satts' mouth guard may have cushioned the blow, but because the punch came down from a height it ripped everything apart. Satts half-hit the deck, and when he came back into line he went to say something and his mouth fell apart.' McCarthy meted out his own sense of justice when he hit

Bucknell across the chest in a ball-and-all tackle and then drove him into the SCG pitch on the point of his spine. Bucknell left the field at halftime.

McCarthy became a regular member of the Australia Test team in 1970. On the sidelines, injured, when the first two Ashes Tests were played, McCarthy was called into the deciding Third Test of the series in Sydney. He scored Australia's only try in the 23–17 loss, which saw the Ashes return to Great Britain. 'The selectors used to pick the nucleus of the top teams, either Saints or Souths, and build the team around them. This year they chopped and changed the teams and there was no combination among the Australian players. Great Britain improved as the series continued. In the World Cup at the end of the year, the selectors picked eight Souths guys and built the team around them. That's why we won.'

McCarthy knew that Ron Coote would do a great job as World Cup captain. 'I would rate Ron in the top five players of all time,' he says. 'He wasn't a talker, he was a doer.' McCarthy also felt for his friend Graeme Langlands who was the nominal captain only to be ruled out with injury. 'Chang broke the scaphoid bone in his hand. It's a small fish-shaped bone that holds the thumb together. It doesn't have a lot of blood flow through that area so it takes a long time to heal. The medico wanted him to do a push-up but Chang said no. He had played injured for years, getting needled up so he could play, and had never had to do a physical before. I told him to clench his fist and do it that way, but he refused and was ruled out.'

Two pieces of McCarthy magic contributed to the upset 12–7 win over a previously undefeated Great Britain team in the World Cup Final at Leeds. The Lions were leading 4–2 approaching halftime when McCarthy hit opposing lock forward Malcolm Reilly in a ball-and-all-tackle close to the Great Britain tryline. Reilly, the most damaging of the Great Britain forwards during their successful Ashes campaign that year, lost control of the ball and McCarthy fired the pass to Ron Coote who sent footballing priest Father John

'Big Jim' Morgan powers past St George defender Billy Smith at the SCG.

Bob McCarthy gets a rub down and some last minute advice from coach Clive Churchill before a big match at the SCG. It was Churchill who gave McCarthy a roving commission to stand out wide in attack and to drift back into the centre in defence. The rest is history.

TOP: Former Newcastle centre-turned-forward Bob Moses tackled by a Wests' defender while playing for Souths in the 1960s.

BOTTOM: Ron Coote is surrounded by Balmain defenders in the 1969 grand final. Souths lost the match 11-2 in a major upset.

'The Sweet Taste of Success' ... John Sattler savours victory in the 1971 grand final win over St George with (from left) coach Clive Churchill, Bob McCarthy, Eric Simms, Denis Pittard and John O'Neill.

OPPOSITE TOP: Souths players visit fan Don Lane on the set of his *Tonight Show* in the mid 1960s. From left: Ivan Jones, Brian James, Ron Coote, Eric Simms and Jim Morgan.

BOTTOM: The club's international players meet Souths officials to consider defying an edict from the ARL to stand down from club duties prior to their departure on a short tour of New Zealand in July 1969. From left: Denis Pittard, Elwyn Walters, Michael Cleary, Bob Honan, John Sattler, Club President Dennis Donoghue, Club Secretary Charlie Gibson, Ron Coote and Bob McCarthy.

South Sydney, 1968 Premiers: (Back row) Bob Moses, Ron Coote, John O'Neill, Jim Morgan, Arthur Branighan, Mike Cleary. (Front row): Elwyn Walters, Bob Honan, Denis Pittard, John Sattler (c), Brian James, Bob Grant, Eric Simms.

Ron Coote, the epitome of sportsmanship, helps fallen St George captain Graeme Langlands to his feet following Souths' 16-10 win over the Dragons in the 1971 grand final. It was Coote's last game in the red and green jersey.

Cootes in for the try. With Australia leading 7–4 in the second half, McCarthy chimed into the backline and lobbed an overhead pass to Lionel Williamson who barged over in the corner. Simms converted from the sideline and Australia withstood a late challenge to win the World Cup.

After the highs of 1970, McCarthy played in Australia's shock 24–3 loss to New Zealand the following year. 'Carlaw Park was disgraceful,' he recalls. 'At high tide, the water seeped up from underground and it rained heavily and the mud was like treacle. The Kiwis really gave it to us, though. A New Zealand strapper was working with us and told us that Kiwi forward Robin Orchard had a broken toe, the left one. Bob O'Reilly stomped on Orchard's foot in the first scrum; Orchard yelled "wrong one!" and it was on.'

The day started out wrong and only got worse. 'At breakfast there was no toast with our bacon and eggs and we asked for the hotel manager,' Bob recalls. 'The manager said that the Australian officials had banned toast. We couldn't believe it. When [tour manager] Dick Dunn came down he said that [coach] Harry Bath had banned it. Harry came down for breakfast and we said, "Where's the toast?" He said it was a well-known fact in English football that on wet days you didn't eat toast because it weighed you down in the mud. He had to be kidding! It was pouring rain, but we blew up and Harry said, "Have your toast, then!" After we came off the field battered and beaten the first thing Harry said was, "I told you the toast would beat you!"'

The 1971 season produced Souths' last grand final appearance and McCarthy had the distinction of scoring the final try of the match. As he put the ball down under the posts to secure Souths' win, McCarthy punched the air with a victory salute. Maybe it was a subconscious farewell gesture to the crowd because Souths have not played in a grand final since, but he almost missed the historic moment. 'I was on the ground with a cramp. Satts ran past and said, "Get up Macca, we need you!" As I got to my feet Coote made the break, I cut across inside and scored. A simple philosophy led to most of my tries … be where the ball is. That's what I was taught as a kid. All the good players follow the ball.'

As players started to leave the club, Souths slipped to fourth place in 1972 and then missed the play-offs in 1973. 'The club committee got lazy,' McCarthy says. 'For years, champion after champion came out of the junior ranks and Souths thought it would be a never-ending story. The kids coming through in the 1970s were good, but there were no more Cootes or Branighans.' Or McCarthys, for that matter. 'There wouldn't be any more internationals come through until the 1980s when Terry Hill, Jim Serdaris and Ian Roberts arrived,' he says. 'Still the club couldn't hang on to them.'

In 1973, McCarthy was named vice-captain to Graeme Langlands on the Kangaroo Tour. 'We won eight straight games and were labeled the best Kangaroos side ever but Great Britain caught us with our pants down and smacked us 21–12 in the First Test. All of a sudden they were bagging us in the press, saying Chang had to stand down.' Langlands suffered a tour-ending injury before the Second Test and McCarthy was named captain. 'Just before half-time the Pommies held me up in a tackle and Brian Lockwood took a running jump, kneed me in the back and dislocated my shoulder. I stayed on the field and shortly after half-time Bob O'Reilly put me through a hole, someone ankle-taped me and I came down hard as I scored the try. My shoulder was at right angles. [Trainer] Alf Richardson got it back in but it popped out in a scrum and I was replaced by Ken Maddison.' Australia won the match 14–6, and ultimately the Ashes, but McCarthy's tour was over.

The shoulder injury gave him trouble all through the next season but famed conditioner George Daldry got him fit for the Second Test of the Ashes series in Sydney. McCarthy's final appearance in the green and gold was in Australia's Ashes-deciding Third Test victory at the SCG. Having taken over as club captain following the departure of John Sattler, McCarthy led the Rabbitohs back into the semi-finals in 1974. Beaten by Wests 24–8, Souths slumped to last the following year.

'We won four out of five games and were joint leaders of the competition in 1975,' McCarthy says of that dire year. 'Lurch O'Neill came back from Manly and Bob Honan and Keith Edwards came out of retirement, but we didn't buy well and the forwards were getting old. Clive Churchill was frustrated. We led many games at halftime but just couldn't finish off. I came to training one night and [Souths President] 'Nipper' Nilson said Clive had resigned. I said not to put another coach in and they asked me to take over for the final five games of the year.'

McCarthy rates the last game of the year against Manly as was the worst game of his long career. Manly won by a then-record score of 54–0 and Souths were handed the wooden spoon. It was only four short years since the club's last grand final victory. But even in the darkest times, McCarthy can see the lighter side. 'Harry Eden got sent off in that match and then George Piggins was sent off for swearing at the referee, Kevin "Bilko" Roberts, a former Souths halfback. George actually dropped Bilko off at the game. He gave George a chance to apologise and he swore at him again. I offered to apologise on George's behalf but it was too late. After the game Bilko was waiting outside the ground for George to pick him up. I said to him he must be joking. George was already back at the Leagues Club.'

At the end of a horror season, McCarthy wasn't in the mood to negotiate contracts. 'I said to [Souths Secretary] Charlie Gibson I was happy to play for the same money and he said I wasn't as good as I used to be. I knew that, that's why I only wanted the same money I was on the previous four years. He said he'd think about it and I thought, bugger it, I'll just retire.' McCarthy was at Giles gymnasium at Coogee when Peter 'Bullfrog' Moore visited him and asked him to play for Canterbury. 'I told him I couldn't play against Souths. He said he had all these young kids coming through, the Mortimers and the Hugheses, and he asked me to think about it. Gary Stevens said I should give it a go and Souths didn't seem interested in keeping me so finally I said yes. Charlie Gibson rang straight away and asked if it was true I was joining Canterbury. I said yes, and he said Souths would match the offer. I told him it was too late, I'd agreed to the deal. He asked me if I signed anything. I said no, but I'd given them my word.'

McCarthy, who became a life member of the Souths club in 1975, still holds the record for most first grade games with 211 appearances between 1963 and 1975.

At Canterbury, McCarthy made his mark, captaining the club into the semi-finals in 1976 and scoring 19 tries in 40 appearances for the club. Graeme Hughes, who was a promising young forward at the club, later wrote that McCarthy not only taught Canterbury how to win but how to bond as a team. A shoulder injury in 1977 saw him contemplate retirement again but a phone call from newly-appointed Souths coach Jack Gibson changed his mind. McCarthy was, at first, skeptical. 'I told him the club thought I was too old two years ago and asked if I grown young all of a sudden. He said the club needed a ball-running forward. I told him they got rid of a bloody good one in 1975. I wasn't that keen, but Souths had a contract ready for me so I came back. Gibson rarely spoke another word to me that year. We played Canterbury in the pre-season final and he asked every player, "How are we going to beat Canterbury?" He skipped right past me and I had captained them for the past two years! I spoke to Harry Eden about it, he worked for Jack, and he said, "Macca, he's working on you! I bet you really want to show him now." We won the final 10–3 and I set up both tries. After the game he thanked every player and skipped right past me again. I was growling!'

After another shoulder injury, McCarthy was happy to retire at the end of 1978 but Bob Fulton talked him into playing a trial for Easts in the pre-season competition. The 34-year old was still training well but after a reserve grade trial he told his wife Judy that it was time to give it away. He later coached Brisbane Souths to a premiership in 1981 ('the club hadn't won a premiership since 1948,' Bob says proudly) and Combined Brisbane to a win in the midweek Panasonic Cup in 1984. The Brisbane Broncos sounded him out for the coaching job in 1988 and asked him how he would handle Wally Lewis. 'No problems, I told them. I coached Wally in 1984. Paul "Porky" Morgan said I had the job but they changed their mind. They asked Jack Gibson who he would pick and he said Wayne Bennett.'

It was then that he got another call from Peter 'Bullfrog' Moore. 'He asked me to take on the coaching position at the Gold Coast–Tweed Heads 'Giants'. Moore was going to be the CEO of the new club. I asked if he had any players and he said no-one at the moment, but he would be bringing five Canterbury players with him, including Steve Mortimer. I said no, but Satts rang me and Bob Hagan rang me. I eventually signed on as coach and Peter Moore stayed with Canterbury.' McCarthy says the club went for big name players in order to make an immediate impact and came up short, rather than grading locals and slowly building a following. 'Nobody wanted to see the Gold Coast getting hammered by Parramatta, but we beat Brisbane at home, 25–22,' he says with some satisfaction.

McCarthy was keen to come back to Souths and waited for Frank Curry to finish his contract in 1993. 'George Piggins said I could have the coaching job but Alan Jones was coming in as football operations manager and if I didn't get along with him I would have to take a walk. They were banking on Jones bringing sponsors and players to the club. We won the pre-season competition, beating Brisbane 27–26 in a nail-biter at Albury. Four-quarter football really suited our young team. Just as the Broncos were winding up, it would be time for a break. But rather than celebrating as a team, the young blokes went into town to the local disco and I had a beer with a stranger at the Albury-Wodonga Motel bar.' Times had changed, and with Alan Jones running the show, McCarthy left the club citing 'health reasons.'

When Souths was excluded from the NRL in 1999 McCarthy marched with the other ex-players and voted for George Piggins when the club was privatised in 2005. He hopes George will come back to the club one day and stand for the Leagues Club Board. 'Now, at least, we're a viable football club, we can win a competition and can afford good players like Greg Inglis.' A City selector since 1994, McCarthy took over as Chairman of the NSW and Australian Selectors in 2000. The NSWRL conducted a review of its State of Origin operations and asked McCarthy why the Maroons have won the last five series. 'I gave five reasons ... Slater, Inglis, Lockyer, Thurston and Smith.'

Would he do it all again? 'I'd love to be playing now' he says. 'It's a different game now, there are no more cheap shots but there are no more ball-playing forwards either. I wouldn't have to play 80 minutes a match, nor would I play for 16 seasons. I would take the big money for 10 years and then sit on a boat in the Mediterranean.' Both of McCarthy's sons, Darren and Troy, also fared well in the game. Darren won a premiership with the Bulldogs in 1988 and Troy played with the Gold Coast before finding premiership success as a coach of the Tweed Heads Seagulls in 2007.

'My daughter Cassandra has my grandchildren wearing Parramatta jerseys because she lives out west,' he laments, 'but they wear Souths underwear underneath.'

PAUL SAIT
(1969–71)

South Sydney junior, Paul Sait, came of age as a first class match-winner in the month after the Rabbitohs won the 1968 grand final against Manly. A handy utility player, he was the ideal squad member for the major premiers' short tour of New Zealand at the end of what had been a breakthrough year for the 22-year-old. In New Zealand, Souths defeated champion Kiwi club Mount Albert, club team Ponsonbery and a Combined Māori outfit before being challenged to a match billed as the 'Australasian Rugby League Championship' by premier Brisbane club, Brisbane Brothers. With an $8000 prize at stake, Souths flew to Brisbane to take on the northern champions during a heat wave on 20 October 1968. Bob McCarthy takes up the story:

'Brothers Brisbane had Dennis Manteit, Johnny Gleeson and Peter Gallagher, who captained Australia on the 1967–68 Kangaroo Tour, in their team and had recently beaten St George in an end of season tour match. I rang Changa Langlands and asked what the hell happened up there and he said that the team had all been on the drink the night before but Brothers were definitely beatable. We were offered $300 a man, which was big money in those days, and we beat them 55–15 in 90-degree heat (about 32 degrees celcius). We scored 13 tries to 3 and for two of our tries I didn't even have to move from the shade under the eaves of the old Lang Park grandstand. Brothers made the mistake of kicking off to Paul Sait and he put that big step of his on them and scored untouched in the corner. They then kicked to him again and off he went. I just stood there smiling … what a player. Clive Churchill was yelling at me from the dugout, "Earn your money Macca!" We were all so dehydrated after the game we couldn't get up off the floor.'

Sait was the reserve forward in the match and didn't even come on into the game until the second half when he replaced Ron Coote. Scoring two tries that Sunday afternoon against the locals marked him as a player of the future. The fact that he had the game's best lock forward in front of him at Souths didn't deter him either. Sait merely moved into the centres and wreaked his own special brand of havoc in the champion Rabbitoh backline.

Paul Joseph Sait was born in Matraville on 4 June 1947. His uncle Bob Sait played for Souths (1954–55) and Easts (1959) and Paul says his family followed Souths all their lives. A local junior, he started his rugby league career with Maroubra Junction and then played for Matraville Tigers. From the time he left school he never played in a team that did not make the grand final. 'I represented Souths' Jersey Flegg and President's Cup before being graded as a lock in 1967,' he tells me on the phone from his home in Kurnell where he is recovering from his second knee replacement surgery. 'Ray Branighan and me played all our football together—until he went to Manly, of course—all the way through the junior rep teams and into grade at Souths. Almost every grand final Ray played in, I played in. In 1970 we made our international debuts in the World Cup and we played for Australia in six consecutive years (1970–75). We were that close we were almost joined at the hip.'

Sait played 16 third grade games in 1967 before moving to second grade and playing in Souths' losing grand final team against Balmain. The following year he appeared in 12 first grade matches, scoring five tries, but was dropped following Souths' shock 23–15 loss to Manly in the major semi-final and had to settle for a win in the club's second grade team alongside Ivan Jones, Bob McCarthy, George Piggins, Gary Stevens and, of course, Ray Branighan. It was a different story the following year.

'I grew up dreaming red and green,' Sait says. 'I just wanted to be a Souths player ... to wear that red and green jersey. My goal from the start was to get to first grade. Ray and I came into the top grade a couple of years after Macca and Cootey, and Eric [Simms] and Gary [Stevens]. We were the next wave of juniors, so to speak. Although they were only a couple years older than me, I idolised Bob McCarthy and Ron Coote as players—I used to watch them from the hill at the Sydney Sports Ground in 1964. It was the biggest thrill for me just to be graded at the same club as them. But I was a backrower, the understudy to Ron Coote, and I just couldn't get into first grade in front of that international pack of forwards so Clive Churchill finally put me in the centres.'

Sait showed good early-season form in the centres, often with Ray Branighan on the wing or as his centre partner. Sait had good leg speed and could step off both feet, a rarity in the game when most big-steppers favoured one foot. He instinctively knew how to mark his man, to get on his outside in attack or force his opposing centre back inside in defence. 'I feel a bit guilty playing out in the backs,' he told pressmen in 1970. 'I come home from a match and I say to my wife, Dulcie, "I don't think I've done enough to earn my money". I like to get involved ... to be in the thick of things.' Sait was hard, aggressive and intimidating. 'I learned the hard way coming through the lower grades, how to play the game. In the second grade grand final against Balmain in 1967 you had someone like Bobby Boland up against you ... you learned pretty quickly.'

Sait started working for Randwick Council in the 1960s and lifted weights with Gary Stevens in his spare time, so fitness was never a big issue for him. His good early form as a centre drew rave reviews from the great Reg Gasnier, who was writing a weekly newspaper column at the time. Gasnier called Sait one of the game's most 'talented all-round players' and state selectors also started taking notice. In the fourth match of the interstate series, which was played in Newcastle on 28 June that year, Sait joined clubmates John Sattler (captain), Elwyn Walters and Bob McCarthy in the Blues' forward pack. The incredible thing was that Paul Sait was playing reserve grade at the time.

I struggle to remember any other player who has been selected to represent his state from reserve grade. Max Krilich, the veteran Manly hooker, was selected for City Seconds from reserve grade in the early 1970s (World Cup rake Freddy Jones was the club's top hooker at the time) and no doubt established players coming back from injury may have made the leap from reserve grade to rep duty during the 1920s or 1930s, but Sait's stellar career was only in its infancy in 1969. 'I was very nervous before the match at Newcastle. I brought my parents up to watch the match but I started vomiting in the dressing sheds. That started Changa Langlands throwing up and that set the team off.' NSW won the match 22–12.

Sait made 10 first grade appearances during the 1969 season but with Souths breaking all records in first grade, he could not force his way into the club's top team in the lead-up to the semi-finals. Resigned to playing a third straight second grade grand final, Sait was left without a date on grand final day when minor premiers Souths lost both finals, to Balmain and Manly respectively, and were knocked out of contention in the reserve grade premiership. Instead, he sat on the bench in first grade alongside George Piggins and the Branighan brothers hoping to get a run in the second half of Souths' grand final showdown with Balmain.

It was well known in Souths' ranks that Bobby Moses was coming back from a rib injury and may not last the match. Sait was the logical replacement when Moses was forced from the field at half-time. By the time Sait came on the field the momentum of the match was all Balmain's way. 'It was frustrating,' he says. 'The ref did us no favours, with the Balmain players going down injured all the time.'

Sait never got the opportunity to use his big step and Souths never got warm in the second half. Approaching full-time he barged across the line and the Tigers' players piled on top of him. Referee Keith Page quickly ruled no try and ran back to the quarter-line. When the players peeled off Sait had the ball on the ground over the line and stood up, nonplussed at the ruling.

Sait played all 24 matches of the 1970 season as a centre three-quarter and also represented City Seconds against Country, played for Sydney Colts against Great Britain before taking his place in Souths' grand final winning team. A bad case of the 'flu almost proved his undoing, however. Before Souths' semi-final clash against Manly, Sait asked to be stood down from training because of the effects of a bad cold. Souths' selectors had installed a 'no train, no play' policy to overcome a perceived lack of discipline in the club and Sait was told to train in the rainy conditions. After fifteen minutes of running around Redfern Oval, Clive Churchill told him to go home to bed.

In the 1970 grand final, he was so intent on marking Manly's Bobby Fulton he did not see the incident in which captain John Sattler had his jaw broken. Six weeks later he was partnering Fulton in the final of the World Cup.

On grand final night, Sait was one of eight Souths players selected in the Australia's World Cup squad. He made his debut in the green and gold jersey as a second row forward against New Zealand in Wigan and appeared in all three matches of the competition as a forward. But in the Final against Great Britain at Leeds, he was chosen as a centre. 'Once again, it was the only place I could get into the team,' Sait laughs, but coach Harry Bath opted to put the robust Souths player in the centres to mark Englishman Syd Hynes and promoted hard-working Ron Costello into the forwards pack. 'As long as I was in the team, I didn't care,' Sait says. 'They could have picked me as hooker. It was a huge thrill, with so many Souths players in the side.'

Not surprisingly, Sait roomed with Ray Branighan in England, the kid with whom he played most of his junior football. After he returned from England, Sait told the press, 'The training the squad did, before they left and when they were there, by the time you finished training or playing, all you felt like doing was having a meal, a few beers and a yarn and then flaking. I remember after we lost to France (in the third match, 16–15) we had our liberty cut down even further and training stepped up ... We were a young side and every single player was breaking his neck to make the [team of] thirteen.'

'We knew we could beat the Englishmen, even though they were favourites and not many people gave us a chance. They had beaten us 11–6 in our first game when they got their win through a late try and Eric [Simms] didn't have a good match with his goal-kicking. In the final our tremendous fitness played off.' It was the end of the season in Australia and the start of the season in England. 'England were only 70 per cent fit,' Sait said.

The 1970 World Cup final, known as 'The Battle of Leeds', is remembered as one of the most vicious Anglo-Australian sporting contests on record. Early in the match Syd Hynes hit Bob Fulton with a stiff arm tackle and Sait immediately came in and gave him the same punishment. Minutes later, as Sait ran the ball out from the Australian line, he was targeted by the Great Britain forwards for a 'square up' and was left dazed and bleeding after a high shot. Wearing a head bandage for the remainder of the half, Sait injured his right knee when he rushed up to tackle Great Britain fullback Ray Dutton. Minutes before halftime he collapsed under the weight of his buckled knee as he supported Fulton in attack. He limped on for the remainder of the half before being replaced by his Souths' teammate Ray Branighan.

'Every time an Englishman got the ball—and they had it most of the game—there were two or three Australians tackling. Watching the second half from the sideline, I could see the Englishmen tiring and the Australians getting on top.' The match finished in pandemonium, with players trading punches after Australia's 12–7 win. Sait looked like a professional wrestler in his Australian tracksuit top and playing gear, tearing feuding players apart. 'I damaged my knee cartilage in the final and had it operated on when I got home. It took me six weeks to get over the injury and that set me back at the start of the 1971 season. They obviously do those operations much quicker these days. I've just had my second knee replacement and I was only in hospital three days … and I walked out. The technology they have today is just amazing.'

Paul Sait epitomised the new breed of professional footballer who played the game at the highest level for almost a solid 12 months. In four seasons, he had missed only one match and had amassed almost 100 grade games. 'First grade footballers gave up a great deal—leisure time with their families, restriction of their social life, the physical toll on their bodies from training and playing …' he was quoted as saying in 1970, 'Then there is the psychological strain of holding your place in the team, getting worried about being injured…'

The chunkily-built, 5 foot 10-and-a-half-inch international was disappointed in his form when he returned to the field in 1971 and he quickly realised his days as a dashing centre were numbered. 'As a professional footballer, if you get hurt you just have to get back to training. I always had to train hard in the off-season to keep my weight down but I lost a bit of speed and came back in '71 in the second row.'

Australian selectors picked him in the touring team for New Zealand but in hindsight, his selection as centre in the one-off Test against the Kiwis may have been a miscalculation. No doubt coach Harry Bath had memories of Sait's brave stance against Great Britain the previous year, but Sait was coming back from a knee operation and his attacking skills were nullified in the Carlaw Park mud. New Zealand won the match 24–3 but Sait remains philosophical about the overseas tours. 'Despite losing the Test, it was still a good tour. Every tour I went on—World Cup in 1970 and 1972, New Zealand in 1971 and the 1973 Kangaroos—was a great experience in their own way.'

By the end of the year, Sait was at peak fitness and took his place in Souths' grand final team in the centres. 'Grand finals are always hard,' he says. 'You battle all season to get into a grand final but once you get there it's a whole different story.' His initial break led to Ron Coote's second half try and helped set up a winning 11–0 lead. But then the team started to disintegrate. 'I was only young—24 years old —and was just starting to get into the rip of things. Losing all those good players was hard for the club but we just had to step up and take control.'

When Ron Coote left for Easts at the end of 1971, it gave Sait a chance to come out from underneath the champion lock's shadow and be a leader at the club for the remainder of the 1970s. 'By the end of my career I played centre, lock, second row, front row and even five-eighth. I'd play anywhere as long as I was in the team.'

Sait missed the domestic Test series against the Kiwis in 1972 because of injury but after Souths were knocked out of the minor semi-final by St George, he joined teammates Bob McCarthy, Gary Stevens and Elwyn Walters in Australia's World Cup squad. 'The referees weren't much good over there but it was a great experience being in France. I missed the final with an injured knee and coach Harry Bath wouldn't put me on the field after I failed the fitness test. I sat up in the broadcast box with 'Tiger' Black and spoke on the radio for about 10 minutes and watched the final from there.'

The 1972 World Cup final finished in a 10–all draw but there would be no second chance for Sait, or Australia for that matter. Instead of replaying the match, organisers awarded the trophy to Great Britain because of a superior record in the competition.

Souths missed the semi-finals in 1973 but Sait, McCarthy, Stevens and Walters again toured together overseas with the 1973 Kangaroos. At age 26, Paul Sait was at the peak of his prowess on the frozen English rugby league fields and with Ron Coote declining to tour because of business reasons, Sait appeared in all three Tests against Great Britain as lock forward. He played in four of the five Tests on that Ashes-winning tour, only surrendering his position to Cronulla's Greg Pierce in the First Test against France in Perpignan because of an injured wrist. Keen judges have rated Australia's Ashes-winning forwards—Arthur Beetson, Elwyn Walters, Bob O'Reilly, John O'Neill, Bob McCarthy, Gary Stevens, Paul Sait and Ken Maddison—as some of the finest packs to tour England.

The following year, with Ron Coote returning to Test duty, the champion Australian pack reprised their Ashes-winning form and defeated Great Britain in the Third Test. Sait played in the first two Tests, but when Bob McCarthy returned from injury, Sait moved to the reserve bench. The following year, with Souths falling from grace and heading for the competition cellar, Sait, Gary Stevens and John O'Neill, who had returned to the club from Manly that year, represented Australia in the domestic leg of a revamped World Series competition. By the end of the year, only George Piggins was chosen to tour England for the return leg of the competition. It was the end of an era for Souths.

'After making first grade I just wanted to win a competition with Souths, which I achieved in 1970,' he says. 'Despite all the players disembarking I was happy to stay. I had offers from Canterbury, Norths and Cronulla but Souths offered me a four-year contract and I was happy to see out my career there.' Lurch O'Neill and Bobby McCarthy came back to club but after they retired and Gary Stevens left in 1976, Sait and George Piggins were the last of the premiership winners to remain at Souths and helped the next generation of kids to come through.

Although the club did not reach the heights of their golden era, Souths remained competitive during the latter half of the 1970s and maintained a keen rugby league following. Sait captained the team under the coaching of John O'Neill in 1977 and shifted to front row. 'Lurch was the first to admit that he was a little bit out of his depth but we all gave him a good hand and helped him through it.' Jack Gibson coached the club in 1978. 'Jack was mad on fitness. He used to make you run 15 kilometre fitness runs. I used to train with Gary Stevens in the off-season, so that helped me get through it.'

'I was hoping to get picked in the 1978 Kangaroo Tour as a prop forward,' Sait admits, 'but I was carrying a lot of injuries by then and my heyday had passed.' So had South Sydney's, the nursery of rugby league champions.

But by the end of 1978 his career was winding down and he decided to retire the following year. 'Souths wanted me to play on and I probably could have broken the club record for most matches but I didn't want to. Bobby McCarthy has that record and he deserves it. My knees were gone by then but I went into coaching and took Wests Wollongong to two premierships in 1980–81. I came back to Souths and coached lower grades in 1982–83 but I gave it away when I couldn't go any higher. I coached pretty much the way I played ... getting players to move the ball about.'

Souths was a like a big family, Sait says, and they bonded like a family and that's why they won so many competitions. Whenever Souths had a barbecue on a weekend, the wives and children went too. Paul and wife Dulcie raised three children in Matraville—Virginia, Paul Jnr and Christopher—before moving to La Perouse where their family has grown to include eight grandchildren. 'Both boys played a bit of football and Chris coached La Perouse A-Grade to a couple of premierships as well as several NSW Aboriginal knockout teams. He's done well.'

Paul Sait, the big-stepping South Sydney centre-come-forward, has had both his knees replaced—the first in 2003. Now retired from the Council, the 'tough bastard' who John Sattler still holds in the utmost respect in the champion South Sydney teams of the late 1960s and 1970s, lives in Kurnell, in 'Sharks' territory and is surrounded by his grandchildren.

GARY STEVENS
(1970–71)

Gary Stevens apologises as he shakes my hand at the front door of the Malabar home he built forty years ago. We were meant to catch up earlier that morning but he phoned to ask if I wouldn't mind rescheduling the interview to that afternoon. Clem Kennedy, the stalwart Souths man who shaped the career of many of the club's juniors as a six-time President's Cup winning coach (1960–65) had passed away and his funeral was being held that morning. Stevens, who remains supremely fit and gives a rock hard handshake as I enter his home, is still in his suit pants and white shirt as he walks me into the foyer.

'Clem was a great man,' he says, apologising again as he takes me on a tour of his bar room which is lovingly decorated with memorabilia from his career and that of his grandfather, the former Test forward Arthur Oxford. 'A lot of Souths' boys were at Clem's funeral,' Gary says. That's where the members of the Rabbitohs last great era catch up in numbers—reunions and funerals.

Some years ago, Tom Brock, the gentlemanly South Sydney historian who left $200,000 to the club when he passed away in 1997, told me that Gary Stevens' career was a lesson to any young player that international success does not happen overnight. Stevens, who made his first grade debut as a 21-year-old in 1965, did not establish a regular first grade position as second row forward until some five years later and did not make his international debut until he was almost 29 years old. What Tommy Brock didn't tell me is that Stevens is one of the nicest people you would meet on a long walk. Generous with his time, his scrapbooks and his memories, Gary shared his career with me that afternoon as we look out over The Coast Golf Course from a stylish glass gazebo attached to the back of his house.

'You know, we had almost a dozen juniors in those grand final teams,' he tells me. 'Many of us played against each other as youngsters, came into grade together at Souths and went on to be internationals. It was a great time to be at Souths in the 1960s.'

Gary Richard Stevens was born on 4 January 1944 in the Sydney suburb of Pagewood. Gary says thoughts of following in his grandfather's footsteps as an international—or following older brother Wayne to grade at Souths for that matter—was the furthest thing from his mind. 'My father came from Broken Hill and never played the game,' Gary says, 'so rugby league wasn't a big part of our lives growing up. I saw all the old photos of my grandfather Arthur in a scrapbook, and I knew his sons played for Souths and Easts, but I had no idea of what playing for Australia even meant. I grew up in Pagewood, not far from Maroubra Beach, and as a teenager I got into surfboard riding in a big way.'

Stevens didn't know it then but he would create history by becoming the first grandson of a Test player to also represent his country in rugby league. Arthur Oxford, his maternal grandfather, played four Tests between 1919 and 1924. A noted goal-kicker in his day, he played for Souths from 1915–21 and Easts from 1922–29. Stevens represented Australia in 1972, somewhat late in his career, but went on to make 11 Test appearances during the next two years.

'I played football at St Charles Primary School and later at Christian Brothers, Waverley and won a couple of premierships but I left school at age 14 to work with my father as an apprentice carpenter. I just loved surfing on the weekend so I gave football away for a couple of years in the early 1960s.'

The surfing craze was really taking off in Sydney at the time but older brother Wayne talked Gary into coming back to the game with the Pagewood club. 'The club's gone now,' Gary says, lamenting the fate of many clubs in the South Sydney district. 'I then went to the Chelsea club for 12 months and represented President's Cup in 1964. I played a few grand finals that year, including two with Chelsea and one with Souths' President's Cup team.' Stevens was named 'Rookie of the Year' and was graded in Souths' third grade. He finished the year in the Rabbitohs' premiership-winning reserve grade team.

Stevens contemplates the fact that he was not a regular first grader for several seasons. 'I spent a lot of time in the lower grades but I stuck it out when many players went to other clubs. I wasn't interested in going anywhere else. I was a Souths man.'

He says his discovery of weight training, years before it was fashionable in sport, was the key to his success. 'When I was 13 I read about fitness training in a magazine so I started lifting weights. When I went into grade at Souths, friends would say that I would get too muscle-bound and I wouldn't be able to play. I was very light for my age but they said that I was mad for training in a gym … you just didn't do that at the time. But without weights I wouldn't have been successful. I used to train at Billy Moore's gym at Mascot. That's why I could pick up bigger players and drop them on their heads.'

Stevens started his career in the centres in junior football and moved to lock/five-eighth in the senior grades. 'I shifted into the back row at Souths but without weight training I wouldn't have been able to keep up with the bigger forwards. Bobby McCarthy was more than 16 stone and my best weight was 13 stone 4lbs.' He played in just 34 first grade matches between 1965 and 1969, appearing in three consecutive reserve grade grand finals (1966–68, the first two with brother Wayne on the wing) and won titles in 1966 and 1968.

He was on track to make his first grade grand final debut in 1967 but a shoulder injury left the door open for Alan Scott to come into the team.

'I used to get a "man of the match" award almost every second week in reserve grade but I wasn't a good ball player so I didn't get much of a run in first grade. (1964–66 first grade coach) Bernie Purcell was known as a ball player, as was [reserve grade coach] Les "Chicka" Cowie in his day. They didn't see defence as the most important part of the game, like they do today. Defensive players will win you more games than you can lose … as they used to say, "attack for show, defence for dough".'

Souths had an 'international' forward pack in the late 1960s with Sattler, Walters, O'Neill, McCarthy and Coote maintaining the standard during the club's run of five straight grand finals. Gary Stevens finally provided the missing ingredient in that champion pack in 1970–71 and joined the ranks of the club's Test stars the following year. 'It was very competitive at Souths, but I never gave up. I enjoyed my football too much to give it away. I was keen on winning and I loved the training. They used to say not to train the day before a game but I thought that was ridiculous. I was always fit, even in the off-season. Sometimes I couldn't help myself. I racked up huge tackle counts, including 56 in one game, which was a record at the time. If an opposing player had the ball I just wanted to hit them as hard as I could … not hurt them … just hit them.'

But there were frustrations along the way. 'I played against Balmain in the 1969 semi-final and we beat them 14–13 to qualify for the grand final. Bobby Moses came back from injury and I was dropped for the grand final, which Balmain won.'

But his perseverance paid off at a time when many others would have sought a first grade position with a rival club. 'Every year I had to fight for a spot but it made me more determined. Souths lost the 1969 grand final and I was in first grade from the get-go the following year.'

The 1970s was Stevens' time to shine. The perfect second row foil for Bob McCarthy, Stevens raked up huge tackle counts in his matches. His philosophy was simple—tackle low. There was no point going high on a player when size was against you, he says. He got his first taste of representative duty in 1970 when selected for Sydney Colts against the visiting Great Britain team. The curious tour match, played at Cronulla's Endeavour Field, saw the Sydney boys captained by former English halfback Tommy Bishop. Stevens played well in the 26–7 loss to the tourists, and was unlucky not to join a swag of Souths' teammates on the end of season World Cup tour.

His initial first grade grand final experience was certainly an eye-opener. 'We hated Manly,' Stevens admits, 'and we always had tough games against them.' As soon as John Sattler was hit and momentarily went down on one hand, Stevens knew his captain was hurt but didn't realise the extent of the injury. 'Bobby McCarthy said to look out for Satts because he was bleeding from the mouth. I did a bit of tackling for him and I could see it was a bad break ... his bottom teeth were all over the place. People who have had a broken jaw can't believe that you could play a rugby league grand final with one. Well, John Sattler did.'

None of the players could have known that the 1971 grand final was the end of an era. Stevens says the majority of players were not privy to what was going on behind the scenes at the club with contract renewals. Stevens had a fine game in the grand final and came of age as an attacking player, making the break that led to Ray Branighan's try just after half-time. 'St George came back in the grand final, as only good sides can. We led 11–0, then Satts belted one of their players and they came back at us hard and made a game of it.'

But three players in that team—Branighan, O'Neill and Coote —would not wear the red and green the following year. Stevens was dumbfounded at the club's lack of urgency to re-sign players. 'We had just won our fourth title in five years and wanted to stay together. It was such a shock to us when the club couldn't come to terms with the players. I still can't fathom how Souths went bad [financially]. We were the top side, the leagues club was always full … someone must have been doing something wrong. The club started to struggle financially but the club committee still didn't confide in us. Manly won two premierships and Easts won another two with some of our most influential players. It's fair to say that we could have won four more titles if we'd kept our team together.'

As Souths' champion team began to slowly fall apart, Stevens says there was no animosity between the players. 'We've known each other for forty-odd years and have never had a blue. Back then we'd go for a drink after training, although I was never a big drinker, and socialise together with our wives and kids. Even when players went to other clubs we used to get together after training or go out to dinner. There were no hard feelings. We were still mates. And we remain so today.'

That bond was forged on the rugby league field but also in the workplace. 'After I got my ticket as a carpenter I worked for a company owned by LJ Hooker for a couple of years and then started my own building company with John O'Neill. He was a "chippie" when he came down to Sydney from Gunnedah in the mid 1960s so I asked him to come into business with me. We later formed a company with Jimmy Lisle and Bob Honan—Dominant Constructions—and renovated terraces in the inner city. Ivan Jones worked with us, as did Bobby Grant and Bobby Moses. We hired people we knew, including lots of young blokes from the club, and we also had our own building projects as well.'

Souths were beaten in the 1972 minor semi-final, thus ending their run of grand final appearances, but Gary Stevens' international career was just beginning. In October, he joined teammates Elwyn Walters and Bob McCarthy in the Australian squad that went to France for the World Cup competition. 'Playing for Australia came right out of the blue,' he admits. 'You'd hear rumours that selectors were looking at you, but at 29 years of age it wasn't on the radar for me.' He considers all the factors working against him at the time. 'I wasn't young, I wasn't a good ball player and I'd spent five years in reserve grade. It goes to show that you never toss in the towel.'

The following year he toured England and France with the 1973 Kangaroos. 'I roomed with Paul Sait on tour. Our nicknames were "Salt and Pepper", we were together so much. Paul and I knocked around with Bob O'Reilly for much of the tour.' Stevens has great memories of the traditional Kangaroo Tour of England and France. 'Hard games, playing in the snow and getting sent off in a minor match,' he smiles. 'I'm a placid sort of a guy,' he says before adding without a hint of irony, 'I didn't want to hurt anyone, other than trying to bury them. I rarely got cautioned. I got sent off for punching Englishman Brian Lockwood on tour but I was exonerated. I guess that doesn't count then.'

Australia had lost the Ashes in 1970 and were hell-bent on winning them back in 1973. 'I was injured for the First Test [which Great Britain won, 21-12] but played in the final two Tests of the series. [Englishman] Phil Lowe killed us in the First Test and my job was to tackle him out of the Second Test at Leeds. Bobby McCarthy was captain, Paul Sait came in as lock and Elwyn Walters was the hooker. We won the Test (14–6) and then held them out in the decider. The Souths players really stood up on that tour.'

The 1974 Ashes series in Australia proved to be a turning point in Stevens' career and ultimately had huge ramifications for his later life. Overlooked for Test duty in the 12–6 win over Great Britain in Brisbane, he came back into the team for the Second Test in Sydney. There were five Souths juniors selected in that Test —reserve back Ray Branighan, then playing with Manly; lock Ron Coote, then playing with Easts; backrowers Paul Sait and Gary Stevens; and reserve forward Bob McCarthy. 'We had the "old firm" back together,' Stevens says, 'but I don't remember a minute of the match.'

Early in the match, Stevens was knocked senseless in a high tackle attributed to fiery Welshman Jim Mills. 'I suffered severe concussion but I stayed on the field. I have a photo of me getting up off the ground so I know I played the match. We lost the Test but luckily the selectors stuck with me for the Third Test in Sydney.' Fired up by the deeds of captain-coach Graeme Langlands, Australia won the deciding Test of the series, 22–18, and retained the Ashes won in England the previous November. But the undiagnosed effects of Stevens' head injury would come back to haunt him decades later.

'Gary was incredibly tough,' Stevens' second row partner Bob McCarthy told me. 'We were playing in a match together at Souths and he came up to pack into a scrum with a grimace on his face but I didn't think too much about it. At the next scrum he still had a pained look on his face and I asked what was wrong. He said he had dislocated his elbow—it was sticking out at right angles. I told him to go off the field and he asked me, "Do you mind?" Can you believe that? Do I mind?'

Gary Stevens played the final international match of his career during the Australian leg of the World Series competition in 1975. His good early season form saw him play successive Tests against New Zealand, Wales and England. Stevens and John O'Neill pulled out of the English leg of the competition at season's end because of their business commitments following a downturn in the building industry. Neither would play for Australia again.

Souths finished with the wooden spoon in 1975. 'There was so much conflict in the club—getting rid of Clive (Churchill) midseason, getting rid of the players—we were just stunned. Then Bob McCarthy left at the end of the year, which should never have happened.' Stevens took over as captain in 1976, playing in 21 of 22 matches with Souths finishing in tenth place on the table. 'We improved a couple of places on the competition ladder,' he says with some satisfaction, but then it was his turn to leave the club he loved.

'Souths pretty much let all their internationals go ... Ronny, Lurch, Ray, Elwyn, Denis and Bobby all went to other clubs. Then I left at the end of 1976. The club's retention committee could have said,

"We're struggling financially but we'll look after you in the future," but they said nothing. If they had have said "we will pay you when we come good", a lot of us would have stayed at Souths. 'I signed a four year contract with Souths for $10,000 payable over eight years … with no interest!' he laughs. 'I got the final payment two years after I finished my career with Canterbury.'

In 1977, Stevens joined Bobby McCarthy in the blue and white of the Bulldogs. 'At age 33, I was thinking of retirement but Bob said to come over to Canterbury. I played only a handful of games in 1977 because I caught hepatitis.' It was the era when players went down injured and were treated with a sponge in a bucket of water. 'The Magic Bucket' they used to call it, players would share from the communal sponge regardless of injury. When Balmain pair Neil Pringle and Wayne Pearce also came down with hepatitis in the next three seasons, the League finally got rid of the sponge in the bucket.

'It was the only thing we could put it down to,' Gary says. 'I don't know how I could have caught hepatitis. I was still super fit but I was always tired. I used to come home from training and tell my wife I must be getting old. I'd go for another run, which was the worst thing I could do. I was killing myself. Then I was diagnosed with hepatitis.'

Stevens came back for the last three games of the year and then played most of the 1978 season. 'Canterbury stuck with me during my illness. The guys were fantastic young blokes. I was like a grandfather to them. You could tell the club was going places; they were a young team learning how to be professional. The discipline they had in the club was unbelievable. We never had that at Souths, but then we didn't need it because we had so many champion players.'

After 14 seasons in the game Gary retired as a player and concentrated on his considerable building interests. Dominant Construction went by the wayside in the early 1970s, but he still had the successful building company he formed with John O'Neill. The company now employed over 40 people and was involved in multi-million dollar construction projects. Gary also had his own family company, 'Stevens and Sons' and won a lucrative contract to oversee the maintenance at News Ltd premises in Surrey Hills, and later Chullora. His family company still operates there.

'It's been a Stevens' family operation for more than thirty years. My brother Wayne used to run the News Ltd operations, my younger brother also worked with us and also my three sons. I told my boys—Brad, Jason and Aaron, the youngest—to work out what they wanted to do but if they didn't get a job, then they worked for me. They all went to "Tech" and got their ticket as carpenters. The older boys have moved on but Aaron now runs the business.'

Stevens also got involved in Giles gymnasium in the late 1970s, a local landmark overlooking Coogee Beach. 'Les Motto, who was working with us at Souths, used to train there and the three of us—John, Les and me—went into managing it together. The beauty of it was a lot of old footballers used to come in and train—Changa Langlands used to go there and all the other St George boys, and because we had other income from football and the building game, we didn't charge everybody. It wasn't a money-making concern for us. We had a 20 year lease with a 20 year option but when the lease came up, another gym came into the area and complained to the council that we weren't charging people. We made enough to cover overheads, but we never got the money back that we spent on it. We put two stories on top of the existing property and completely renovated the place. The council got rid of us in the end and pulled it down.'

In the 1980s, Stevens bought the Courthouse Hotel in Redfern for $850,000 with former teammates John O'Neill, Bob McCarthy and Richie Powell. Although the investment was not a success he was later part of a group that secured 40 hectares of land at Lake Conjola on the NSW South Coast. Every Wednesday night he and wife Kay would have dinner with Ron Coote, John O'Neill and George Piggins and their wives, and talk invariably turned to business. The four subdivided a section of lakefront land each but Gary never built on his block. Instead he has a holiday house on the other side of the lake and hosts his children and grandchildren, two families at a time, at Christmas and Easter.

'I play a little golf at Mollymook but I'm just a hacker,' he says. 'We fish and canoe on the lake, and bike ride through the scrub down to Milton. We never stop.'

Gary and wife Kay's four children, including daughter Melanie, are all married and live close by and the Stevenses now have 15 grandchildren. Gary bought his first block of land at Malabar in the early 1960s before moving closer to the golf course. 'Malabar was like the end of the earth for some people. They used to ask, "Are you the poor member of the building partnership? What are you living there for?" Now people pay millions for a block of land.'

Despite all the upsets and upheavals at the club over the years Gary Stevens remains a Souths man. 'I don't get involved in politics,' he says, 'and football has changed so much because of the money in the game. That's thing that has killed rugby league ... money. Players today are full-time professionals but they don't do anything else with their lives and when their careers are over at age 30, they think, "What am I going to do now?" The years from age 20 to 30 are the most important years of your life. That period sets you up for the future.'

Gary Stevens, a self-made millionaire, could teach the current generation of 20-somethings a lot about hard work and setting yourself up for life. But he is not a political animal and it is easy to see that his loyalties are torn between his close relationships with George Piggins and his brother, Wayne Stevens, who was on the Souths' Board of Directors when members voted to sell control of the club in 2006, and his love for Souths. 'I don't like to comment on the club too much because I'm not involved in it now,' he says. 'I marched with everyone else to save the Rabbitohs and supported George when Souths were readmitted in 2002. We all believed in what we were doing and I'd do it again. George and Wayne are now gone from the club and although I think Russell Crowe is a champion bloke, and without him we might not have a club today, I'm not sure that individuals should own a football club. Souths was always the "people's club". That's my opinion.

'But I can't say I'm not a Souths man—I am. I will be until I die.'

He acknowledges, though, that times have changed. 'No club looks after their junior leagues like they did in the 1960s,' he laments. 'There's no connection between Souths Juniors and Souths' senior club anymore. A lot of our players are established stars who are brought to the club; they're not local juniors coming through the ranks. It's a worry.'

And with that he takes me back to his bar room to have a look at the memorabilia on the wall. Stevens has lovingly restored his grandfather's Australian and NSW representative jerseys from almost a hundred years ago and has them beautifully framed beside his Souths' jerseys. There is a great colour photo of Stevens, O'Neill, Coote and Piggins dressed in black tie at a club fundraiser in the 1980s, their faces beaming in celebrations of good times and lasting friendship, and Gary says that he likes to look at the photo now that his friend Lurch O'Neill is no longer with them. He also has several jerseys, signed and framed, ready to hang on the wall or to give to his children.

He then proudly shows me an original oil painting of Souths' internationals for which he paid $10,000 at a club fundraiser. 'Russell Crowe was the under-bidder. When he saw that I was bidding for it, he backed off which shows what a good bloke he is.'

In another room is a home gymnasium, which Gary uses four times a week to stay in such great shape. He is now retired from his building business, he says, because his short term memory is going on him. It all goes back to that day at the SCG in 1974 when he was hit in a stiff-arm tackle playing for his country. 'I developed a clot on my brain which doctors think affected my short-term memory. I can remember what happened years back but I have difficulty remembering what I did 10 minutes ago.'

He says this matter-of-factly without a hint of sentiment or regret. 'Physically, I'm perfect. I enjoy life and I keep myself fit. I walk the golf course out the back every day … training is like opium for me. I'm addicted to it.' There is another reason he trains so hard, he admits. 'You see, I don't want to be a burden on anybody.'

Gary Stevens looks back on his time at Souths with great fondness. 'I never had a cross word with anyone, just a lot of laughter and good times. And they're still my mates today.'

RAY BRANIGHAN
(1970–71)

Ray Branighan wants to set the record straight. 'I loved Souths, I loved the opportunity of playing with Souths, and I loved the players we had. People still hate the fact that I left Souths but they don't know the real reason and what went on behind the scenes with the club committee. The truth is I never went to Manly for the money ... and [Manly Secretary] Ken Arthurson didn't approach me on the 1970 World Cup Tour about joining the Sea Eagles either. I rang him at the end of 1971 because I was disenchanted with the way Souths' committee were handling my contact negotiations. I wasn't on big money at Manly but I stayed with the club because they looked after me and my family. You'd go to a club function or a barbecue and the officials would talk to you, get your wife a drink and look after you, and that went on for seven years.'

Branighan was the first South Sydney international of that era to leave the club, signing a contract to play with Manly on Christmas Eve 1971, but he was not the last. 'Basically, if you get enough knives in your back you're going to die from a loss of blood ...'

Raymond John Branighan was born on 5 December 1947. A Moore Park junior, he represented NSW Under 6-stone team as a 12 year old and his path to grade at Souths was set in motion. 'I was in the second row back then,' he remembers. 'Johnny Hipwell [later a rugby international] was in that team, as was Alan Dagwell [1975 NSW rep from Newcastle], who was billeted with us at Revesby, and [future Canterbury and Parramatta halfback] Terry Reynolds. I grew up with Pauly Sait in the junior league, playing H Grade to C Grade with him, and we came to Souths about the same time.' A silk-screen printer by trade, Branighan worked at Bankstown at the time older brother, Arthur, was making his reputation as a promising centre with the Rabbitohs.

In 1967, the younger of the Branighan brothers received notification that he was in Souths' President's Cup squad, but living in the Canterbury district with his parents, and knowing that Arthur had already been denied a place on the strict residential qualification rules of the time, it was pointless trying out for the team. Instead he was graded in Souths' third grade team as a five-eighth. Ray finished the season as a centre in Souths' second grade grand final team which lost to Balmain. He made his first grade debut the following year.

'I played a couple of first grade games as a replacement before my first "run on" game. My first time on the field in first grade was at Redfern Oval against Parramatta. Ken Thornett was the fullback that day and I thought he would kill me.' Parramatta won the match 18–14 and although Branighan scored a late try, he was to fare no better in his official first grade debut three weeks later.

'That was an easy one,' Ray laughs, 'against St George at the SCG in front of 35,000 people.' St George won the match, 28–19, but Branighan backed up a week later and showed his goal-kicking prowess in Souths' 20–6 win over Balmain. 'I was always a goal-kicker as a junior but that pretty much stopped at Souths because of a man named Eric Simms. [Former club great] "Wacka" Graves gave me a lesson when I came into grade but I couldn't understand a word he was saying.' Branighan kicked three goals against the Tigers, but it was his last appearance in the top grade for the year. He finished the season as a centre in Souths' grand final-winning reserve grade team. 'It didn't worry me too much when I got dropped. I was 20 years old and playing with all these fabulous players.'

But Branighan was a fast learner. 'I learnt pretty quickly that when two players were running at you to always cover the man in support because at the last moment a fellow called Ron Coote would come across and tackle the man with the ball.'

Although he was a specialist five-eighth, Branighan was used as a utility back during his early grade career. He made nine first grade appearances in 1969, but again finished the season in reserve grade with the club easily securing the minor premiership. Inexplicably, Souths lost both lower grade semi-finals and missed qualifying for a fourth consecutive grand final. While the first grade team was heading for a shock loss to Balmain in the first grade grand final, Ray sat beside his brother Arthur on the reserves bench. 'I remember that day very clearly,' he says. 'Saturday 20 September, 1969 … the day after my daughter Rayner was born.'

It took Ray Branighan three seasons to become a regular member of Souths' first grade team, and even then it was as a winger. In 1970, playing fullback in the absence of the injured Eric Simms, he kicked 14 goals in the opening two matches of the season—the 38-5 win over Penrith and a 29-6 win over Parramtta—but did not kick another goal all year. Branighan's form on the flank was a revelation in the early part of the season and he was selected for City Firsts. On the first day of training he worked up the courage to front coach Harry Bath. 'I'd had a couple of games on the left wing and asked Harry if I could play there. [St George legend] Johnny King was the other winger in the team and he was a left winger. Harry said, "No, just do your best, son."' Brnighan then made his State debut in the final match of the interstate series in August. Played in Newcastle, he kicked three goals in NSW's 32–15 victory and all of a sudden he was in the picture for World Cup selection at the end of the season.

After playing the majority of the season as a winger, Branighan maintained his place in Souths' team for the semi-final and grand final. 'The selectors were a bit fickle,' Ray recalls. 'I was graded as a five-eighth and had made my reputation as a centre/five-eighth in reserve grade but in first grade I was a winger.' Taking on Manly in the grand final, Branighan scored a try before half-time to send Souths to the break with a 12–6 lead. 'One try in the Members Stand corner of the SCG is worth 20 anywhere else,' he says. 'Two of my grand final tries were scored in that corner.'

Branighan doesn't remember anything particular about grand final celebrations, saying, 'Souths were never that great at looking after the players after winning a grand final.' After the 1970 grand final victory he waited nervously at home for the announcement of Australia's World Cup team. 'I couldn't hear any news of the team so I got on the phone and rang the sports department of a newspaper and they read out the team. I thought it was alphabetical order and when they went past the Bs I thought, oh well, that's it. I didn't make it. And then they read out my name towards the end of the list.' What did he do then, I ask?

'I went outside, threw up, and rang up again to just to make sure.'

Branighan was over the moon with his selection but Souths' committee quickly brought him back down to earth. 'At Souths there was a tiered system for contract money which had been implemented by Bernie Purcell when he was coach. Because I represented City, NSW and Australia during that year, I thought I would get a contract upgrade. Souths said no, it didn't start until the next year. I was already married with a young family and I actually had to borrow money to go overseas and represent my country.'

Souths supplied a record-equalling eight players for the Australia's World Cup team in 1970. 'And five of them were Souths juniors,' Ray points out, 'Coote, Sait, McCarthy, Simms and Branighan. Bobby Grant was desperately unlucky not to tour while Satts would have been a certainty.' The final against home nation Great Britain at Leeds ended in a 12–7 boilover to Australia. 'Great Britain was the best team in the competition by far but we never gave up,' Branighan says. 'Simms was fullback in the final, Lionel Williamson and Mark Harris were on the wings, and Fr John Cootes and Paul Sait were the centres, which put me on the bench. Saity was injured at halftime and I came on as a centre. That final, and the 1973 grand final, were the toughest games of my career.'

In 1971, Eric Simms broke his collarbone in May and Ray Branighan moved to fullback and took over the goal-kicking duties. Although not entirely comfortable at fullback, Branighan scored four tries and kicked 14 goals in five matches for a personal total of 40 points. When selected for NSW at the end of the month, Branighan was retained at fullback and replaced the injured Graeme Langlands. The following month he was in New Zealand with the Australian team. Branighan played all three games on the week-long tour, including the shock 24–3 Test loss, again as a winger. 'At Carlaw Park the mud was above your ankles. [Kiwi forward] Henry Tatana was kicking goals from everywhere. The ball was so heavy with water and mud I couldn't reach the posts from 30 yards out when I tried to kick it.'

For the second consecutive year, Branighan scored a try in Souths' grand final success. 'A minute into the second half, Gary Stevens went down the left hand side, passed to me and I luckily pushed off Billy Smith and scored as Graeme Langlands came across.' The try gave Souths a 4–0 lead which laid the foundation for the 16–10 win. But Branighan was not happy at the club. Souths had key players coming off contract—Ron Coote, John O'Neill as well as Branighan—and the club committee was delaying contract renewals to the start of the 1972 season when they hoped that the internationals would stick with the club.

Branighan remembers the weeks leading up to Christmas as tense and frustrating. 'In that two weeks, the "dummies" we thrown both ways ... Souths said they weren't going to give me any more money, I said see you later and they thought I'd just sign up for next year. I was between a rock and a hard place. I never wanted to leave Souths but the situation had become too awkward. I had two children by the end of 1971 and we were struggling financially. I couldn't believe Souths' attitude. My wife Fay said she didn't care who I played for, but not to play for Souths, even though she was, and remains, very close to the wives of the Souths players.' It was then that Branighan reached out to Ken Arthurson. 'At the 1970 World Cup, Arko only ever said one thing to me—if ever I had any problems with anything, to give him a call and he would help. I was having hassles with Souths so I rang him up from a public telephone near my work and I told him I was getting out of the club. Arko said, "If you want to come over here I can offer you so much money ... no more, no less." John O'Neill wasn't even in the equation then and I never spoke to anyone about leaving the club during the season.'

Leaving Souths lifted a huge weight off his shoulders. 'I never signed a contract with Manly ... it was a verbal agreement between me and the club. After I agreed to terms, I asked Arko not to say anything for two weeks so I could wind up things with Souths. They were absolutely stuffing around with Lurch O'Neill—making meetings with him and then not turning up—so I had a beer with him at the Clocktower Hotel and he was telling me all the problems he was having so I told him that there was a guy on the other side of the harbour who would love to talk to him. I didn't speak to Arko about Lurch going over; he did all the talking for himself.'

For forty years Manly supremo Ken Arthurson, later the Chief Executive of the NSWRL and ARL, has been painted as the villain by Souths fans for luring their star players to his club. Bob Moses may have left Souths to secure a place in first grade but both Branighan and O'Neill willingly left the club because of the committee's attitude. 'Souths thought they owned you. If you were a junior, they thought that it was their God-given right to offer you nothing and expect you to stay while offering other players from outside the club the big money. Souths cut off their own noses to spite their face ...why did Cootey leave, Elwyn Walters leave, Bob McCarthy leave and Gary

Stevens leave? The same reason I left. Souths took too many things for granted.'

When Ray Branighan and John O'Neill arrived at Manly, it was the dawn of a new era on the north side of the harbour. Manly had built up their ranks the previous year by signing Malcolm Reilly from Great Britain and champion winger Ken Irvine from Norths, but had been bundled out of the preliminary final by St George. Branighan faced his former club in a trial match at North Sydney early in 1972. 'I was lining up a kick at goal and Satts stood in front of me and just gave it to me,' he laughs. 'He wouldn't shut up, saying "What have we here?" I was no chance of kicking it … 100 to 1.'

'Manly had a great attitude,' says Ray. 'They were good blokes, easy to get along with, but it was very different. At Souths, whichever grade trained first would call out to the other squads coming onto the field, "Where are we drinking tonight?" The call would come back, "The George" or "The Cauli". You'd get to the pub later that night and all the players would be there.

'At Manly, we went to training at Brookvale Oval and then headed for the pub. There'd be Ken Irvine, Bobby Moses, Freddy Jones, Lurch O'Neill, me and one or two others … in the whole club! Halfway through the year we said if they weren't going to pull together off the field, what's going to happen on the field when the shit hits the fan? By the end of the season we had the whole three grades there. You didn't have to have a drink—you could have an orange juice or twenty schooners if you wanted to—but you had to turn up. At Manly, it was strange to begin with but then it felt very, very good.'

Manly captured the minor premiership in 1972 and duly qualified for the grand final against Easts. As is often the case when high profile players move to another club, injuries saw Branighan miss the representative season and limited him to just nine appearances in the latter half of the year—but as a centre in a champion team. Souths fans have often maintained that it was a case of 'Souths versus Souths' in the 1972 grand final and I ask Ray if it was weird playing against former club mates Jimmy Morgan and Ron Coote. He gives an interesting insight into the psyche of a professional rugby league player. 'You didn't play against faces, you played against colours,' he says. 'There were no friends out there, just opponents.' He sees a weird kind of synchronicity in playing such an integral role in Manly's maiden premiership title. 'Manly came into the competition in 1947 and I came into the world the same year,' he laughs. 'It seemed right.'

Although the club had a budding champion in the form of teenage fullback Graeme Eadie, Manly coach Ron Willey chose Branighan as the number one goal-kicker in the grand final. Eadie was injured in the major semi-final and Branighan took over the goal-kicking duties and landed five goals in the 32–8 thrashing of Easts. In the grand final a fortnight later he scored a try—his third in as many grand final appearances—and kicked six goals for a personal tally of 15 points in Manly's 19–14 win. Ray's memory of the match differs from that of his former Souths' teammate Ron Coote. 'Easts were never in it … we won pretty easily—sorry, "Solid",' he smiles, referring to Coote by his nickname. 'Easts ran with the wind in the first half but the score was 4–all at the break. We then ran to a 19–4 lead before they came back into the game late in the match.'

Branighan went to France in 1972 for his second World Cup competition—a tournament remembered for a number of bizarre incidents that have since passed into rugby league folklore. In the match against France, Branighan was awarded a try by the English referee who was then overruled by a French touch judge. The Frenchman originally said that Branighan had scored off a forward pass but when he was informed by officials that these were not grounds to over-rule a try, he put his flag in the air and said Branighan had stepped into touch. Australia won the match 9–4 and qualified for the final against the unbeaten Great Britain team.

'I still don't know how it all worked out in the final,' he says. 'I had a kick at goal with a couple minutes to go that just shaved the post but after a period of extra time the score was 10-all. We all came off the field and thought it was either a replay or we retained the World Cup because we were holders of the trophy since 1970. Instead they gave it to Great Britain on count-back because they headed the World Cup competition table. To this day I can't fathom why we didn't win it.' Compounding the defeat was the denial of a spectacular flying try by Australian captain Graeme Langlands off a Dennis Ward kick. 'It was the try of the century,' Ray recalls. 'The French referee ruled Changa was off-side. Only a player as good as Changa could have scored a try like that. There was only one Changa Langlands. You could have selected him in the front row and he still would have been a champion.'

In 1973 Branighan made it four consecutive first grade grand final appearances when minor premiers Manly defended their title against newcomers Cronulla. The game was one of the toughest—if not the dirtiest—grand finals on record. In the first half, Manly and Cronulla staged pitched battles across the SCG, then settled down to play football. Was Branighan aware of a 'vibe' in the Manly camp before the match? 'We were quietly confident of beating them but there was a "get square" from Cronulla that we knew nothing about before the match. Malcolm Reilly was the target … he had cut [Cronulla hooker] Ron Turner's mouth in a high tackle earlier in the year and the injury needed a lot of stitches. Malcolm was targetted from the kickoff. Then Turner's boot caught Reilly in the back as he kicked downfield. He went off for a needle but knew the injury would not recover. Malcolm apparently said he'd go back on but if he had to come off the field he'd take as many others with him as he could.'

When referee Keith Page retained control, Manly scored a try in each half, courtesy of Bob Fulton, before Cronulla came back with a late try. The Sea Eagles won the match 10–7 to claim back-to-back premierships. "'Bozo" Fulton was brilliant that day—nobody could guess what went through his head in a match—but so was [Manly captain] Freddy Jones, who was the best hooker-forward I saw before the Benny Elias era when the role of the hooker changed. Freddy doesn't get many raps these days but he made Bozo's first try out of nothing and his ability to dictate where the ball needed to go was just amazing.'

After Branighan returned from the 1973 Kangaroo Tour, where he played 13 games and all five Tests (as winger, centre and fullback against France), Manly's reign as premiers quickly ended. The 1974 season is memorable in that it provided Ray with his first Test appearance at home in a pivotal time in Anglo-Australian Test history. After missing the First Test of the series in Brisbane, Branighan was on the bench in the Second Test in Sydney. '"Wombat" Eadie got smashed by the Poms and I went on ... he didn't want to come off.' Great Britain won 16-11 and Branighan was selected on the wing in the Ashes-deciding Third Test.

'Right on halftime, Great Britain put up a midfield bomb and it was swirling around in the air and I spilt it. I dropped it cold and Richards, the Pommy winger, kicked the ball ahead. I've never seen anything like it—the ball bounced end on end all the way inside the sideline and he ran all the way down and touched down for a try.' Branighan's mistake gave Great Britain a 16–10 lead at half-time and the Ashes were halfway home to England. 'In the dressing room at half-time [Australian captain-coach] Changa Langlands never mentioned the mistake. I spoke to him later and he said he never came across in cover because he had confidence in me to catch the ball and he thought I had it covered.' Australia won the match, 22–18, and retained the Ashes.

Branighan's last game for Australia was as a reserve in the final match of the domestic leg of 1975's World Series competition. 'I was a reserve against England at the SCG and the match finished 10–all.' With Manly bowing out of semi-final contention in meek fashion, Branighan was overlooked for the English leg of the World Series competition at the end of the season. He did, however, receive a visit from a ghost from the past.

'At the end of 1975, Souths wanted me to return to the club. Eric Simms had left and they wanted me to take over as fullback and goal-kicker. Before we started negotiating a contract they said to me, "Now, don't be stupid and ask for too much money … this is Souths and we can only offer so much." I signed with Manly for another three years. Souths weren't the greatest negotiators and they still didn't know how to treat the players. Gary Stevens was captain in 1976 and won the club's best and fairest award. At the end of the season the club didn't want him and he ended up playing for Canterbury.'

Branighan stayed with the Sea Eagles and enjoyed success with a new coach with a new approach. 'Ron Willey was an old-style, aggressive coach—he was good for his time but "Cranky" Frank Stanton—"the shithouse with a red roof"—was the best coach I played under by a country mile. I actually played against Frank in second grade in the late 1960s and we became great mates. He had a good, aggressive team but the patterns we played were very smart. We were rarely beaten at Brookvale Oval. Branighan was in vintage form in the early part of the 1976 season when he snapped his medial ligament. 'It was on my son's birthday —20 June,' he says, plucking another date out of the memory bank. 'It was against Wests at Lidcombe Oval.' Manly won another grand final that year but Branighan resisted the temptation to come back for the match. 'I could have played in the grand final—Manly wanted to rush me back—but I said not for one game. It wouldn't be fair to the other players and it wouldn't be fair to the club if I broke down after two minutes.'

Although he missed out on a premiership title in 1976, by a quirk of history, Branighan finished his Sydney career with another premiership title two years later. 'I was playing at Leichhardt Oval and I tore my Achilles tendon and groin. I was out for a while and when I came back during the semi-finals I couldn't get back into the team because they were going that well. I came off the bench for the minor semi-final replay against Parramatta, which we won 17-11, but then I was named on the bench for the grand final against

Cronulla. It was one of the few times I could have killed Frank [Stanton] because I didn't get on the field and the match finished in an 11-all draw. In the grand final replay I got a token 10–15 minutes late in the game when the match was won.' Manly's 16–0 grand final victory was Branighan's swan song to Sydney.

'I'd had enough; I couldn't have got through another year of the training. It was big difference to Souths a decade before. When it was raining at Souths we used to run around the brewery and even then Lurch O'Neill took his taxi money. Manly had Reg Austin as the trainer. It was a totally different world we'd do twelve 400s just to start and there were no shortcuts.' The 1980s were coming fast and it was time for Branighan to move on. 'I didn't want to leave but my body told me it was time.'

An offer came from former Manly clubman Ron O'Connell to take on a captain-coach role in Ayr, Queensland. 'I could have gone to Newcastle but there was a good chance of them punching the Christ out of me so I took the family up to Ayr and it was fabulous. It was an unusual set-up. Ayr had four teams in the local competition and they played every other team five times. I played for all four teams, changing from club to club after a round [three games] of football. That's what they wanted me to do up there. Then a district representative team ('Burdekin') was selected and played in the Foley Shield competition against other districts such as Ipswich and Toowoomba. I coached Burdekin in the Foley Shield.'

Branighan was such hot property, the clubs in Ayr decided to auction his services to the highest bidder at the end of 1979. 'I told them if I didn't play with Brothers I won't be there next year ... we won the Ayr Premiership and were beaten in the Foley Shield grand final.'

Ray Branighan moved his young family back home to Malabar where he has lived for the past 35 years. Now retired after taking a redundancy from working for Aristocrat gaming, his only involvement in the game now is helping a mate of son, Reece, coach an Under 6s team. 'I don't watch a lot of football on television—the salary cap is a circus and the game is too much like grid iron for me—but I get a real buzz from watching those kids.' He smiles as he proudly displays the Tommy Bishop Shield the team won last year. 'I'm their punching bag,' he says with a look of contentment on his face.

GEORGE PIGGINS
(1971)

If there is an image that best defines the career of George Piggins, AM, it may not be the one of him doing the lap of honour with Souths after the 1971 grand final or standing on the steps of the Town Hall addressing a crowd of 80,000 rugby league fans as Souths fought to be readmitted into the NRL thirty years later. It would be his solo try in the club match against Wests at a packed Lidcombe Oval on 2 May 1976. Taking the ball under his arm, Piggins beat player after player in a determined run to the tryline. Replayed on Channel 7 that Sunday night, commentator Rex Mossop bellowed, 'George only knows one way and that's hard. By heavens, he's barrelled his way over, right through the meat of the Western Suburbs pack.'

It was the same type of determination George showed as coach of the club in the late 1980s, as club Chairman in the 1990s and in getting Souths readmitted into the NRL in 2001.

George Leslie Piggins was born on 14 October 1944 in Mascot, NSW, in the heart of South Sydney territory. One of seven children born into the modest home of a railway worker, George learned lessons early in life about family, friendship, community and hard work. 'But without rugby league my life could have gone the wrong way,' he tells me. 'It taught me discipline and respect. Playing E Grade for Mascot, Jimmy Griffiths, with 15 kids of his own, would come down and coach us to keep us off the streets. I played for nothing, just for the sport. I started out as a second row forward and switched to hooker as a teenager in 1959.'

He never had the luxury of watching Souths play as a kid, he says. 'I played on the weekend and there was no TV coverage at the time. The footballers were local stars and kids in the district wanted to be part of that ... Satts, McCarthy and Coote were already household names back then at a time when TV didn't even come on until midday. Now TV's taken over the whole game.'

Piggins won the 'best and fairest' award for President's Cup in 1964 and was graded with Souths the following year. 'Our coach, Clem Kennedy, won six or seven President's Cup premierships in a row. That's how strong our juniors were back then because they had so many to choose from. Clem had this great 'club' feel about him. Only the War stopped him from being one of the greats of the game, but he still played for Australia in 1946, the year Souths finished last in the competition. He must have been some player! That's what he gave us ... the passion to play for Souths. Bob McCarthy, Ronnie Coote, Eric Simms, Gary Stevens, Pauly Sait, Ray Branighan and me came out of the Souths juniors and all of us played for Australia. It will never happen again.'

Playing for Mascot in Souths' junior league was for enjoyment, but securing a contract with Souths was about the money. 'When I went into grade I got the chance to maybe earn the deposit for a house or the opportunity to buy into a small business. Souths had great second grade and third grade teams and I was happy playing there. Lots of good players didn't get the chance to play a grand final ... Alan Heiler, Dennis Lee, Colin Dunne and Wayne Stevens, for example. They could hold their own and did not disgrace that red and green jumper. That's what made us such a great club.'

Frank Facer, the Secretary of the champion St George club, offered

Piggins a contract after watching him play in a trial match. 'Saints were the premier club at the time, although it wasn't a first grade spot, but it didn't interest me. I wanted to play for Souths, but I also had to earn a quid. I already had a wife and kids, so I needed the weekend overtime on the wharfs. I worked out I was going to get more money working on the waterfront on Saturday and Sunday than playing grade for Souths. They offered me £300 and I said I wanted £1000 a season. That was a lot of money in those days and they said, point blank, "Well, you're not going to get it." I told Souths "fine, I'll just play for Mascot with my mates," and they said "no you'll play for us or nobody". With that, I went.'

Several weeks later Souths officials rang Piggins and offered him the money he wanted. As a hooker, there was nothing flash about his playing style. 'I had the determination to get the ball, I suppose, but the skill you picked up along the way. I had good props alongside me, but in the era of unlimited tackles, if you weren't prepared to mix it then you weren't going to win the ball.' Piggins remembers an early third grade match against Parramatta at the Sydney Sports Ground in 1965. 'I locked horns with an opponent and after he headbutted me, I chased him down the sideline and kicked him. The referee said it was his first game in grade and he had been instructed not to send anyone off. "If you do it again I'm going to have to," he told me. The next day in the newspapers they wrote how could he leave a madman like me on the field?'

In 1966, Souths brought down former Tweed Heads hooker Elwyn Walters from Brisbane as an understudy for veteran rake Fred Anderson. 'There was competition between us for the top spot in the sense that he gave it his all and I gave it my all, but my relegation to reserve grade had nothing to do with Elwyn,' George says. 'I always believed you should get picked on your merits and I wasn't given that opportunity. In 1966 Elwyn was the reserve grade hooker and I was the third grade hooker all year. On grand final day, they moved Elwyn to the second row and played me at hooker and we won the premiership. Well, that didn't sit well with [reserve grade coach] Les "Chicka" Cowie. He and I didn't see eye to eye for years. One night after training I told him to come around the back and we'd sort it out. One thing I'll say about him, though, he was a good Souths bloke. Towards the end of my career we became good friends.'

When Anderson relinquished the top job at the end of the season, Walters gained the inside running ahead of Piggins, only to break his arm in a club game. 'I played 16 straight matches that year,' he remembers. 'We beat Saints twice that season but I got sent off against Norths late in the year. I was kicked in the calf by their hooker Rossy Warner and I retaliated and we both got sent off. I wasn't suspended, but we lost to Norths that day. I was picked the following week against Penrith but got dropped for the semi-finals. I basically never got a look-in for the next five years.'

Piggins reveals that his falling out with reserve grade coach Les 'Chicka' Cowie, who later became a selector, and a comment from leading referee Col Pearce to coach Clive Churchill kept him out of Souths' first grade team for several seasons. Pearce told Souths coach Clive Churchill that the club wouldn't win a premiership with George Piggins as hooker. Piggins, he said, was worth '10 penalties to the opposition'.

'Col Pearce was barking my name and he had a few allies listening to him, even in our own camp,' George says ruefully. He played in Souths' losing reserve grade grand final team in 1967 but won his second premiership title the following year in the 17–7 win over Manly in the reserve grade grand final. Piggins appeared in just eleven games during the next three seasons (1968–70) and sat on the bench in first grade when Souths fell to Balmain in the 1969 grand final and John Sattler played on with a smashed jaw in the 1970 grand final against Manly.

Piggins must have been incredibly patient or incredibly loyal. 'I wasn't patient at all,' he says. 'I did well out of it; I was always paid well. The money Souths were paying me was equivalent to a first grade wage.' Piggins later revealed he was on $4000 a year in the late 1960s, which was the same money as many of the internationals at the club. He may have been a very tough negotiator at contract time but Souths knew his value as a tough ball-winner in an era when scrummaging was an essential part of the game. 'Football wasn't your whole life; it was just a small part of it so you had to put it in the right perspective.'

He finally got his chance to play in a first grade grand final when Elwyn Walters broke his collarbone in the semi-final win against Manly in 1971. 'Right up to the end of grand final week, Souths were thinking of putting a young bloke in the team. They thought I gave away too many penalties. A lot of it was warranted but the bad press cost me a lot in my career.'

In the grand final against the Jack Gibson-coached St George team, Piggins won the scrums 15–14 and turned the tide of the match on several occasions by raking the ball back with his foot in the play-the-ball. 'It was something I used to do if the opportunity arose. Possession was the key in those days. Players had to drop the ball from the knees when they played the ball so the opportunity to strike for the ball was there. [Souths and later Manly international forward] Ian Roberts used to be good at it too, but the game's changed now and you're not allowed to strike for the ball anymore.'

Late in the grand final, with Souths hanging on to an 11–10 lead against a determined Saints team, Piggins raked the ball back on the half-way mark. At the end of the next set, Bob McCarthy scored under the posts to wrap up the 16-10 win. Piggins proved to the skeptics that he was a first grade match-winner. 'Graeme "Changa" Langlands said St George talked about me raking the ball back in the ruck all week and the first person I took it off was him.'

Piggins more regularly appeared in first grade in the 1971-73 seasons, with international hooker Elwyn Walters often shifting to second row and prop. His battles with Manly's Great Britain international Malcolm Reilly were some of the most vicious encounters seen on a rugby league field. In July 1973 Piggins and Reilly locked horns in a 'match of the day' at the SCG. 'There was no feud between us, because you only played each other twice a year and you barely spoke a handful of words to each other,' Piggins recalls. 'In that particular game Reilly's boot connected with my face and ripped open my lip. I got up to challenge him and we faced off and threw a few punches. Referee Laurie Bruyeres told us to break it up and as I let go, Reilly hit me with an elbow so I picked him up and dumped him on the ground. As I was wrestling with him his fingers went into my eyes, so I said "You want to gouge, I'll show you a bloody gouge," and we both got sent off. When I saw him on Phillip Street both our faces were covered with scratches and bruises. "What happened to you?" he remarked when he saw me. "You did," I said'.

But one by one Souths' established Test stars left the club. 'Most of the internationals left for the money because they wanted to support their families and you couldn't blame them. They didn't have the transport business I had or the building business Gary Stevens and Lurch O'Neill had. In the end, Souths made their own bed,' he says of the demise of the club's golden era. 'The Leagues Club was flying, the football club was flying and we had a winning football team but with that comes winning match payments. The Club directors thought it was time for Souths to be a "megaclub" and they went for a big Leagues Club renovation. It was a recipe for disaster.'

Elwyn Walters left Souths and joined Easts at the beginning of the 1974 season. The following year Piggins represented NSW, and in 1975, Australia. Piggins remarried, to his childhood sweetheart Nolene, and success in his career was mirroring his success in life and business. Did he feel vindicated after receiving such belated recognition, I ask him? 'You look back on life and you realise you have to be dedicated in whatever you do. I was just as dedicated in what I was doing at work. My trucking business was taking off and there was no comparison between what I was earning with rugby league and what I was earning with the trucks. It was chalk and cheese. My not playing first grade was not always about football; there was a lot of politics involved in it. I sat on the bench for a lot of first grade matches and I still turned up to work on the trucks on Monday. Life went on.'

In spite of Souths' disastrous 1975 season, Piggins was selected in Australia's World Series squad alongside teammates Paul Sait, John O'Neill and Gary Stevens. He made his international debut in the 24–8 win over New Zealand in Auckland and made 3 Test appearances during the international leg of the competition. 'But for my wife, Noelene, and my father, I wouldn't have played for Australia. I had four or five semi-trailers on the road and that was more important to me. But I always had the belief in myself. I played for The Rest against the 1973 Kangaroos in a charity match at the beginning of 1974 and coach Jack Gibson spoke to me about playing for Easts. My answer was no, but I knew I must have had some ability for Jack to ask me. It was because I was in such a good position in my business that meant I didn't have to chase a dollar in rugby league. I owned my own home and I was getting a good quid so I wasn't interested in playing for another club to further my career. I was a Souths man.'

At the end of the 1975 season, George Piggins won a belated Australian jersey when Australia took on New Zealand in September. Australia won 24-8 in Auckland and he then travelled to England for the remainder of the World Series competition. 'Only for my wife, Noelene, and my father I wouldn't have played for Australia. I had four or five semi-trailers on the road and that was more important to me. I actually wanted to pull out of the England tour but I'm glad I went.'

With Paul Sait winding up his first grade career, it was the end of the line for Souths' grand final heroes from their last golden era. As it turned out 1979 was Gibson's last year with the club with Souths declining to reappoint the 'super coach' just as they were on the verge of making the semi-finals. 'Jack would tell the selectors what he thought and they couldn't swallow their egos. Gibbo may have changed the face of coaching but he started by getting rid of the selection committee. In saying that, he would listen to anyone who had anything to offer.'

Piggins, it turns out, had a lot to offer Sydney's coaching ranks. By the mid 1980s, he had sold his trucking business to TNT, invented a device that made loading trucks easier and invested in a sports store, a nursery and several racehorses. 'Souths asked me the day Clive Churchill was buried in 1985 if I would take over the coaching reins. I had just got my horse trainer's license and I didn't really want to get involved. But I thought about it again, and football had given me a lot in my life that I felt it was time to put something back into the game.'

When Piggins took over as Souths coach he conducted open trials at Redfern Oval during grand final weekend. 'I thought the SCG was a Mecca' and lots of people would come to the city. If they had kids with any talent they could drop into Redfern for a trial and we might be able to pick up a couple of players. We got four or five kids in the first year and we maintained those kids right through that period. We also brought in a couple of good players to augment the team, such as Phil Gould and Phil Blake. A kid like Paul Roberts could have been anything, had we got him to the club earlier.'

Under Piggins in 1986 Souths finished second on the competition table, a point behind minor premiers Parramatta. 'We had a team of youngsters but in the end we were a class centre off winning the competition. We made the most of what we had, though. We bought Phil Gould from Canterbury because he had a great football brain and I thought he would be good for us. Although I had only retired six or seven years before, I was smart enough to realise the era in which I played was long gone and the 1980s were something different again. I had Phil run the side one night because I just wanted to see how they trained. It was still the same game I knew but the terminology had changed. You weren't going to score a try going anyway but forward and natural ability in the team had to be able to express itself. You couldn't put it into a player. There were players who could be selfish and you had to knock that out of them without knocking their confidence. It was still a team game.'

In 1987, Souths made the finals for a second successive season but the loss of two competition points for playing an illegal replacement (Scott Wilson) in an Anzac Day match against Manly cost the club a place in the 1988 play-offs. The following year Souths captured the minor premiership. 'It's a simple game,' Piggins says. 'You don't have to be Einstein as a coach. You have to be a good judge of ability and character. Craig Coleman was a great organiser but it was difficult to get Craig to see beyond the halfback spot. Hooker would have been a good option for him but when I bought it up he said that it would ruin his career. If he couldn't see what I could see, then it was easier to leave him where he was rather than force him to be something he didn't want to be.'

In 1990, the wheels fell off and Souths finished with the wooden spoon. 'The worse that can happen to a football team is to be successful when you have a club that's broke,' he says. 'There was no money and we had kids playing with Souths for the same reason I went there, which was to get a start in life.' He could see the same thing happening to Souths that occurred at the end of 1971. The players started to get good offers from rival clubs and one day Ian Roberts came to him and spoke of an offer from Manly. 'I told him if he was my son I would drive him over the Harbour Bridge to get it.' Roberts signed with Manly, just as Ray Branighan and John O'Neill had done twenty years before him.

After standing down as coach, Piggins became president of the football club and chairman of Souths Leagues in the 1990s. Souths was operating well under the allocated salary cap when the game reunited following the Super League war in order to survive the cull the NRL was conducting at the end of 1999. 'I'm an uneducated person but all I wanted was truth reflected on the balance sheets. We may have "robbed Peter to pay Paul" in supporting the leagues club, but as far I was concerned Peter and Paul were brothers. There was no robbing anybody … we just wanted to keep the club afloat.'

When Piggins took over as Club Chairman, Souths were $1 million in debt. 'I talked to Souths Juniors about a possible takeover and I sold the club's Narellan golf course property for $1.2 million and paid off the club's debt to the taxman. Without doing that, Souths football club does not exist today. I was told I wouldn't find a buyer, I was told I couldn't get the Board to agree but I did it. After clearing the debt we had to build on that success. We were told we needed a bigger carpark space so we entered into a contract with a builder. We looked like getting somewhere.'

Souths Leagues turned a loss into a $1 million profit under Piggins' chairmanship. '[NSW Premier] Bob Carr's poker machine tax came in and we recorded a $300,000 loss. The builder needed his money [$250,000], we gave $1 million to the football club and Optus gave us $500,000. Kerry Packer gave us $750,000 over three years because he was a closet Souths fan. Later we asked for $250,000 back from the football club and they gave it to us as a loan. We wanted it in the form of the repayment of a gift. The Leagues Club paid back their debts and the members retained control.'

By the end of the 1990s, Souths was staring at exclusion from the NRL. 'The fundamental injustice was that someone as wealthy as Rupert Murdoch and News Ltd could turn around and take a sporting organisation that had been run by committees—and owned by the community—out of the rugby league competition. It was something that the average bloke, whether they lived at Penrith, Newcastle or Perth, should be able to be part of. No government should allow one person to take over a community icon like a rugby league club. All Murdoch wanted to do was to take the game off us and we weren't going to hear anything about South Sydney again.'

When the axe fell on Souths, on 15 October 1999, Piggins immediately started a very public fight-back. 'It was just getting enough people enraged enough to say, "Hey, this isn't right … we are entitled to watch Souths play in the competition." That's why

80,000 people marched on the Town Hall. It was so gratifying to see the former players, the fans and the little old ladies from Redfern, marching up George Street.'

Many wanted the club to merge with another NRL club, even members of the high profile 'Group 14' who reunited the junior and senior clubs in the fight against News Ltd, but Piggins never lost his nerve. 'Why merge and take away a club that had existed for 90-odd years? Why would we want to merge with Cronulla or Easts? Why didn't they want to merge with us? Because we were going to be swallowed up and all they wanted us for was our junior league. We did the only thing that was possible which was to stand alone on our own feet.'

Souths won the right through the courts to compete in the 2002 NRL premiership and News Ltd had the sense not to appeal the decision. 'The thing that drove me on was I felt that we had one chance to combine South Sydney and the South Sydney Juniors and by doing that, you would have seen rugby league as it was in the 1960s and 1970s with community-based ownership and involvement. The fans could go to the club and share in the wins and the excitement.' But Souths Juniors did not want to take over the senior club and that dream quickly died. Piggins' plan for a $41 million redevelopment of Redfern Oval as a playing venue also came up against strong opposition from Sydney Council.

After an uneasy return to the 'Big League', former Souths lawyer and director Nick Pappas took over the running of the football club and Piggins remained Chairman of the leagues club. 'Nick said he had the big end of town. I tried to explain to him—this not business, this is community—but in the end I said "fine, do it." He ran it for two years before he realised what I meant. It's not as easy as it looks. You have to have a leagues club pulling in big money, the fans to come in droves and sponsorship by the truck load. We never had that and we struggled. But when they said they were going to sell the Club, I didn't agree with it.'

In 2006, actor Russell Crowe and businessman Peter Holmes a Court offered the members $3 million for a majority 75% takeover of the football club. 'When Russell asked me if I would support his bid for private ownership I had only one question to ask: "What happens when you get sick of owning Souths? Are we going to end up in Perth, Brisbane on the Central Coast or merged with another club?" In the end they didn't grab it, the members voted to give the club away. It finished for me once they gave up on Redfern Oval as a base for our home games. The fans wouldn't be coming back to the leagues club and all of our sudden the whole geography of a having a community-based club had changed.' Piggins resigned as Chairman of the leagues club and walked away from the club.

Five years after losing power, is he now able to gain a little perspective on what was a very bitter parting with the club he helped to save? 'Nothing happened that I didn't think would happen. In this day and age you need at least $15 million to run a club. That's a frightening concept. Private owners could do $45 million in three years and not see too much for their investment. Life's changing so much, and TV and global sport is changing so much that people like me don't really understand it. Whether TV rights alone can support the game, only time will tell. Can the next Fox deal pay all our footballers into the future if we don't grow our product internationally? It's a bit like racehorse ownership. There's no guarantee for a return on your investment.'

Success has to be planned, he says. 'We lasted 17 years. I'd like to see what the present owners have put into the club in the past five years compared to what we put into the game on the budget we had. People still ask how we did it.'

Piggins admits that if he had his time again he wouldn't have taken up the challenge of running Souths. 'It got to the stage where people who were involved in Souths weren't in it for the same reasons I was. I was doing it because it was the right thing for the community. I thought it was great for the youth of the area because it kept them off the street and away from drugs. Sport is a fantastic thing. Our biggest mistake was going fully professional with young players not having to go to work. If my grandson, and he could be anything as a player, had to choose between playing first grade and an apprenticeship, then I'd suggest to him to get a job. In my time, if you got graded, you went to work and came to training ... not the other way around. Players did that for the best part of 90 years.'

Where does Souths exist now, I ask him, in the head or the heart? 'On the TV screen,' he says without hesitation. 'I sit down and watch Souths every time they play. Look, a lot of personal stuff went on [during the takeover bid]. I'm over it, but I had five court cases and I won all five. I'm 66 years of age and I have no intention of getting involved in rugby league again. I'm a spectator, and for most people my age that's all they are. The direction the game is taking is disappointing. Watching rugby league on TV can be frustrating ... it's all about tries, tries, tries. The man with the whistle controls the game.'

'The modern game is set up for the elite kid who gets the bulk of the publicity, rather than the average first grader. The elite kid isn't the club, he isn't the community. He's part of it. A good player may lift six or seven other players to play better and he may attract sponsors but it can't be at the expense of local juniors. His contribution could be enormous, but you have to have good financial controllers in a club because, at the end of the day, if you go broke ... ?' His voice trails off and he gives an exasperated shrug of the shoulders.

While human nature can be fickle, George Piggins still counts among his closest friends the men he played with at Redfern Oval forty years ago. 'I still follow the South Sydney district and I still support the South Sydney juniors. I returned to Redfern Oval and kicked off for the juniors' grand final match last year. I grew up with all those guys and the juniors are an important part of my life. Unfortunately, the juniors can't find enough players for their local competitions. We've taken the whole game in a completely different direction and its going to be quite a fight for the Independent Commission to reclaim that and for the game to survive.'

At the end of our interview he says, 'Souths were once great and hopefully will be great again, but it will be a different game to the one I played. In saying that, I'd like to see the kids in the current squad do well.'

When Souths made the 2014 Grand Final, Piggins hadn't seen his team play live since the beginning of the 2006 season. Asked if he would attend the match, Piggins suggested 'if someone donated $100,000 to charity', he would go. John Singleton, the TAB, and a Sydney car dealer did better than that, collecting a total of $120,000 in donations, which was to be shared between the Men of League Foundation, the Sydney Children's Hospital and food rescue charity, OzHarvest. When Souths defeated Canterbury 30–6, there was no prouder man in ANZ stadium.

George Piggins ... once a Souths man, always a Souths man.

… NOT TO FORGET
JIM MORGAN, KERRY BURKE, KEITH EDWARDS AND CLIVE CHURCHILL

Former Newcastle prop 'Big Jim' Morgan had the reputation of being the big match bridesmaid in his five seasons with Souths (1965–69). A smashed cheekbone while playing for NSW in a midweek interstate clash dented his representative hopes in his first season in Sydney. After playing in the 1965 grand final loss to St George, the following year he was a non-playing reserve in Australia's Second Test success in Brisbane and then missed the 1967 grand final through injury. Morgan got his chance to win a premiership the following year against Manly but after being unable to maintain his place in Souths' first grade team in 1969, he left the club for Easts … and promptly played for Australia.

Jim Morgan backed his own ability and reaped the rewards.

David James ('Jim') Morgan was born in Maitland in 1942. The same age as John Sattler, they attended school together at Maitland Marist Brothers. 'We met in third class,' Sattler recalls. 'He sat in front of me and for some reason him even saying the name "Morgan" scared me. I was terrified of him. His parents had the sandwich shop across the road from the school. It was great when he came down to Souths in 1965. He was a good, tough player.'

At age of 21, Morgan represented Country Firsts in 1964 and excelled against the more-experienced City pack. That year he represented NSW Colts against France and was a member of the famous Newcastle team that won the NSW Country Championship and the final of the State Cup. Morgan's signature was chased by St George, Newtown and finally Souths but his Maitland club originally blocked his move to Sydney and he made his debut for the Rabbitohs in 1965 just two rounds before the rep season started. Selected for City Seconds, he played for NSW in his first season with the club but a broken cheekbone limited him to a handful of first grade games before he came back into first grade as Souths charged into the grand final from fourth position. He caught a tropical throat infection on Souths' end of season tour of New Guinea that year and lost almost two stone from his strapping 6 foot 2 inch frame.

In 1966 Balmain's Arthur Beetson was a late withdrawal from Australia's Second Test team, and with Dick Thornett coming into the side, Jim Morgan was flown to Brisbane to be the reserve forward. Australia won a tryless match, 6–4, to keep the Ashes series alive but Morgan did not make it onto the field. In the deciding Third Test in Sydney, Beetson came back into the team, Thornett was the reserve forward and Morgan was dropped from the squad. He would get his chance against the Poms in four year's time.

The 1968 grand final win was the peak of Morgan's 58-game career with Souths. Taking his place in the front row of a champion pack, he played a pivotal role in the Rabbitohs' 13–9 win over Manly. The following year, however, Morgan suffered an early season injury and found it difficult to regain his place in first grade. Coach Clive Churchill moved John Sattler to the front row to accommodate young forwards Gary Stevens, and later, Paul Sait and Morgan found himself in reserve grade.

1969 was an unhappy season for Morgan. His final match for Souths saw him sent from the field in the second grade major semi-final against Manly after one of the 'wildest brawls seen at the SCG.' His three-match suspension resulted in his missing the final against Balmain (which minor premiers Souths lost) and any chance of playing in the first grade grand final.

Morgan was the first of the Souths' tight-knit family to move to another club when he signed with Easts in 1970 in order to secure a first grade position. Press reports of the time quoted him as having 'regrets', but he knew he was doing the right thing for his career. After representing City and NSW in 1970, Morgan was called into Australia's First Test team against Great Britain and produced the game of his life. Scoring two tries on debut in Australia's crushing, 37–15 win in Brisbane, Morgan had his nose smashed after a vicious head clash with opposing prop Cliff Watson.

John Sattler recalls, 'It was one of the worst injuries I've ever seen. Jim was a tough bastard. He got himself into a bit of trouble because he had this habit where he'd get up to play the ball and give the marker a bit of a nudge or put his forehead on him. He did that to Cliffy Watson and he just smashed Jim with a "Liverpool Kiss."' Morgan missed the Second Test but made his comeback in the deciding Test of the series at the SCG, which saw the Ashes lost to Great Britain. Morgan's fearless confrontation of the Great Britain forwards ultimately went against him at the end of the year when Australia's World Cup squad was selected. Australia had a new coach in Harry Bath, and new tactics, and Morgan's Test career was over.

After playing in Easts' grand final loss to Manly in 1972, Morgan followed coach Don Furner to Queanbeyan. In 1974 he toured New Zealand with the Combined NSW Country team, represented NSW against Queensland and then led NSW Country to an upset win over a star-studded City team in 1975. Morgan ran a successful garbage disposal business in Sydney, often servicing the sites John O'Neill and Gary Stevens renovated in the 1960s and 1970s. After his football career finished, he returned to Sydney, lived in Woolloomooloo and raised his growing family. In 1986 he coached the Roosters' reserve grade team to a premiership.

'Big' Jim Morgan was living at Palm Beach on Queensland's Gold Coast when he suffered a massive heart attack while surfing at Tallebudgera beach in October 2005. His funeral at Mary Immaculate Church, Waverley, was attended by a large crowd of family and friends.

Parramatta junior Kerry Burke was fated to be the only Souths player in the elite squad of 25 grand finalists between 1967 and 1971 whose only appearance was in the 11–2 loss to Balmain. Burke played in 35 games for the Eels before joining Souths in 1969. A strong defensive centre, he was part of the selection merry-go-round which saw the club use a number of centres during that year. A talented utility player, he also played halfback in reserves and filled in at fullback, centre, wing and five-eighth in first grade over the ensuing years. After playing nine matches in the Rabbitohs' top grade in 1969, including the 14–13 win over the Tigers in the major-semi final, Burke was retained as Bob Honan's centre partner for the grand final. He left Souths at the end of 1972, having appeared in 36 first grade matches, and later moved to Queensland. Burke ran a newsagency at Southport on the Gold Coast for several years, before shifting to Brisbane.

Keith Edwards, a Souths junior born in Kingsford in 1946 and raised in Randwick, played rugby league for the Maroubra Lions but gave the game away as a teenager to concentrate on cricket. A talented wicket-keeper for Randwick, he came back to league at age 18 when friends talked him into trialling for Easts' President's Cup squad. Selected for the Roosters, Souths wouldn't give him a clearance to be selected in the squad on the basis of residency.. Although he didn't play a single game in the competition he was still graded in third grade in 1968.

A six-foot, blond-haired winger-centre, Edwards made the

transition from A-Grade cricketer to first grade rugby league player in consecutive years. 'I was something of a late bloomer to the game,' Edwards says. 'I was also an A-Grade tennis player. I was athletic, but certainly not academic. Wes Hall, the famous West Indian captain, came to Randwick in 1965 and I was the first grade wicket-keeper. I represented NSW Colts at age 18 but I gave the game away in 1968 to concentrate on rugby league.'

Edwards made his first grade debut in the 16–4 win over Manly at the SCG in May 1969 when seven Souths players were on tour with the Australian team in New Zealand. 'I won a premiership with Souths' third grade team that year which remains my greatest personal thrill,' he says. 'We played Canterbury, who were hot favourites, and we slaughtered them 25–11. Jeff Withers, my centre partner that day, had a blinder. Rod Gorman captained the side from the forwards and Kevin McDonald, an old Saints man, was the coach.'

When Mike Cleary dislocated his wrist in 1970, Edwards was thrown into 'the deep end' he says and appeared in 11 first grade matches only to break his arm in the last game of the season. 'Mike Cleary was playing well in reserve grade and he came into the side for the semi-finals,' he recalls. When Cleary left the club for Easts at the end of the year, Edwards played the majority of the season on the wing. 'I was a reliable winger,' he says with a self-deprecating laugh, 'not so much fast, but not too many could get past me … except Ken Irvine! Playing first grade was a childhood dream. Dad took us out to Redfern Oval to watch Clive Churchill when I was a kid and here I was playing with all these great players.'

The fact that Edwards was the one of only three players in Souths' 1971 grand final team who wasn't an international (Gary Stevens and George Piggins, who took Elwyn Walters' place in the grand final, later played for Australia) never weighed on his mind. 'It was great playing with so many champion players, but I don't think Clive was too keen on me. I suppose he didn't have to say too much to me because he had all those internationals in the team to worry about,'

Keith laughs again. 'I used to play injured just so I could retain my place in the side.'

Paradoxically, he doesn't have overly fond memories of the 1971 grand final win. 'I was disappointed because the game was played in the forwards. Very little of the ball got out to the backline ... whether Clive instructed the forwards to keep the ball in the middle, I don't know, but I thought Souths would have spun it out more.'

Edwards played in 74 games for Souths up to the end of 1973 and then suddenly retired. 'Souths were consistent in 1972, making the semi-final, but overall I could feel us slipping away. We missed those internationals we lost and we didn't have the same unity as a team. My then wife and I bought a self-service station in Alexandria and I just felt that playing and training would take up too much time from running the business. I went back to Souths in 1975 because I thought I could balance my business and playing duties.'

Edwards appeared in 11 matches in 1975 but admits that there just wasn't the same atmosphere at the club. 'Clive left and there wasn't the same bond there anymore and we came last. I was 28 years old and I'd made a bit of money from the game. It was time to retire.' Living in Coogee, where he raised a family, he talks to George Piggins on a regular basis, runs into locals Gary Stevens, Ray Branighan and Bob McCarthy, and enjoys Souths' player reunions. He admits that he's not a huge fan of the way the game is played today.

'I go back to when the game changed to the limited tackle rule [in 1967]. It took away a lot of the skills in the game such as how to hang on to the ball, how to tackle and cover defend. Once money and commercialism came into the game plus all the rule changes over the years, we basically changed the game from how it had been played since 1908. The game they play today has little to do with the game we played. If you break the first line of defence there's no cover defence coming across and more than likely you're going to score a try. Where are the Bobby McCarthys and Ronnie Cootes of today? Those days are done. Commercialism has overwhelmed reality. The kids who play the game today are living in a different era, but good luck to them.' And good luck to Keith Edwards, a true gentleman.

The final piece of the South Sydney jigsaw puzzle belongs to Clive Churchill—the champion player of his era and, according to most historians, the greatest player ever to grace the game. He capped his brilliant career by coaching the Rabbitohs to five consecutive grand finals. Those same writers, however, remain divided about the extent of Churchill's contribution to Souths' success. Some would have us believe that the champion team coached themselves, others who were closer to the club say that Churchill was the right coach at the right time for the right club. The record, which show that his teams made the grand final five times in nine seasons, speaks for itself.

Clive Bernard Churchill was born in Newcastle, NSW, in 1927. A keen swimmer and boxer, he was a star schoolboy player at Marist Brothers, Hamilton, and captained school teams to five consecutive premierships. A brilliant attacking fullback with the speed of a winger, he came to Souths from the Central Newcastle Club towards the end of the 1947 season and made his Test debut against the Kiwis the following year. After touring England and France with the 1948–49 Kangaroos and New Zealand in 1949, he became Australian Test captain in 1950. That year he led Australia to a memorable Ashes victory at the SCG, defeating Great Britain in a series for the first time in 30 years.

That same year, Souths captured the Sydney premiership. Although he was not captain at Souths (fellow Test forward Jack Rayner held that honour) Souths won five premierships in six seasons (1950–51 and 1952–55). The only blot on their record was an upset 22–12 loss to Wests in the 1952 grand final when Churchill and several other stars were already on voyage to England with the 1952–53 Kangaroos. Churchill also missed the 1955 grand final with a broken arm, but not before he kept Souths' premiership hopes alive with a last minute goal in the match against Manly—his broken arm limply hanging by his side. During this period, Churchill appeared in 99 consecutive rep matches and captained Australia in a record 27 consecutive Test matches (including the 1954 World Cup).

Clive's widow Joyce met her future husband when he was working at the Kensington Service station he leased in the mid 1950s. 'I'm an Eastern Suburbs girl, but my family were all big Souths fans. We started talking football and that's how it all started. I went home and said I had met Clive Churchill and my family couldn't believe it. I said I might even bring him home for dinner. My mother was very nervous when she met him.' Joyce met up with Clive in England when he was touring with the 1956–57 Kangaroos and they married in 1958. The following year their only child, Rodney, was born.

The late 1950s was a difficult time in Churchill's career. He was overlooked as captain on the 1956–57 Kangaroo Tour and his Test career was effectively over. After two controversial seasons as captain-coach of Souths he went to Queensland in 1959. 'Clive was shattered when his international career ended,' Joyce tells me, 'but he went into coaching and never the left the game.' Churchill coached Queensland to interstate success in 1959 and then went to England and France as coach of the 1959-60 Kangaroos. After a final stint with Moree in 1961, he returned to Sydney and coached Canterbury in 1964, but the club finished last in the premiership. Two years later, he returned to Souths. 'Clive was over the moon to get the coaching job at Souths,' Joyce says. 'He was always a Souths' man at heart.'

Michael Cleary had not been too impressed with the standard of training when he came to rugby league from the amateur ranks in 1962. 'We only trained for an hour, twice a week, under Dennis Donoghue and it showed in our results. I was training for the Commonwealth Games so I always did my own training anyway. Bernie Purcell created the nucleus of the Souths stronghold. The ability Clive Churchill had was to keep blokes happy. He was like a little blowfly. He took it very seriously but we didn't have to be flogged at training because we were such a happy team. Training was still on Tuesdays and Thursdays, but we all trained on the other days with Clive and we'd go to Centennial Park and did a few hours running around there and kept fit.'

John Sattler says, 'With the team we had we all knew what we had to do. Clive was a real father-figure to us. He kept everybody in a good frame of mind. If somebody had the shits he'd have a chat with them or go and kick a ball to them. As his captain, he and I would talk but he didn't give instructions as such. Nothing was said too much in the dressing sheds. Ten minutes before we went out Clive would say, "You've been training all week for it and all year for it. You know what you've got do. All the best fellas." He never ever call me John ... he'd say, "Good luck, captain".'

When Clive and Joyce went to see John Sattler in hospital on grand final night in 1970 after he broke his jaw, the sight of Satts in a hospital bed with his jaw all wired up reduced them both to tears. 'As soon as we walked in and saw John we both broke up,' Joyce says. 'We loved Satts so much, seeing him in that state really upset us.'

Gary Stevens and George Piggins are quick to acknowledge the contribution coach Clive Churchill made at Souths and in his career. George Piggins states, 'Clive Churchill was one bloke on a committee. He prepared the team that was selected for him. Souths were a good team and he was able to put that side together and keep them happy. But Clive was also a good people person. He was a good judge of ability and a great judge of footballers. He enhanced the championship genius of that first grade team and never over-coached them'.

In his 2002 biography *Never Say Die*, George Piggins states: 'In fact, Churchill was the shrewdest of league men with a wonderful football brain. He coached with a light touch because he knew he had the troops and didn't have to interfere too much ... He won four premierships in five years and should have won a fifth. Sure, he had a championship team, but he handled that side just right, expertly and without fuss. His manner and style were light years away from those of some of today's ego-driven, overpaid coaches ...'

Not that Churchill shied away from the odd innovation or two. 'There's a great story about Clive and George Piggins in the early 1970s,' Ron Coote recalls. 'Jack Gibson brought in tackle counts and Clive thought he'd do it too. He got a mate who was a taxi driver and knew nothing about rugby league to tally the tackle counts one day. At halftime Clive told us what he thought we'd been doing wrong and then he said, "I've got the tackle count here … O'Neill you've done 13, Piggins you've done 2—where've you been hiding? Sattler you've done so-and-so…" and he went right through them team to Eric Simms. Well, George started taking his boots off. Clive asked, "What are you doing, George?" and he said, "Well you can go and get f****d if you think I've only done two tackles!"

'Quick as a flash Clive said, "That's it! I'm throwing the tackle count away!"'

Despite losing most of his star players, Clive stayed on at Souths until 1975 before resigning late in the season, frustrated and disheartened at the club's stance. "This is what happened in sport and you have to cop it on the chin," Joyce remembers Clive saying. 'It was a happy time—it was a happy club—and the girls all mixed together. We still go out for lunch, Noelene and George Piggins, my very best friends, and Bobby and Judy McCarthy. They're lovely people and we've all stuck together. They were all Clive's boys. There was lots of affection there and we went out with them and drank with them and this is why they got on so well together.'

The Churchills use to run the bottle shop at the Duke of Gloucester Hotel in Randwick before opening a little bottle shop of their own on Frenchman's Road. One night in the early 1980s, Clive was bashed during attempted robbery. 'It definitely contributed to his poor health,' Joyce says. 'He was beaten across his back and they found a lump on his spine on which they couldn't operate. He developed cancer and within a couple of years he passed away. He fought it right to the end … I've never seen anything like it. He kept saying that he was going to beat it and he was such a tough man—

and such a healthy person, I never knew him to have a headache or a sick day—but it beat him in the end. It was sad, because he has missed out on so much.'

In 1985, shortly before his death, Churchill was informed at a gala dinner held in his honour at Randwick Racecourse that the newly built grandstand in the corner of the SCG where winger Ron Roberts crossed for the try that gave Australia the Ashes in 1950 would be dedicated to him. In a perfect arc of symmetry the proposal was put forward by Pat Hills, the former South Sydney Patron, Labor politician and the then Chairman of the SCG Trust, and announced by The Honourable Michael Cleary, the then Labor Member for Coogee. The 'Clive Churchill Stand' is a reminder to the Australian sporting public that rugby league once ruled the SCG in winter and Churchill, the 'Little Master', was the King. Suffering the ravages of his cancer, Churchill blamed his lack of hair on his Irish barber, 'Kim O'Therapy'. It brought the house down.

One of the original four postwar 'immortals' named by *Rugby League Week* in 1981, Clive Churchill was appointed a Members of the General Division Order of Australia (AM) for services to sport. He died on 9 August 1985 and his funeral was one of the biggest Sydney has witnessed. Former players John Sattler, Ron Coote, Bob McCarthy, Gary Stevens and George Piggins were pallbearers along with Clive's son Rod. His casket was covered with a South Sydney jersey.

Joyce Churchill and her son have maintained Clive's legacy, attending Centenary of Rugby League celebrations and presenting the 'Clive Churchill Medal' for the man of the match in each year's grand final. 'I've tried my best,' Joyce says. 'In 2008 I attended 22 functions. They sent me everywhere. Russell Crowe looks after me too, making sure I get to the home games OK, and I appreciate that. It's great Souths are still going strong and so am I. Not bad for an 84-year old.'

In 2008 Clive Churchill was voted the greatest player in the game's history and was named captain and fullback in the ARL Team of the Century. 'Clive would have been so proud and humbled. It was such a great honour. Rod and I just broke up when it was announced. I told Clive all about it—I had a little chat with him and told him I was so proud of him.'

PART 4:
FORTY LICKS
(1972–2011)

Despite the loss of internationals Branighan, O'Neill and Coote to rival clubs, Souths started 1972 confidently by defeating Easts in the final of the pre-season competition, 11–10. The Rabbitohs lost only two first round matches and headed the competition at the halfway mark of the season, but the manner in which St George crushed them at the SCG, 24–7, exposed a notable lack of depth in the club. Bob Honan tried a novel approach to contract negotiating that year, offering the club a package deal that included Eric Simms, Bob Grant, Gary Stevens and Bob McCarthy in an effort to keep the nucleus of the side together, but Souths officials baulked at the idea. Souths stumbled in the second round of competition, winning five of 11 matches before limping into fourth place in the play-offs. When St George defeated them in the minor semi-final, 14–10, Souths' golden era had come to an end.

The 1972 grand final between Manly and Easts was the first time since 1948 neither Souths or St George were not fighting out premiership honours. It was the start of a new era in the game dominated by 'silver-tail' clubs Manly (which won four premierships during the decade) and Easts (1974–75 winners). Diehard Rabbitoh fans may have viewed the Manly-Easts grand final as 'Souths versus Souths' but the cold hard fact was if the club had been able to keep its 1971 premiership-winning team intact, it would have been hard to beat in 1972.

John Sattler left for Queensland at the end of the season, Bob Honan signed to play with Easts (but retired before he could wear the tri-colour jersey) and Souths narrowly failed to make the play-offs in 1973. On 30 June 1973 South Sydney Leagues Club closed its doors. Years of financial mismanagement, over-expansion and the effects of a recession combined to take the club to the brink of bankruptcy. For three months the future of the South Sydney football club hung in the balance, but after strenuous fundraising efforts from the 'Save Souths' Committee, the club reopened its doors in September. The issuing of debentures raised $230,000 and the restructuring of the leagues club accounting practices meant that Souths had a future – at least for the time being.

At the end of 1973, Elwyn Walters left for Easts after the return of the Kangaroos and Denis Pittard joined Parramatta. Souths returned to the semi-finals in 1974, losing to Wests in the minor semi-final, 24–8, at the Sports Ground. With the establishment of the '13 Import Rule' in 1975, John O'Neill, Bob Honan and Keith Edwards came back to the club (Souths used only 11 imported players that year), but after a promising start, the club crashed to lose 11 of 12 matches and Clive Churchill resigned. When Souths were thrashed by Manly in the final match of the season by a record 54–0 margin, the once-proud club claimed the wooden spoon. It was only four years since the salad days of the 1971 grand final. Bobby Grant retired, Eric Simms moved to the country and Bob McCarthy, caretaker captain-coach of the club following Clive Churchill's departure, signed with Canterbury when Souths failed to make him a suitable offer for 1976.

Johnny King, the former Saints winger and 1974 Amco Cup-winning coach with Western Division, was the new Souths coach but found little success and stayed for only the one year. John O'Neill fared no better in his year at the helm in 1977. Captaining Souths also proved to be something of a poisoned chalice in the late 1970s; Gary Stevens led the club in 1976 and then joined McCarthy at Canterbury. Jack Gibson coached Souths in 1978–79, with George Piggins and Paul Sait the last remnants of the club's golden era. Inexplicably, Souths let the 'super coach' go just as the inexperienced team was on the verge of making the semi-finals.

Bill Anderson took the club back to the semi-finals in 1980, with captain 'Rocky' Laurie, wingers Ziggy Niszcott and Terry Fahey, and forwards Peter Tunks and Gary Hambly very much to the fore. Souths won the midweek knockout Tooth Cup in 1981 and Ron Willey, who had coached Manly to premierships in 1972–73, returned Souths to the play-offs in 1984. George Piggins' tenure as coach in the late 1980s constituted the club's last successful era before it was excluded from the NRL premiership in 1999. Souths qualified for the semi-finals in 1986 (in second place), 1987 (fifth place) but missed the finals in 1988 when the NSWRL deducted two competition points for playing an ineligible replacement in the Anzac Day win over arch rivals Manly.

The 1989 season was the high-point of Piggins' time as coach, with Souths capturing both the minor premiership and Club Championship. Players such as Mario Fenech, Phil Blake, Craig Coleman, Les Davidson, David Boyle, Michael Andrews, Wayne Chisholm, Ian Roberts, Paul Roberts, Tony Rampling and Jim Serdaris forged new success at Souths, but success was fleeting and produced no premierships. In 1989 many were predicting a rematch of the Souths-Balmain grand final from twenty years before, but Canberra crushed that dream in the preliminary final, defeating Souths 36–12, before going on to beat the Tigers in a classic grand final match.

The following year Souths went from first to last in the first grade minor premiership and club championship, winning just two matches. Hit by another financial crisis, which saw history repeat when Ian Roberts signed with Manly, the disastrous season led to Piggins' resignation and sparked a mass exodus at the club. Souths would tinker towards a slow death during the 1990s, finishing no better than ninth in a decade which saw them remain loyal to the ARL during the Super League war, only to be placed on the chopping block when the game reunited under the NRL banner in 1998. The highlight of the decade was the club's win over Brisbane in the 1994 pre-season competition with Bob McCarthy at the helm. The link to the club's past was potentially an exciting one, but McCarthy found his coaching role compromised by new operations manager Alan Jones and diplomatically resigned. Within five years, Souths was staring at rugby league oblivion.

As president of both the football club and struggling leagues club, George Piggins deliberately operated under the existing salary cap in order to keep the club solvent. He vowed to fight any move to axe the club from the proposed 14-team competition in 2000 and resist any pressures, external or internal, to secure the $6 million on offer to merge with another club. When the axe was finally lowered, on 15 October 1999, Piggins immediately started court action against the NRL and News Ltd, part owners of the game. Souths fans and people who loved rugby league could not comprehend why the NRL would want to go forward without the most successful, iconic and recognisable Sydney rugby league club in the game's history. Not only was it bad business but it alienated many people still aggrieved by the Super League war.

What followed was two years of fundraising, public rallies and court cases. Although several early decisions went against Souths and News Ltd then appealed the decision to allow the club to compete in the 2002 premiership, on 6 July 2001 the court dismissed the appeal and Souths were able reenter the competition. But Souths had lost a lot of momentum in not being able to field a team for three seasons (local juniors Craig Wing and Braith Anasta represented Australia with other NRL clubs), the leagues club was still struggling and the football club was operating on a shoe-string budget. In their first season in the NRL, Souths were headed for the wooden spoon before Canterbury-Bankstown was stripped of all its competition points for salary cap rorting.

It was a tough initiation for the Rabbitohs being back in the 'big league'. The club exhausted a succession of coaches—Craig Coleman (2002), Paul Langmack (2003–04), Arthur Katinas (caretaker 2004) and Shaun McRae (2005–06)—and parted company with chief executive Paul Dunn midway through the 2004 season. After finishing last in 2003 and 2004, the arrival of successful Super League coach Shaun McRae did not improve the club's stocks. At the end of 2006, which saw the club capture its third wooden spoon in five seasons, McRae was replaced by his assistant, Jason Taylor.

Earlier that year, Academy Award-winning actor Russell Crowe, a Souths sponsor and supporter, and businessman Peter Holmes a Court, tabled their $3 million bid to secure a majority 75% share to Souths members. In March 2006, football club members voted to support the plan for privatisation of the club by a 75.8% majority (the takeover needed at least a 75% majority). George Piggins stated at the time that $3 million dollars undervalued the club, but with his plans to return games to Redfern Oval stalling because of Sydney Council opposition and a suggested takeover by the successful Souths Juniors Club failing to materialise, members supported the Crowe-Holmes a Court bid. Piggins, the man who had saved Souths, severed all ties with the club—but not the South Sydney district.

With the signing of Roy Asotasi, Nigel Vagana, David Kidwell, Daniel Irvine, Jeremy Smith and Reece Simmonds, plus the promotion of Jason Taylor to coach, the 2007 season produced a return to semi-final football for the first time since 1989. Souths' supporters returned too, with chief executive Shane Richardson moving the club's home games from the Sydney Football Stadium to ANZ Stadium at Homebush Bay. Seventh position on the competition ladder meant Souths took on second-place Manly in a qualifying final against Manly at Brookvale Oval. The scores were locked 6–all at half-time but the grand final bound Sea Eagles ended Souths' best season in almost two decades by winning 30-6.

On Australia Day 2008, the Rabbitohs lost 26–24 to the Leeds Rhinos in front of 12,000 fans at the University of North Florida in Jacksonville, Florida. It was the first time first-grade rugby league teams from Australia and England played each other in the United States and it showed the lengths co-owner Russell Crowe would go to publicise his club and the game of rugby league. That May, Executive Chairman Peter Holmes a Court resigned as CEO and the experienced Shane Richardson returned to the role. The South Sydney Rabbitohs celebrated their centenary year in rugby league fielding teams in the NRL Premiership, the Toyota Cup National Youth Competition and the NSW Cup (with affiliate club, the North Sydney Bears).

Craig Wing returned to the club in 2008 but his early-season injury against former club the Roosters was an indication of the luck the club experienced that year. Souths lost the opening seven games of the season, although the club rallied late in the year to win eight matches, they eventually finished 14th in the competition. Souths lost a lot of hard-won ground but on a positive note, two of the club's 'little men'—Chris Sandow and Isaac Luke—breathed new life into the club with some refreshing performances. Peter Holmes a Court also relinquished his 'hands on' role at the football club, with the experienced Shane Richardson reinstated as chief executive, and premiership-winner John Lang was brought in as coaching co-ordinator.

Souths started the 2009 season with a convincing 52–12 win over archrivals the Sydney Roosters but the great start to the season could not be built on. The Rabbitohs eventually won 12 of their 24 matches to finish in tenth place. Coach Jason Taylor was sacked after being involved in an altercation at 'Mad Monday' celebrations (Taylor later won a payout from the club) and was replaced by John Lang after three mixed seasons with the Rabbitohs. Times had changed at Souths, and the new owners have set the highest professional standards for success.

With experienced forwards such as Roy Asotasi, Mick Crocker and Luke Stuart joined by new signings Sam Burgess, Dave Taylor and Ben Ross, coach John Lang had a forward pack which could match it with any other team. 21-year-old Great Britain international Sam Burgess, rated the most exciting forward prospect to come from England since Malcolm Reilly, had a great season but Ben Ross' future was in doubt after he suffered a serious neck injury early in the season. 2010 produced an uneven effort—Souths missed the final eight by a solitary win.

The arrival of former Melbourne international Greg Inglis in 2011 did not guarantee immediate success for the battling Rabbitohs. The club won 11 matches and lost 13, ending John Lang's stop-gap tenure as coach just outside the final eight for the third successive year. The departure of live wire halfback Chris Sandow to a huge deal with Parramatta was a setback. An undeniable match winner, Sandow finsihed on top of the point-scoring list, while winger Nathan Merritt completed a rare double for the club when he topped the try-scorers' table.

The signing of coach Michael Maguire, who had guided the mighty Wigan club to success in the 2010 English Super League, and the 2011 Challenge Cup Final, hastened a new era for the club. Gone was the inconsistency, underperformance and poor attitude that had undermined the Souths efforts for the past decade.

At long last, four decades after their last grand final success, the Rabbitohs were once again premiership contenders.

REMEMBERING JOHN O'NEILL

(1967–71)

John O'Neill could never understand why his teammates called him 'Lurch' when he first came down to Sydney from Gunnedah in 1965. At 6 foot 2 inches (about 188 centimetres) and 16 stone (101 kilograms), with a cold stare that could put opposing forwards in a trance, O'Neill conceded he only bore a passing resemblance to the ghoulish doorman from the then-popular Addams Family television show. In a newspaper article at the time, O'Neill recalled, '[One of the Souths players] said out there on the field he looks a bit like Lurch doesn't he? When someone sticks a brand on you and everyone starts calling you by the nickname you either accept it or cop a fight or two. I accepted it; it doesn't worry me anymore but it took a long time to get used to.'

John Bernard O'Neill was born in Griffith, NSW, on 9 May 1943. After moving to Gunnedah, he was a first grader at age 16 and played his first representative match for Northern Districts in 1961 as a second rower against Newcastle. A Country Firsts representative in 1964, he played for NSW Colts against France later that year. 'Ron Coote, Bob McCarthy, Bob Moses and Les Johns played in that game … not a bad quartet to play with,' he later remarked. It was this match that led to Souths making O'Neill an offer for 1965.

O'Neill was a 21-year-old carpenter when he left the family home at Gunnedah and ventured to Sydney. He linked up with another 'chippie' at the club, Gary Stevens, and formed a building company renovating houses. He married his girlfriend, Clare, whom he met at Tambar Springs when they were teenagers, and raised three daughters together; Michelle, Julie and Cindy.

In 1965 there were a number of new faces at Souths—Jim Morgan and Bobby Moses from Newcastle, Ivan Jones from Brisbane and O'Neill from Gunnedah. 'Get a load of the bush boy haircuts,' was one remark when the quartet turned up for pre-season training at Waterloo Oval. 'I can still remember those big eyes of his getting bigger whenever someone told a story,' John Sattler recalls fondly. '"Yeah?" John would say. He was a big, raw-boned country boy. He was until the day he died. He was as tough as teak and if he made up his mind to do something, that was it! Nothing changed it. He was like that in business as well.'

O'Neill quickly earned his stripes with Souths fans that year, playing in all 21 premiership matches alongside Jim Morgan and clubmen Dennis 'Sluggo' Lee and Richie Powell. O'Neill at full charge was a fearful sight for opposing forwards. One press report stated, 'In his first match with the Rabbitohs, he showed the granite toughness, the crashing runs and the punishing tackles that have made him one of Sydney rugby league's most rugged props.'

But there were lessons to be learned. Two matches he played in that year, against St George at the SCG and Balmain at the Sports Ground, were two he would never forget. 'There was I, a kid from the bush, a country hick, stacked up against probably the best props in Sydney,' he later said. 'I copped the lot but I must have done all right because Souths kept me in the team.' In the match against defending premiers St George, which Souths won 14–4, hooker Freddy Anderson warned him, 'If Norm Provan had connected with that stiff arm he threw at you, your head would have been over the goalposts.'

A hardened Tigers outfit defeated Souths, 20–7, the following week. The word had got out about the young country prop that had terrorised Saints' star forward pack and in the match against the Tigers, O'Neill was knocked out cold early in the contest. 'Bobby Boland did it,' O'Neill later recalled. 'I went down in the scrum and something hit me. Next thing I know I was looking up at the first aid man. It kind of upset me … years of [playing] football and never before out like a light. But Bobby was really nice about it. He patted me on the shoulder and said, "Sorry I had to do that, Lurch, but you were going too well. Had to slow you down a bit.'

O'Neill learned quickly but he was still young for a prop forward —'raw-boned,' as John Sattler called him—and he was not yet ready for the rigors of representative football. Taking on St George in the grand final in front of 78,000 people after qualifying in third place on the competition table was another huge learning curve for O'Neill and for the entire South Sydney club. Missing the play-offs in 1966 was another lesson for the young Souths outfit, but the ensuing years would be golden for the Rabbitohs.

O'Neill made his NSW debut in 1967 and shifted to loose-head prop in the grand final when Jim Morgan succumbed to injury and second rower John Sattler was promoted to prop. O'Neill scored the opening try of the grand final against Canterbury after only eight minutes of play. Going to dummy half after a long break, O'Neill crashed over from close to the Canterbury tryline to give Souths an early 5–2 lead. Grand final success that year did not lead to further representative honours for O'Neill, however, and he would have to wait another three years for his Test jersey.

In the 1968 grand final, O'Neill and Bobby Honan both had their noses broken in the first half. 'O'Neill was in a fearful mood at halftime in the dressing room threatening to get even with the Manly player who got him in a high tackle,' Clive Churchill told journalist Mike Gibson. 'I'll get square,' O'Neill said. 'He got me cold'. Souths officials and coach Clive Churchill took him aside and quietened him down. 'We couldn't afford to risk him being sent off,' said [Club President] Denis Donoghue. When Souths won 13-9, O'Neill did his lap of the SCG with a Manly jersey draped around his neck and blood splattered all over his face as badge of honour.

O'Neill played hard on and off the field. His building business with Gary Stevens had taken off and he was now renovating terrace houses in the inner city. Other Souths players such as Ivan Jones, Bobby Moses, Bobby Grant and Jim Morgan worked on the projects (Bob Honan and Jim Lisle were also involved behind the scenes) and doubled as drinking buddies and card partners. 'We knocked around a bit in those days,' Ivan Jones told me. 'Three larrikins—John O'Neill, Bobby Moses and me. John and I clicked straight away ... the biggest fella on the field and the smallest. Lurch never backed off an inch, and ended up having one of the great careers in the game.'

At that time O'Neill was a demon for playing a game of cards at the time—euchre, bridge, poker, Rickety Kate—and often held court at the Cauliflower Hotel after work and football training. At the end of the 1968 season, Souths' first grade squad sailed to Perth on the *Oriana*. When the ship got underway, O'Neill, Bobby Moses, Club Secretary Charlie Gibson and some others sat down for a game of poker. They were still going strong when the ship arrived in Melbourne and sailed into the Great Australian Bight. Seasickness couldn't stop them, and they finally called it a day three hours before berthing in Perth. The following year the club booked a cruise to Noumea and Suva. O'Neill and Moses missed the briefing conference in the Souths boardroom because they were playing cards at the 'Cauli'. When informed of that they were missing the meeting, O'Neill remarked 'What's the panic? The ship doesn't sail until tomorrow.'

The 1969 grand final loss to Balmain never sat well with any of the Souths' greats, but especially for O'Neill, the fiercest of competitors. 'To this day I can still remember the late John O'Neill saying, "We've got 'em buggered, we've got 'em buggered. C'mon! C'mon!" Michael Cleary recalls. 'He was still saying it at the end of the game when

Balmain beat us. The whistle had gone, the game was over and they completely had us stuffed.' O'Neill would never concede defeat.

By the end of the decade, O'Neill's once lean frame had filled out to more than 17 stone and the 'bush boy haircut' was now fashionably long. Bob McCarthy laughs at the memory. 'The official program had me playing at 14 stone 10 lbs, but that was my Jersey Flegg weight. I was almost 16 stone by then. John used to always have a go at me about it. The program had him at 17.2 stone and I wasn't far behind him. "Why don't you tell them your real weight?" he'd complain. I used to just laugh, "I'm not telling them anything … people might think I was a fat prick, like you!"'

'Lurch was a lot quicker than people realised,' Gary Stevens recalls. 'He was very mobile for a big guy, and quick with the fists and quick to anger. I partnered Bob McCarthy in a game against Parramatta one day and Lurch thumped someone in the opposition scrum and suddenly the opposition forwards started to look at us like daggers. Macca said, "Great work son, they've been quiet all match," and we ended up copping it from them.'

O'Neill was again passed over for Test duty in 1970 (his former prop partner Jim Morgan played two Tests against Great Britain that year, having shifted to Easts) but there was no denying his selection following Souths' win over Manly in the grand final at the end of the year. O'Neill punished the Manly forwards after Sattler had his jaw broken and was selected in Australia's World Cup squad on grand final night. Clive Churchill told the press O'Neill had 'developed into a classic front row forward … [a] good ball handler who played close to the ruck and knows how to niggle forwards and lead them into indiscretions. He's a past-master of the softening up process. Just watch the way he ran with the ball and how he hits a tackler. And keep an eye on him when he is making his tackle—you'll see that it's generally the tackled man who comes off the second best.' Manly's John Bucknell could attest to that.

Not that everything was free beer and backslapping on grand final night. O'Neill and Michael Cleary fronted officials back at Leagues Club when they learned that the officials had failed to check on John Sattler, who was in hospital having his jaw wired, and had dined at an inner-city restaurant while the players feasted on 'sandwiches and cold pies' among a sea of fans. O'Neill later claimed he 'cuffed' one or two officials that night when they tried to defend their actions. As a result Cleary was placed on open transfer the following year and Souths' officials stalled contract negotiation with O'Neill, who achieved his highest honour with selection in Australia's World Cup squad.

'I was that keen to go I was scared to cross the street in case something happened,' O'Neill told journalist Tony Adams in the book *Hit Men*. 'That's how much it meant to me.'

Having lost the Ashes earlier that year, Australia were underdogs for the World Cup final against Great Britain in Leeds. 'Our coach, Harry Bath, said we had to starve them off the ball,' Bob McCarthy remembers. 'He suggested Ron Turner, our hooker, put mercurochrome in his hair and rub it in the eyes of the Great Britain hooker. It burns like hell, Harry said, and they used to do it in the old days in English club football. Ron Turner said, "Harry, you can't do that!" John O'Neill said that he would do it but Ronnie Coote said no, we wouldn't do it. We had tried everything; punching them from the second row, screwing the scrum, but nothing worked. We went for another plan to upset their front row ...'

World Cup captain Ron Coote takes up the story. 'Harry Bath got one of his mates down to our training—a hooker for Great Britain who had played something like 400 games in English club football —to give us some tips about how we were going to win the ball. He told Lurch he had to grab Dennis Hartley, the opposite front rower, by the fat around his ribs. Lurch had big hands and he had big fingernails too and he just kept grabbing Hartley by his guts. A lot of the trouble in the scrums and the fights among the forwards came from that. It was a win-at-all-costs game. I can still hear the Pommy yelling out to the referee, "He's nipping! Sir! He's nipping here!" That's why they kicked Lurch in the leg and ripped a big piece out of his shin.'

The Great Britain forwards threw everything at O'Neill, hoping that he would lash out and be sent off in the final. At one point in the hectic finish to the match, O'Neill was kicked in the head when Malcolm Reilly hurdled a tackled player. O'Neill finished the match with a gashed cheek and a split shin, but he never lost his cool and Australia recorded a famous victory. O'Neill used to laugh at the postscript to the match. A couple of minutes before the end of the final, and with the result still very much in the balance, Dennis Hartley sidled up to O'Neill in a scrum and said, 'Hey John, want to swap jumpers at the end of the game?'

'Can you believe that?' O'Neill told his teammates, shaking his head. Hartley's ribs were red raw on one side.

The 1970 World Cup tour also continued one of the game's fiercest rivalries. Champion St George halfback Billy Smith, the 'wild man of rugby league' in the era, was named vice-captain to Ron Coote for that tour. Smith had never forgiven O'Neill since breaking his jaw in a trial match in 1969, but while they were playing together in the Australian team they had put their feud on hold. In France one night after the World Cup was won, O'Neill took umbrage at Smith's suggestion that he tone it down while the team was dining at a restaurant. Smith suggested they go outside and settle their differences in the alley and stunned teammates watched the pair slug it out in the cold Perpignan night.

As fate would have it, Souths took on St George in the opening round of the 1971 season at the SCG. As O'Neill took the ball up five minutes into the match, Smith hit him across the forehead with a stiff-arm tackle. Unknown to O'Neill, the two teams and the crowd of 27,000, Smith fractured his arm in the tackle. Staying on the field, he was then picked up and driven in a tackle by Gary Stevens. At the last moment, Smith thrust his arm out to cushion the blow and shattered the arm in five places. He still played on until half-time. 'We hated each other with a vengeance,' Smith told me in an interview in 2003. 'But we became the best of mates after we stopped playing against each other.'

O'Neill returned from England with the reputation as being the best prop in the world but he lost a lot of the discipline he found on tour trying to maintain that reputation. John Sattler remembers, 'Keith "Yappy" Holman, the old Test halfback, was a referee at the time and he wouldn't shut up during a match, telling us how to pack the scrum and penalising us. Later, Yappy, was standing between two packs, reading us the riot act when Lurch lost it and called out "now" and charged forward to pack the scrum with Holman still in the middle. Holman pointed his finger at us and said, "Do that again and you're both off!"'

In the match against Parramatta that year, O'Neill was sent from the field for kneeing his World Cup forward partner Bob O'Reilly in a tackle and was suspended for three weeks. In his return match against Saints at the SCG, he again used knees in the tackle and split opposing forward Barry Beath's forehead open. Sent from the field, O'Neill was vilified in the press and turned up to Phillip Street with teammate Bob Honan in support, fearing the NSWRL Judiciary would rub him out of the game. He was subsequently suspended for five weeks and missed the Australian tour of New Zealand. His burgeoning rep career had quickly hit rock bottom.

O'Neill returned to the field in the run to the grand final, with Souths always in control against St George. But when his contract came up for renewal at the end of the year, Souths officials showed they had long memories and delayed negotiations over Christmas as punishment for his standing up to them. When teammate Ray Branighan revealed to O'Neill that he was leaving the club to play for Manly in 1972, O'Neill made the decision to contact Manly secretary Ken Arthurson to see what the Sea Eagles could offer him. He would play in maroon and white for the next three years.

In 1972, O'Neill missed the Test series against New Zealand

but played his part in Manly's maiden grand final success before travelling to France for the World Cup. The following year he made his seventh straight grand final appearance—and his eighth in nine years—as Manly defended its premiership against a plucky Cronulla team. That 10–7 win over the Sharks has since gone down in history as one of the hardest grand finals on record. O'Neill told Tony Adams, 'The 1973 grand final was boots and all. Of all the grand finals I played in, that's the one people ask me about. It's the game they all remember. And it's not because of the quality of the football … At one stage, their little halfback Tommy Bishop, who was a cheeky bugger, kicked me in the shins. I started chasing him but he ran and hid behind Cliff Watson. I nearly caught up with him a few times, but he was too slippery. Games like that were hard, but they were great to play in.'

On the 1973 Kangaroo Tour O'Neill suffered a broken cheekbone and missed the Ashes series against Great Britain. Playing against Widnes in the fifth match of the tour, O'Neill scuffled with local forward Bob Blackwood in a tackle. Blackwood quickly got to his feet, played the ball and busted O'Neill's cheekbone with a headbutt. O'Neill couldn't retaliate because he already had an injured hand and Blackwood was sent off for the incident although the damage was done. O'Neill missed the English leg of the tour but made his comeback in the Test series against France.

Souths' teammate Bob McCarthy soon joined him on the injured list. McCarthy, Australian Test captain in the Second Test, dislocated his shoulder scoring a try. '[Kangaroos Tour Manager] Charlie Gibson took me to the hospital and there was a mile of people in front of me,' McCarthy recalls. 'So much for the free public hospital system. When Charlie went back to the game, he left me in the queue with [Cronulla lock] Greg Pierce, who was the duty boy that day. I asked Greg to get me up the front of the line but he said there were too many people. I was still in my football gear and covered in mud when Charlie Gibson came back to the hospital after the Test was finished.

The pain was so bad I told him to get me in to see a doctor or I was going to throw myself under a bus. Charlie started swearing at them and got me in to see the doctor, who gave me a needle.'

Back at the hotel and covered in mud, John O'Neill offered to run McCarthy a bath and clean him up a bit. 'I was lying in the bath in agony and he was kneeling beside the bath washing the mud off my legs and I thought to myself, "This is a bit queer!"' McCarthy is laughing hard now as he recalls the incident. 'When he got to the private parts, he threw me the sponge and said, "I'm not that good a mate, you can do the rest yourself." I told him he had me worried there for a minute.'

In 1974 O'Neill joined former South Sydney teammates Ray Branighan, Ron Coote, Bob McCarthy, Gary Stevens and Paul Sait in Australia's Ashes-winning Third Test team but when his three-year contract ended with Manly's semi-final defeat at the end of the year, it was no surprise to see him back at Souths in 1975. 'Lurch didn't really feel comfortable at Manly,' John Sattler says. 'He would always come back after the game to drink with the Souths boys. He said he couldn't get over the Manly fellas. They never got together to have a drink after training. They just went home. He changed all that. Terry Randall told me once that Lurch O'Neill taught Manly how to win the tough matches.'

Rabbitoh fans hoped that O'Neill's return would be the signal for a return to the club's halcyon days and after a promising start to the season he joined Gary Stevens and Paul Sait in Australia's World Series team. But the season ended in disaster, with O'Neill injuring his shoulder and the team capturing the wooden spoon after Clive Churchill resigned as coach with five games remaining. O'Neill played in just eight matches for Souths in 1976, taking his first grade tally to more than 200 games (151 for Souths) before he announced his retirement as a player.

'They were great days,' O'Neill told Tony Adams in the early 1990s, 'but they went too bloody quick.'

The veteran of 10 Test appearances (including 8 World Cup matches) O'Neill surprised many when he put his hand up for the vacant coaching position at Souths. With Bob McCarthy and Gary Stevens leaving Souths for Canterbury, O'Neill only had Paul Sait and George Piggins for leadership at the club. George Piggins recalls, 'Lurch took over the job but soon realised he didn't have the time to devote to it. He had a very successful building business and quickly realsied he couldn't turn up at five o'clock in shorts to coach a bunch of footballers. He had to prepare, get the team ready for its next match. John probably thought, "What have I done here?" He picked a job paying a $1000 a year when his business was turning over millions.'

Souths won only three games in 1977, finishing second last, and O'Neill went to see premiership-winning coach Jack Gibson about taking over the coaching reins at the club the following year. In the 1980s he concentrated on his considerable business interests as a director with Gary Stevens in a building company that employed around 40 people and had, among their many projects, a multi-million dollar re-fit of the Coogee Bay Hotel. The pair also ran the Giles Sporting Centre in Coogee and invested in the Court House Hotel with Bob McCarthy and Richie Powell in Redfern. O'Neill had the foresight to sell out before the deal soured, and retained a vigorous business regime right up to the diagnosis of his illness. In the mid 1980s he invested in acreage at Lake Conjola on NSW's South Coast with former teammates Ron Coote, George Piggins and Gary Stevens, and built his dream house there on the water.

The rugby league public, however, knew little about O'Neill's toughest battle. In the mid 1990s he was diagnosed with bowel cancer. In 1998, journalist Paul Kent wrote a small snippet in the *Daily Telegraph* when O'Neill re-entered hospital. 'As footballers go, former South Sydney prop John O'Neill was tough. Even his nickname—Lurch—was tough. Sad to see then, that O'Neill isn't doing so well after entering St George Hospital this week to have cancer removed from his body. O'Neill never changed from the boy who used to concern his poor mum while she ran the corner shop in Gunnedah and he played in the big smoke. Back then, the ABC match of the day was on Saturday afternoon and O'Neill was often on telly, turning the opposition into a pile of blood clots. Still, whenever anyone walked in for two-bob's worth of mixed lollies, they were always met with Mrs O'Neill's, "Did you see what they did to my Johnny today?"'

The once commanding frame of John Lurch O'Neill was skeleton-thin when he succumbed to cancer in August 1999, aged 56. He was buried on 9 August, the same date Clive Churchill died 14 years before, and the funeral service at St Mary's Cathedral was attended by a large crowd of mourners from all walks of life.

'It was very sad when John O'Neill passed away,' Ron Coote reflected when I caught up with him at Lake Conjola. Across the water is the home he built with wife, Clare, who still lives there. 'He's been gone 11 years now. We were very close. We used to sit on the verandah after a hard day's work down here. He never looked after himself. I told him to go and have a colonoscopy but he wouldn't go. When he finally did have one and they diagnosed cancer he said he wished he'd listened to me. You know, when you're over 40 you're supposed to do it every two years. I did, and I said to him that he should too. He had an operation but he didn't change his lifestyle too much. He was always a big drinker ... three years later the doctor said to him, "It looks like you've beaten this. Everything looks good. But on your way out you'd better go and have a blood test, just to be sure." The blood test came back and the cancer had returned. He had five years from when he was first diagnosed until he died.'

His friend George Piggins devoted a chapter to O'Neill in his 2002 biography, *Never Say Die*. Piggins wrote, 'John was a funny bugger and when you had him as a friend, he was a friend for life, as his old mates from Gunnedah could testify. He was as close to them when he was a star footballer and successful city businessman as when he first left town to try his luck in Sydney. He had time for everybody. When I think of him, I think of a bloke who never lost his country qualities, but was very "South Sydney" too. Friendships meant a lot to him, and he would go out of his way to make sure they were sustained; the Gunnedah crowd, football mates from tours, the blokes at Souths he had played with.'

'The cancer was probably the only thing that ever got over the top of him. And I think he tried just about everything to beat that too in the way of natural therapies. Clare took him to clinics in Melbourne and his youngest daughter, Cindy, would go all over the place to get him the right organic foods to eat … he died at 56, a young man still.'

When Souths and Manly named their respective 'Teams of the Century', John O'Neill was selected in the front row of both teams. In 2008 he was named in the Top 100 ARL Players of all time, alongside Souths teammates John Sattler, Ron Coote and Bob McCarthy. Gary Stevens says, 'With John, his word was his bond from the get-go. His illness hit everyone hard. It was frightening, really, but he fought it to the end. He was a good party man, Lurch … he had the lifestyle of ten men.'

IN SEARCH OF '21'

March 2011: Shane Richardson sits in Souths' football club offices in Chalmers Street across the road from the refurbished Redfern Oval and points to a sign on the wall behind him that simply says '21'. 'Our number one priority is to win our 21st premiership. Every day that's what we think about and that's what I'm here to do. We've set ourselves up really strongly financially—we don't have poker machines and we don't rely on that sort of income so we've had to stand on our own two feet—but we turned over $17 million last year and we still made an $880,000 profit. We are a different world away from where I took over seven years ago.'

The South Sydney football office is a hive of activity. A bell rings every time a new member is signed and the whole office cheers. 'Our staff turnover is the lowest in the NRL,' Richardson says with some pride. 'They believe in what we're doing and everyone works as a team. We only have 22 full-time staff but we have a tight-knit team, a really good working premises, great training facilities across the road and a strong membership base. We're ready for our 21st premiership and when we win it, the club will go through the roof. It's a real business model based on rugby league being a business—not a heroin addict needing a quick fix. And I think we're getting better and better at it.'

Souths currently have a three-year business plan in place as part of a ten-year vision for achieving future success. Among other things, Souths want to be the best run sporting club in Australia and be recognised as Australia's number 1 sporting brand. They also want to be 'Number 1' in terms of corporate social responsibility and assisting charities such as 'Souths Cares' and the Number 1 club for player development with at least 20% of players undertaking university degrees. They want to be independently financially secure and double net profits and sales of merchandise. They want to create a strategic alliance with female supporters across the code and grow membership to 30,000 ticketed members and 10,000 non-ticketed members. They want to lead lobbying and debate at NRL level on such matters as player retention, player draft, player imaging and fixed scheduling. But most importantly the Club wants to deliver the next golden era of premiership success with at least three premierships in the next 10 years.

'One of our marketing strategies was to be everybody's second team,' Richardson explains in quick, staccato style. '80,000 people marched to get Souths back into the NRL and they weren't all Souths supporters. They were rugby league supporters. When we make the grand final it will be the greatest sporting event in Australia's sporting history. That's how we see it. It's a different world we're creating here for the 21st century.'

Richardson, who has been the CEO of Cronulla, English Super League club Hull and 2003 premiership-winners Penrith during the past 17 years, has been with Souths since 2004. His track record is impressive. 'When I went to Penrith they had just won the wooden spoon in 2001 and the leagues club was putting in $4.5 million to run the football club. My task was to get us back on track football-wise and, at the same time, to run a successful business. The first year we cut our debt from $4.5 to $2.5 million and the next year we won a premiership and broke square. [Penrith Chief Executive] Roger Cowan's vision of the Club was all about poker machines and the view that rugby league couldn't survive without poker machines.

I never believed that. I have always believed that rugby league is a great sport in its own right, so we never saw eye to eye on that. Cowan wanted to use the club as an example that the NSW State Government was going to destroy rugby league through increased poker machine taxation. I had seen the same argument used with cigarettes and alcohol sponsorship, and I formed the view that league could not live off poker machines forever.'

Souths was facing the same economic realities when Richardson joined the club in 2004. 'The problem with the club was we never moved with the times. We had this great district rugby league club, which we still do, but we never put together a business plan that was based on making money without poker machines. Whereas, in the 1980s, all our competitors leapt ahead of us because of the cash influx from poker machines, we never really had that luxury, year after year. We got to the stage where we were struggling to just stay alive.'

The legalisation of poker machine in NSW in the mid 1950s led to the formation of leagues clubs to support rugby league at a district level. Prosperous Sydney leagues clubs became cash cows in the 1960s, able to lure the best players from Queensland and NSW Country centres with big contracts. St George, with its leagues club known as the 'Taj Mahal', was able to fuel the football club's eleven-year reign as premiers. But in the new millennium, that model of rugby league support is no longer viable.

'As the poker machine tax becomes bigger and bigger, clubs will have the increasing situation of not being able to put the money into rugby league. And like a heroin addict, we've been so used to the money coming in that we didn't know any other way of growing our business. We are starting to find other ways of increasing revenue but it's taken a long time to turn the Clubs around. Souths have been on that path now for six or seven years.'

Despite being readmitted into the NRL in 2002 on a wave of public emotion, Souths was still in a perilous financial state. 'The South Sydney Juniors were assisting us but we never had any major influx of money so we had to change the financial model of the club,' Richardson says. 'We had to refocus our efforts on football-related business such as membership and corporate sponsorship, stadium income and revenue from game-day activities. We had to make some really hard decisions on a lot of things but if we hadn't have made those decisions I don't think we would even be here today.'

In the years immediately before the club moved to private ownership, South Sydney struggled to make ends meet. 'Every Friday I couldn't guarantee I had a job,' Richardson says frankly. 'I was staring down the abyss of being in charge of the end of South Sydney as a rugby league club. We had to make some tough decisions on how we wanted to run our business and what plans we needed to create more business. The first part of that was attracting some capital injection and the only way we were ever going to do that was through private ownership.'

When Richardson came to Souths in 2004, George Piggins was still in charge but it was increasingly difficult to keep the Club financially competitive. 'I told George I was going to support Russell Crowe and Peter Holmes a Court. It was a tough time because I have an enormous amount of admiration for George and I've told him that. It was a tough call from me because we wouldn't be here today if it wasn't for George Piggins. Let's be honest, he got us back into the competition … it was his grit, pig-headedness and strength of character that got us back in the NRL. It was just a little bit harder for him once we got back into the competition. I think it was a big surprise to everyone that it happened so quickly. I still think to this day that it caught George by surprise. He never expected to win the battle, it was a battle to the death and he was going to die trying.'

When Souths were readmitted into the NRL in 2002 after News Ltd buckled to the will of people power, Richardson says it was a whole new ball game. Rugby league had moved on but the way that we did things hadn't. Sport as a business had moved on so quickly and Souths didn't move with it. All we were doing was surviving from day to day and George's attitude was as long as we have a team on the field that's all that matters, but that's not what the members wanted and that's not what I wanted. I didn't come to the club to do that; I came to the club to win the 21st premiership with the greatest club of all time.'

Richardson feels for Piggins but says the door will always be open for him to be involved in the club. 'We still have the George Piggins Medal for the player of the year and we'll never change that. The biggest photo on our dressing room wall is of George Piggins. We don't want to ever detract from what he did for the club. We don't want to ditch the past, but instead of going round pubs with a hat in hand and some auction items we now have a business plan. And even then it's a battle. The side has to keep winning—we can't keep selling fresh air—but we're going about it properly and we're building from the bottom up. We have to consistently finish in the top eight and aim for the top four. We have a quality coaching staff around us with [former Australian Cricket team conditioner] Errol Alcott [assistant coach] Gorden Tallis, and [head coach] John Lang, so we're in a really good place.'

Richardson has had to cultivate a good relationship with the majority owners, actor Russell Crowe and businessman Peter Holmes a Court. 'I supported Russell and Peter because I thought it was the best thing for the club. I honestly believed at the time they would have got rid of me within 12 months. For the first two years they probably thought they could run the club a lot better than me. Peter had taken over as executive chairman, we lost $4.5 million dollars and I was within 48 hours of leaving the club. Russell made contact with me when they realised that running a football club is more than just coming up with great ideas. You have to grind away, day to day, and work hard to build the business up and to get credibility. Over the last two and a half years we've done that. We've made a profit, we're on the verge of the finals and we have credibility as a club.'

'The bottom line is, if you're running a business and you're losing money you need to change what you're doing. Millionaires don't become millionaires by throwing money away. I've always believed that rugby league could make money, and we're making a success of it at the moment. It's a different type of business. Every Sunday you have to deal with the emotions of the owners just like you do the fans. There are Boards, and I've worked for 17 years as a CEO with four different boards, and there are expectations.'

Having such a high-profile majority owner in Russell Crowe must come with its own sort of pressures, I put to him. 'Russell may be the public figure of the club but there is true corporate governance at Souths. He doesn't like losing, none of us do, but he doesn't interfere. He's never been inside the football office in the time I've been here but he comes to training three or four times a year and he comes to the games all the time. He's passionate about it, and one of his biggest contributions has been the polishing of our brand and his involvement with our merchandise. He has some great ideas and concepts. Russell's very easy to work, with as is Nick Pappas.'

'The best part about working for the owners is that they are really focused on making it a business and we have real corporate governance. At our Board meetings we discuss our finances and our marketing, not who should or shouldn't be in the team. People on our board are at the top level of business people in Sydney. Russell owns 37.5%, Peter owns 37.5% and the members own 25%, with Nick Pappas as the Chairman. Peter and Russell have two representatives each on the board, the members have two and the Juniors have one. Peter is re-evaluating his involvement (he currently lives in the South of France) but at the end of the day, Peter and Russell have never voted against each other.'

Richardson says, 'It's just the whole way we view our business. We never based our business on rugby league. We based it completely on the AFL model. It broke my heart to do it because I've been a rugby league man all my life but the bottom line is you learn from the best in class and the AFL Clubs are the best. We went to Melbourne

Ivan Jones tries to evade his opposite number Billy Smith in a club match in the late 1960s.

Coach Clive Churchill celebrates Souths' win in the 1967 grand final by throwing his hat in the air at the SCG.

Souths players stood out on the field together and often worked together. Gary Stevens, John O'Neill and Ivan Jones renovate an inner-city terrace in the late 1960s.

Denis Pittard scores a spectacular try against Manly in an SCG match in 1972.

TOP: After many of the club's internationals left the club in the early 1970s Paul Sait and Gary Stevens remained to guide the young team into an uncertain future.

BOTTOM: Souths' 1971 grand final team, the last to win a first grade grand final: (Back row) Bob Grant, Gary Stevens, Keith Edwards, John O'Neill, Ray Branighan, George Piggins.(Front row): Denis Pittard, Bob Honan, Eric Simms, John Sattler (c), Ron Coote, Paul Sait, Bob McCarthy.

TOP: Brian James tries to break the tackle of an Eastern Suburbs defender as Bob McCarthy and Ivan Jones look on.

BOTTOM: Together again—former Souths teammates (from left) Paul Sait, Ray Branighan, Gary Stevens, Bob McCarthy and Ron Coote before the Ashes-deciding Third Test in Sydney in 1974. Australia won the Test and retained the Ashes.

George Piggins (right) stands up to Manly's Great Britain international Malcolm Reilly in 1973. Piggins used the same resolute, boots-and-all approach when he took on the NRL in 1999.

and spent time with Collingwood, Hawthorne and Essendon. We not only looked at club membership but a whole range of things —how they run their business and how they do their corporate hospitality, the way they do their corporate sales and presented deals to businesses.'

Souths have subsequently raised membership revenue from $350,000 a year to $2.7 million and gate-takings have improved markedly since making the decision to move home games from the Sydney Football Stadium (SFS) to Homebush's ANZ Stadium in their heart of the former Olympic Games precinct. 'In 2006 we made $36,000 playing at the SFS. Last year we made $2.6 million playing at ANZ Stadium,' he explains. 'You don't have to be a genius to turn these things around. Sponsorship is up ... and they told us we wouldn't make any money going to ANZ? Sponsorship was worth $3 million at the SFS and today its $6 million. Now we go down to Melbourne and they're asking us about how we run things. We've come a long way from where we were to where we are now and we still have a long way to go.'

One of the more recent 'tough decisions' the club has had to make was the contracting of former Melbourne Storm player Greg Inglis. Fitting the Queensland State of Origin and established Test star under the club's salary cap indirectly led to the departure of local junior Beau Champion—a situation that upset many fans. 'The intent from the word "go" was never to lose Beau Champion,' Richardson says. 'When it came to the crunch, Beau didn't have to go anywhere in 2011. Beau left because he got a three-year deal from Melbourne on more money than he was on with us. We could have held him to his contract for this year but there was no guarantee we could keep him the following year. The way the business is today, you're always trying to improve your team. You can't sit back and rely on your juniors coming through. What we have to do is try and retain our juniors—Beau's the first one we've lost—whenever we possibly can, but at the same time you have to improve your squad in order to win that 21st premiership.'

Isn't it good that Souths is in such a strong position that a player of Inglis' ability wants to play for the club, I rationalise? 'It wouldn't have happened five years ago. When a player comes onto the market you ask yourself whether he will fit into your plans and that's what we did with Greg. We never thought we'd have to lose Beau Champion to get him. Beau actually made the initial phone call to Greg. But if you don't make the tough decisions like private ownership, to move your football club, to change the way we ran our business, to sign a "Greg Inglis", then you're never going to win a 21st premiership. I'm not here for us to be mediocre. The signing of Greg Inglis was a massive boost to our club financially and it will also boost us on the field.'

Other decisions are more cut and dry. Leaving behind the dream of playing home games at Redfern Oval was a simple one, Richardson says. 'As long as our arses pointed to the ground, Sydney City Council was not going to approve Redfern Oval for redevelopment. George Piggins had a view that we could survive there with a crowd of 15,000 at a rebuilt Redfern Oval. We're averaging 17,500 now at the ANZ and we have 20,000 members. Where were we going to put them all? If you're going to dream big, dream big. Instead of taking on Sydney Council, we needed a base at Redfern Oval that would great for us, the local community could use and be proud of. The Council spent $22 million dollars on a community asset. It's the best inner-city training facility in Australia. People said that it had to be enclosed because of graffiti vandalism. It's not enclosed and it doesn't have one piece of graffiti on it because our fans are so heavily involved in the area. They won't graffiti the rabbit! It's a great set up, we have a great relationship with the Council and the locals love it.'

Moving from the Sydney Football Stadium wasn't a tough call either. 'If the SFS wanted to keep us they would have made us a better offer. Their main clients were the Roosters and Sydney Football Club, not Souths. ANZ Stadium came to us, offered us a plan and then they bettered their offer, whereas the SFS barely moved from the original deal. The deal the SFS gave us when we came back to the NRL in 2002 was not a good one but we had to play somewhere so I understand the decision to go there. But we couldn't make money at the SFS and we were going backwards. From our point of view we needed a partner who would help us grow our membership. The ANZ Stadium Trust gets that, whereas the SFS still don't get it. We now have double the number of members the Roosters and Sydney FC have combined.'

'ANZ Stadium helped us and we extended our contract after the first five years. Look at the figures … we were averaging 8500 at the SFS and now we're double that at ANZ. We've grown our members from 3,600 to 20,000 in the same period. The ANZ Stadium Trust has been genuine partners. We had a dream where we wanted to take Souths and they bought into the dream. We'd like to have our own stadium one day for 30,000 people in our own area, so who knows where we'll end up.'

Richardson has also worked hard to mend the bridge between the current Club and South Sydney Juniors. 'George Piggins got on great with the Juniors but he was filthy they never took over the running of the senior club. The bottom line was the Juniors never wanted to take over Souths. Their job has always been to provide socks and shorts and boots and jerseys for the young kids playing in the area and they've done a great job doing that. For them, the senior club was a way for the local kids to progress into grade as it still is today. They supported us in the early days when we were struggling. We had to borrow $500,000 to dollars to start one season and they gave us a loan, which we paid back. They wouldn't just give us the money—it was a business loan—and no-one ever thought we could pay it back but we have.'

'They're very smart men—Steve Fisher, Keith McCraw and Henry Morris—and consequently we have a better business relationship with them because I've never asked them to take over the running of the club. They have their opinions, but that's footy people for you. I respect what they do, how they run their club, but I don't ask them for things they can't give me.'

For Souths outsiders, like me, it seems incongruent that the Souths Sydney Juniors Leagues Club could prosper over the past four decades when the senior club faltered. 'That's easy,' Richardson fires back. 'The Juniors were run really well and the football club wasn't, let's be honest. In the 1970s, and again in the 1990s, South Sydney produced some of the greatest players of their generation but had to let them go because they couldn't afford to keep them because they ran such a poor business. As soon as the leagues club wasn't in a position to put money into the football club, the playing roster just fell away. We had to let people go and instead of having a three-, five- or a 10-year plan that we could build on it was all about surviving from year to year. Meanwhile the Juniors were doing their job and saying, "Why would we want to give the senior club $3 million?" They are specialists in what they do and we have a great relationship with them.

'We recruit for the Juniors now. We bring in six or seven kids a year into the Harold Matthews and SG Ball teams. They're also the sponsors for our National Youth Club (Toyota Cup). We made the grand final last year (Souths were beaten by the Warriors) and of the top 25 players, 19 were juniors. That's a great record in itself. Eleven out of 25 players in our top squad are juniors and we have nine indigenous players in the top squad. We try to keep the history and culture of the club in place. We work with it and add to it and we'll take it into the 21st century.'

Souths are also searching for a new coach for 2012 and another tough business decision will have to be made. Richardson has a close relationship with current Rabbitohs coach John Lang, having worked with him at Cronulla (1995–2001) and having won a premiership together at Penrith in 2003. 'There's not a lot of emotion in the decision,' he says matter-of-factly. 'When we did the deal with John

I told him it would only be for two years. We want to attract the best possible coach who could take us forward again. Once again, it's about significantly improving the team. Whoever we employ, we'll be going through a really rigorous process and employing the best coach available. Our history of selecting coaches in recent years hasn't been about getting the best coach—it's been a situation where we've needed to appoint a coach—but in saying that, they haven't done a bad job. We're in a much better position now.'

Some decisions attract a backlash from the media, such as Souths' signing a sponsorship with Star City Casino after their very public stance on poker machines. Richardson quickly dismisses the criticism. 'With Star City, it's not about the money from poker machines but being associated with an iconic brand, a five-star establishment, that uses us in a mutually beneficial, cross-brand relationship. We have always stated that you don't need poker machines to run a rugby league club but it was never about gambling. It's just that the owners did not want poker machines in the same building as the football club offices. 60% of local people are on public housing here, and we don't think its right to have poker machines here. Russell's idea was to have a nice bistro, bar and lounge for people to relax – like a clubhouse—but he's not involved in the leagues club in any way.'

The Leagues Club is currently closed and will reopen soon on the same premises, as the football club operates as Souths on Chalmers. Richardson is careful to make the following distinction. 'It's not our leagues club. We, as a football club, have no people on their Board, we have no say in their Board and we don't control the funds. Good luck to them, but we have no control over them because if we did they wouldn't be doing what they're doing. I know how to run a rugby league football club. I don't know how to build buildings, how to run a leagues club or serve beer. I'm not employed to run a leagues club or a building site. The football club members and the major equity owners have no interest in the leagues club. Our members may also be a member of the league club individually, but the majority has nothing to do with it.'

Souths on Chalmers is owned by a company called High Concept (Trivest) who is currently in dispute with the builders. Given the jagged history of Souths League over the past four decades, Richardson is keen to divorce Souths' current football club operations from the problematic history of its leagues club. 'Not one part of our 10 year plan has anything to do with a leagues club. When George Piggins was in charge, the football club supported the league club for years and years. They never put any money in to help us ... it was the other way around. The leagues club building was sold off to developers and part of the deal was the leagues club was going to be on the first floor, Woolworths took the ground floor, the football offices are on the top floor and two other floors are for commercial space. We're tenants of the building, just like Woolworths, but the leagues club and football club are separate entities.'

In achieving its future goals, Souths has to walk that fine line of separating the achievements of the past yet acknowledging the legacy of the club's champion teams. 'When you win a grand final there is an unbreakable bond between players,' Richardson says. 'That bond goes beyond your family and it goes beyond your work, because it's a bond you share with 13 or so other players. No-one can ever take that away from you. Once you win a grand final, you never forget the guys who stood beside you on the field. I have enormous respect for the past but you can't live in it.'

Most of the legendary Souths players from the 1960s and 1970s have reconciled with the club, and Richardson says the club is reaching out to the 'lost generation' of players from the 1980s and 1990s. 'There was a gap in between the 1970s and the 2000s in which we really lost a lot of people who could have helped the club. Guys like Les Davidson, Sean Garlick and Craig Coleman have a lot more to do with club now, but at the end of the day they can't run onto the field with the football team and win a premiership for us. We have to stand on our own two feet and be consistent in what we're doing.

The only way to do that is to consistently finish in the top four every year. If you do that, eventually you'll win the premiership. We were two and a half wins from the top four last year and yet we missed the eight. That's how tough it can be.

'You saw what happened to St George last year? When we win it, and we will win it, this town will be painted red.'

And green, I add.

It's a brave new world for Souths and for the game itself … a chance to distance themselves from the mistakes of the past. 'We've gone from the club that no-one ever listened to, to having a strong a voice in Nick Pappas, in the formation of the Independent Commission and I'd like to think I'm one of the more senior CEOs in the game. Traditionally, rugby league has been destroyed by nepotism, cronyism and conflicts of interest. This is a chance for a fresh start for the game and to take it into the modern era. Despite how poorly we've been run in the past, rugby league is still a great game. It's the only way we survived because it's such a great game to watch. We need to take rugby league to the next level and put a class of business around it that will grow the game for next 100 years. The only way we can do that is to have the Independent Commission, through true corporate governance from the top right down to the clubs, but with clubs having a bigger say than they have in the past.'

The bottom line is, and this would be the mission statement of the Souths football office, to win that 21st premiership. 'We're just that far away,' Richardson says as he closes his index finger and thumb together so they almost meet. 'Everything we do here is to win that 21st premiership. When? I don't know, but I know we couldn't do it without a business plan. That's the modern way. Rugby league is a business, but it's also a business where a lot of people take off their head and put on a pumpkin or they make decisions with their heart or on raw emotion. It's an emotional game. It frustrates me when we lose, like it does every other fan, but you just have to keep going.'

Our meeting ends and Richardson walks me to the door. It's late but he has several more meetings before he heads home for the day. 'They're big plans,' he says. 'I'm not here to survive from year to year. These plans have been put into place in preparation for Souths' next golden era.'

EPILOGUE

Ten years after the South Sydney Club were readmitted into the NRL, the Rabbitohs emerged in 2012 as real premiership contenders under the watchful eye of new coach Michael Maguire. The emergence of rookie halfback Adam Reynolds, who ably took over the role vacated by the erratic Chris Sandow and topped the 200 points mark along the way, provided the Rabbitohs with real strike power alongside five-eighth John Sutton. Former Bradford Bulls forward Sam Burgess, alongside brothers George and Luke, settled into the new regime and brought out the best in Dave Taylor, who quickly garnered international honours. The shifting of champion centre-winger Greg Inglis to fullback, however, was a masterstroke by Maguire and for the first time in a generation, Souths had a team other clubs actually feared.

After a slow start (three losses out of the opening four matches), Souths settled on a winning combination, which saw the team in the top four at the halfway mark of the season. Six successive victories ensued before late-season losses to Manly and Cronulla cost the club a shot at the minor premiership. Souths finished in third place on the competition table – the highest placing since the halcyon days of 1989 – but the 24–6 loss to eventual premiers Melbourne was an early indication that the young side might be a season or two from realising their potential. However, an authoritative 38–16 win over Canberra – the club's first semi-final win since 1984 – saw them just one win away from an unlikely grand final appearance.

Cruelly, an injury to Dally M 'Rookie of the Year' Adam Reynolds in the preliminary final at 8–0, resulted in a devastating 32–8 loss to the Canterbury Bulldogs. Dreams of a NRL grand final appearance were put on hold for another year, but they were no longer dreams.

Souths hit the ground running in 2013, winning nine of their opening ten matches to head the competition. The traditional season opener against arch rivals, the Roosters, was an early indication of the belief the Rabbitohs had in their ability to mix it with the League heavyweights, winning 28–10 in a comprehensive performance. The loss of Dave Taylor to the Gold Coast, and captain Mick Crocker to an injury did not undermine Souths' efforts; in fact, John Sutton's captaincy of the side was a revelation and Ben T'eo and Roy Asotasi (in his final season) more than made their mark as a formidable forward pack. The Burgess brothers were even joined by a fourth sibling, Tom Burgess, to make the Rabbitohs a real family affair.

And the public got behind the resurgent Rabbitohs; for the second successive year, Souths attracted a record average crowd in excess of 22,000 supporters at their home games. Several losses after the representative season somewhat sobered fans' expectations, and the last round loss to eventual premiers the Roosters cost the club the minor premiership on the score of 'for and against' points differentials. This was a harbinger of what was to follow. Souths put defending premiers Melbourne to the sword, 20–10, and after a weekend off, took on fourth placed Manly in the preliminary final. Souths led 14–0 at the break and were 40 minutes away from a grand final appearance when the explicable happened. Manly exploited Souths' brittle defence on the edges of the ruck and on the right flank, and went on to win the match 30–20.

A season that had promised so much finished with little to show for itself. But Souths, and their hard-working coach 'Madge' Maguire, were determined to make the 2014 season a case of third-time lucky.

In 2014, Souths were ruthlessly professional in going about the task of winning the club's 21st title. When veteran winger Nathan Merritt struggled for form, the club persevered with him long enough for him to break Benny Wearing's club record 144 tries, but then dropped him from the top side shortly after. There was no fairy tale return for Merritt, his place was taken by young winger Alex Johnston, and he retired to take on a mentor role with the club. Meanwhile, the Rabbitohs had overcome an inconsistent start (three wins from seven matches) to find form in the middle of the season. Greg Inglis continued to go from strength to strength at the back, as did young backs Alex Johnston and Dylan Walker, who would later join him in Australia's Four Nations squad at the end of the year.

There was a sense of urgency about the 2014 season. Sam Burgess, the club's forward leader, successfully sought a release from Souths to return to English rugby in time for the 2015 World Cup. Would he win a premiership for the club before he returned home or would Souths once again falter in sight of grand final glory?

It was an uneasy sense of deja-vu for Souths fans when the Rabbitohs lost to the Roosters in the final game of the regular season, losing their grip on the minor premiership which Manly ultimately gifted to the defending premiers with their last round loss to the Cowboys. But the manner in which Souths stuck to their task against the Roosters, coming back from a potential 22–2 drubbing to post a face-saving 22–18 loss, gave hope for their inevitable showdown in the semi-finals. High scoring wins over Manly, 40–24, and Roosters in the preliminary final, 32–22, made the Rabbitohs the team to beat for the 2014 title. However, they would have to do it without hardworking Kiwi hooker Isaac Luke, who was suspended for two matches for a dangerous tackle.

Grand final favourites. It was uncharted territory for the club and its army of supporters for the past 43 years.

History has a way of repeating itself, and the clash between Souths and Canterbury was a nod to the 1967 grand final that started Souths' last golden era. The Bulldogs had qualified for the grand final under coach Des Hasler just two years before, blowing Souths out of the park in the process, and the 2014 grand final would be no lay-down meziere for the Rabbitohs. When Sam Burgess smashed his cheekbone in the opening tackle of the game, doubts again surfaced. The Rabbitohs led only 6–0 at the break, and Canterbury equalised in the 49th minute, but to use a well-rehearsed line from Souths' owner Russel Crowe's stellar acting career, the 'red and greens' were ready to unleash hell.

It was George Burgess who broke the deadlock, bursting through the middle of the ruck to score under the posts. Reynolds scored in the 64th minute to give the Rabbitohs a 14–6 lead, and a try to replacement forward Kirisome Auva'a made victory inevitable, but still the fired up Souths' team would not be tempered. Tries to Reynolds and Inglis in the final two minutes blew the score-line out to a commanding 30–6. Sam Burgess, in his final match for the club, was a worthy Clive Churchill Medal winner, paying an unplanned homage to 'Satts' in finishing the game with one eye closed.

There is no denying Souths' status now; from rugby league outcasts to premiership champions. The most successful club in the history of Australian Rugby League, now six titles ahead of their closest rivals St George, who technically no longer exist, it was 'Glory Days' once again.

RECORDS AND STATISTICS

SOUTH SYDNEY GRAND FINAL TEAMS

1967 (v Canterbury)
Kevin Longbottom
Michael Cleary*
Bob Moses
Eric Simms
Brian James
Jim Lisle
Ivan Jones
Ron Coote
Alan Scott
Bob McCarthy
John O'Neill
Elwyn Walters
John Sattler (c)
Reserve: Greg Norgard*

1968 (v Manly)
Eric Simms
Michael Cleary
Arthur Branighan
Bob Honan
Brian James
Denis Pittard
Bob Grant
Ron Coote
John Sattler (c)
Bob Moses
John O'Neill
Elwyn Walters
Jim Morgan

1969 (v Balmain)
Eric Simms
Michael Cleary
Bob Honan
Kerry Burke
Brian James
Denis Pittard
Bob Grant
Ron Coote
Bob Moses*
Bob McCarthy
John O'Neill
Elwyn Walters
John Sattler (c)
Reserve: Paul Sait*

1970 (v Manly)
Eric Simms
Michael Cleary
Paul Sait*
Arthur Branighan
Ray Branighan
Denis Pittard
Bob Grant
Ron Coote
Bob McCarthy
Gary Stevens
John Sattler (c)
Elwyn Walters
John O'Neill
Reserve: Bob Honan*

1971 (v St George)
Eric Simms
Keith Edwards
Paul Sait
Bob Honan
Ray Branighan
Denis Pittard
Bob Grant
Ron Coote
Gary Stevens
Bob McCarthy
John O'Neill
George Piggins
John Sattler (c)

GRAND FINAL 'FOR AND AGAINST'

Team	Tries	Goals	Field Goals	Points
Souths	9	15	5*	66
Opponents	4	14	6	52
Canterbury	*0*	*4*	*1*	*10*
Manly	*1*	*6*	*3*	*21*
Balmain	*1*	*2*	*2*	*11*
St George	*2*	*2*	*0*	*10*

* 4 x 2-point field goals, 1 x 1-point field goal

GRAND FINAL POINT SCORERS

Eric Simms (1967-1971) 15 goals, 4 (2pt) field goals, 1 (1pt) field goal – 39 points

Bob McCarthy (1967-71) 2 tries – 6 points

Bob Grant (1970) 2 tries – 6 points

Ray Branighan (1970-1971) 2 tries – 6 points

John O'Neill (1967) 1 try – 3 points

Ron Coote (1971) 1 try – 3 points

Mike Cleary (1968) 1 try – 3 points

GRAND FINAL APPEARANCES 1967-71

5   John Sattler, 1967, 1968, 1969, 1970, 1971
    Ron Coote, 1967, 1968, 1969, 1970, 1971 *
    John O'Neill, 1967, 1968, 1969, 1970, 1971
    Eric Simms, 1967, 1968, 1969, 1970, 1971 *
4   Bob McCarthy, 1967, 1969, 1970, 1971 *
    Elwyn Walters, 1967, 1968, 1969, 1970
    Mike Cleary, 1967, 1968, 1969, 1970
    Denis Pittard, 1968, 1969, 1970, 1971
    Bob Grant, 1968, 1969, 1970, 1971
    Bob Honan, 1968, 1969, 1970, 1971
3   Bob Moses, 1967, 1968, 1969
    Brian James, 1967, 1968, 1969
    Paul Sait, 1969, 1970, 1971 *
2   Arthur Branighan, 1968, 1970 *
    Ray Branighan, 1970, 1971 *
    Gary Stevens, 1970, 1971 *
1   Kevin Longbottom, 1967 *
    Jim Lisle, 1967
    Ivan Jones, 1967
    Alan Scott, 1967 *
    Greg Norgard, 1967
    Jim Morgan, 1968
    Kerry Burke, 1969
    Keith Edwards, 1971 *
    George Piggins, 1971 *

Denotes a South Sydney Junior

SOUTH SYDNEY AWARDS

1967
First grade premiers
Second grade runners up
Third grade semi-finalists
Club Champions
City Seconds: *Mike Cleary, Ron Coote, Brian James*
NSW: *Ron Coote, John O'Neill*
Australia: *Ron Coote, John Sattler, Elwyn Walters*

1968
First grade premiers
First grade minor premiers
Second grade premiers
Third grade semi-finalists
Club Champions
Australasian Club Champions
City Seconds: *Ron Coote, Bob Honan, Jim Morgan, Bob McCarthy, Eric Simms*
City Firsts: *Brian James*
NSW: *Brian James, Eric Simms.*
Australia: *Ron Coote, Brian James, Eric Simms*

1969
First grade runners up
First grade minor premiers
Second grade finalists
Third grade premiers
Club Champions
City Seconds: *Bob Honan, Bob Moses, John O'Neill*

City Firsts: *Mike Cleary, Ron Coote, Bob Honan (res), Bob McCarthy, Denis Pittard, John Sattler (c), Eric Simms*
NSW: *Bob Honan, Denis Pittard, Ron Coote, Mike Cleary, Bob McCarthy, John Sattler (c), Elwyn Walters*
Australia: *Mike Cleary, Ron Coote, Bob Honan, Bob McCarthy, Denis Pittard, John Sattler (c), Elwyn Walters*
Rothmans Medal: *Denis Pittard*

1970
First grade premiers
First grade minor premiers
Third grade grand finalists
City Seconds: *Bob Honan, Bob Grant, Denis Pittard, Paul Sait, John Sattler (c)*
City Firsts: *Ray Branighan, Ron Coote, Bob McCarthy, John O'Neill Elwyn Walters*
Sydney Colts: *Paul Sait, Gary Stevens*
NSW: *Ron Coote, Bob McCarthy (c), Elwyn Walters, Ray Branighan, Denis Pittard, John O'Neill*
Australia: *Ray Branighan, Ron Coote (c), Bob Grant, Bob McCarthy, John O'Neill, Denis Pittard, Paul Sait, John Sattler (c), Eric Simms, Elwyn Walters*

1971
First grade premiers
Third grade finalists
City Seconds: *Bob Honan, Bob Grant, Denis Pittard, Paul Sait, John Sattler (c)*
City Firsts: *Ray Branighan, Ron Coote, Bob McCarthy, John O'Neill, Elwyn Walters*
NSW: *Ray Branighan, Bob Grant, Bob McCarthy, John O'Neill, Paul Sait*
Australia: *Ray Branighan, Bob Grant, Bob McCarthy, Paul Sait, John Sattler*
Rothmans Medal: *Denis Pittard*

SOUTH SYDNEY TEAM RECORDS 1967-71

1967: 22 games, 16 wins, 6 losses. 442 for 272 against – 32 points

1 April   W 23-11 v Wests (Pratten Park)
A.Heiler 2, R.Honan tries; E.Simms 6, K.Longbottom goals.
9 April   W 17-15 v Parramatta (Redfern)
J.Lisle try; E.Simms 6, K.Longbottom goals.
15 April   W 23-15 v Cronulla (Redfern)
R.Moses, B.James, J.Sattler tries; E.Simms 5, K.Longbottom goals, R.Honan field goal.
22 April   L 9-20 v Canterbury (SCG)
R.McCarthy try; E.Simms 3 goals.
25 April   L 15-17 v Newtown (Redfern)
B.James try; E.Simms 5 goals and a field goal.
30 April   W 23-21 v Manly (Brookvale)
R.Coote, M.Cleary, K.Longbottom tries; E.Simms 5, Longbottom 2 goals.
7 May   W 12-9 v St George (Sports Ground)
E.Simms 3, K.Longbottom goals, Simms 2 field goals.
13 May   W 34-19 v Norths (Redfern)
M.Cleary 2, R.Coote 2, R.McCarthy, E.Simms tries; Simms 7, K.Longbottom goals.
21 May   W 39-0 v Penrith (Penrith)
R.Coote 2, B.James 2, R.McCarthy, J.Lisle, M.Cleary, E.Simms, K.Longbottom tries; Simms 4, Longbottom 2 goals.
28 May   L 6-9 v Easts (Sports Ground)
E.Simms 3 goals.
4 June   W 24-15 v Balmain (Sports Ground)
R.McCarthy 2, R.Moses, J.Lisle tries; E.Simms 5 goals and a field goal

11 June   L 6-9 v Wests (Sports Ground)
E.Simms 2 goals and a field goal
18 June   W 23-13 v Parramatta (Cumberland)
R.McCarthy 2, B.James tries; E.Simms 6 goals and a field goal
24 June   W 29-14 v Cronulla (Sutherland)
B.James 2, R.McCarthy, R.Coote tries; E Simms 7 goals
1 July   W 23-10 v Canterbury (SCG)
K.Longbottom, M.Cleary, B.James, I.Jones, R.Coote tries; E.Simms 4 goals
9 July   W 31-10 v Newtown (Henson)
M.Cleary 2, K.Longbottom, B.James, I. Jones tries; E.Simms 6 goals and 2 field goals
16 July   L 13-17 v Manly (Sports Ground)
J.O'Neill try; E.Simms 2 goals, K.Longbottom goal, Simms and J.Morgan field goals.
22 July   W 20-13 v St George (SCG)
B.James 2, R.McCarthy, M.Cleary tries; E.Simms 3 goals, K.Longbottom goal
29 July   L 17-18 v Norths (North Sydney)
R.McCarthy 2, B.James tries; E.Simms 4 goals
6 August   W 14-7 v Penrith (Redfern)
I.Jones, R.Coote tries; E.Simms 4 goals
12 August   W 10-4 v Easts (SCG)
B.James 2 tries; E.Simms goal and a field goal
18 August   W 11-10 v Balmain (SCG)
M.Cleary try; E.Simms 2 goals and 2 field goals
2 September   W 13-8 v St George (SCG) Major Semi-Final
R.McCarthy try; E.Simms 4, K.Longbottom goals
16 September   W 12-10 v Canterbury (SCG) Grand final
J.O'Neill, R.McCarthy tries; E.Simms 3 goals

1968: 22 games, 16 wins, 6 losses. 394 (for) 271 (against) – 32 pts

30 March W 15-10 v Newtown (Redfern)
A.Heiler, R.Coote, W.Stevens tries; E.Simms 3 goals
6 April L 11-15 v St George (SCG)
A. Heiler try; E. Simms 4 goals
15 April W 18-11 v Balmain (SCG)
A.Heiler, R.Honan tries; E.Simms 3 goals, Simms 2 and Honan field goals
21 April W 21-11 v Wests (Lidcombe)
R.Coote, I.Jones, R.Moses tries; E.Simms 3 goals and 3 field goals
25 April W 15-9 v Cronulla (Redfern)
R.Coote try; E.Simms 3 goals and 3 field goals
27 April L 15-25 v Manly (SCG)
R.Coote, R.McCarthy tries; E.Simms 3 goals
5 May L 12-13 v Penrith (Redfern)
R.Coote, B.James tries; E.Simms 2, K.Longbottom goals
12 May W 11-6 v Canterbury (Redfern)
A.Branighan try; E.Simms 3, K.Longbottom goals
19 May W 15-5 v Norths (North Sydney)
M.Cleary try; E.Simms 3 goals and 3 field goals
26 May L 14-18 v Parramatta (Redfern)
R.McCarthy, R.Branighan tries; K.Longbottom 2 goals, R.Grant 2 field goals
2 June L 13-19 v Easts (Sports Ground)
A.Branighan, M.Cleary, R.McCarthy tries; K.Longbottom 2 goals
15 June W 33-8 v Newtown (Henson)
M.Cleary 2, R.McCarthy 2, J.Morgan, J.O'Neill, D.Pittard tries; E.Simms 5 goals and a field goal
22 June L 19-28 v St George (SCG)
M.Cleary, A.Branighan, P.Sait tries; E.Simms 4 goals and a field goal
29 June W 20-6 v Balmain (SCG)
M.Cleary, R.Honan, R.Moses, P.Sait tries; R.Branighan 3, K.Longbottom goals.

7 July   W 18-9 v Wests (Redfern)
M.Cleary, D.Pittard tries; E.Simms 4 goals and 2 field goals
14 July   W 32-9 v Cronulla (Endeavour)
R.Coote 2, B.James 2, A.Branighan, J.Lisle tries; E.Simms 4 goals and 3 field goals
20 July   W 20-4 v Manly (SCG)
A.Branighan, R.Coote tries; E.Simms 4 goals and 3 field goals
27 July   W 19-14 v Penrith (SCG)
R.Sait 2, R.Moses tries; E.Simms 2 goals and 3 field goals
4 August   W 14-9 v Canterbury (Belmore)
B.James, R.Sait tries; E.Simms 4 goals
10 August   W 13-10 v Norths (Redfern)
J.O'Neill try; K.Longbottom 5 goals
18 August   W 22-10 v Parramatta (Sports Ground)
R.Amatto, R.McCarthy tries; E.Simms 6 goals and 2 field goals
24 August   W 24-22 v Easts (SCG)
D.Pittard 2, A.Branighan, R.Honan tries; E.Simms 5 goals and a field goal
7 September   L 15-23 v Manly (SCG) Major Semi-Final
D.Pittard 2, J.Morgan tries; E.Simms 3 goals
14 September   W 20-8 v St George (SCG) Preliminary Final
M.Cleary, R.Honan tries, E.Simms 4 goals, Simms 2 and Honan field goals
21 September   W 13-9 v Manly (SCG) Grand final
M.Cleary try; E.Simms 5 goals

1969: 22 games, 18 wins, 4 losses. 489 (for) 222 (against) – 36 pts

29 March   L 7-16 v Balmain (Sports Ground)
E.Walters try; E.Simms 2 goals

3 April   W 20-6 v Newtown (Redfern)
B.James, R.McCarthy tries; E.Simms 7 goals

11 April   W 43-4 v Cronulla (Redfern)
D.Pittard 3, M.Cleary 3, R.Grant tries; E.Simms 11 goals

29 April   W 20-10 v Wests (SCG)
G.Norgard, P.Sait tries; E.Simms 5 goals, R.Honan, R.Grant field goals

27 April   W 16-12 v Easts (Sports Ground)
R.Branighan, R.McCarthy tries; E.Simms 3 goals, Simms and R.Grant field goals

4 May   W 29-2 v Parramatta (Redfern)
B.James 2, R.McCarthy 2, E.Simms tries; Simms 6 goals and a field goal

11 May   W 18-17 v Penrith (Sports Ground)
M.Cleary, D.Pittard tries; E.Simms 4 goals and 2 field goals

18 May   L 10-14 v St George (Sports Ground)
E.Simms 3 goals and 2 field goals

24 May   W 16-4 v Manly (SCG)
A.Heiler, R.Branighan, P.Sait, J.O'Neill tries; E.Simms 2 goals

1 June   L 12-21 v Norths (Sports Ground)
A.Heiler 2 tries; E.Simms 3 goals

8 June   W 27-7 v Canterbury (Belmore)
R.Branighan 2, K.Longbottom, A.Branighan, B.James tries; E.Simms 6 goals

14 June   W 22-5 v Balmain (SCG)
R.McCarthy 3, R.Grant tries; E.Simms 4 goals and a field goal

22 June   W 24-4 v Newtown (Henson)
R.Honan, D.Pittard, R.Moses, R.McCarthy tries; E.Simms 4, K.Longbottom goals, R.Honan field goal

29 June   W 8-3 v Cronulla (Endeavour)
E.Simms 3 goals and a field goal

5 July   W 16-9 v Wests (Redfern)

R.Honan, R.McCarthy tries; E.Simms 5 goals
12 July   W 31-4 v Easts (Redfern)
R.Branighan 2, A.Heiler, D.Pittard, R.Coote tries; E.Simms 4 goals and 3 field goals, R.Honan field goal
20 July   L 13-22 v Parramatta (Sports Ground)
A.Heiler try; E.Simms 4 goals and a field goal
27 July   W 40-18 v Penrith (Penrith)
M.Cleary, R.Honan, A.Heiler, D.Pittard, G.Stevens, J.Morgan tries; E.Simms 6 goals and 5 field goals
2 August   W 36-15 v St George (SCG)
K.Burke 2, D.Pittard 2, R.Coote 2 tries; E.Simms 8 goals and a field goal
9 August   W 19-15 v Manly (SCG)
R.Moses 2, M.Cleary tries; E.Simms 5 goals
17 August   W 30-10 v Norths (Redfern)
K.Burke, D.Pittard, R.Coote, K.Walters tries; E.Simms 9 goals
23 August   W 24-22 v Easts (SCG) W 32-4 Canterbury (SCG)
M.Cleary 2, B.James 2, D.Pittard2, R.Moses, R.McCarthy tries; E.Simms 4 goals
6 September   W 14-13 v Balmain (SCG) Major Semi-Final
R.McCarthy, M.Cleary tries; E.Simms 3 goals and a field goal
20 September   L 2-11 v Balmain (SCG) Grand Final
E.Simms goal.

1970: 22 games, 17 wins, 4 losses, 1 draw. 479 (for) 273 (against) – 35 pts

28 March   W 38-5 v Penrith (Redfern)
M.Cleary 3, R.Honan 2, A.Heiler 2, E.Walters tries; R.Branighan 7 goals
5 April   W 29-6 v Parramatta (Cumberland)
R.Honan 2, P.Sait, E.Walters, R.Coote; R.Branighan 7 goals
12 April   W 29-20 v Newtown (Sports Ground)
R.McCarthy 2, M.Cleary, G.Stevens, J.O'Neill tries; E.Simms 7 goals
18 April   W 12-2 v Canterbury (SCG)
A.Heiler, R.McCarthy tries; E.Simms 3 goals.
24 April   W 18-7 v Easts (SCG)
R.Branighan, R.Grant, R.Coote, G.Stevens tries; E.Simms 3 goals
2 May   W 14-5 v Balmain (SCG)
R.Branighan 2, R.Grant, R.Coote tries; E.Simms goal
9 May   L 8-16 v St George (SCG)
E.Simms 4 goals
17 May   W 25-0 v Norths (Sports Ground)
R.McCarthy 2, R.Branighan, D.Pittard tries; E.Simms 6 goals
23 May   L 6-25 v Cronulla (Endeavour)
P.Sait, R.Grant tries
31 May   W 24-5 v Wests (Sports Ground)
K.Edwards, G.Norgard, R.Honan, D.Pittard, P.Sait tries; E.Simms 5 goals
7 June   L 6-10 v Manly (SCG)
E.Simms 3 goals
14 June   D 18-18 Penrith (Penrith)
E.Simms 2, K.Edwards, R.McCarthy tries; E.Simms 3 goals
21 June   W 27-9 Parramatta (Sports Ground)
K.Edwards, E.Simms, R.Coote, D.Pittard, J.Sattler tries; E.Simms 5 goals and a field goal
27 June   W 36-20 Newtown (Redfern)
R.McCarthy 2, A.Branighan, P.Sait, D.Pittard, G.Stevens tries; E.Simms 7 goals and 2 field goals
5 July   W 22-11 Canterbury (Sports Ground)

K.Edwards, D.Pittard, P.Brown, R.McCarthy tries; E.Simms 5 goals

11 July   W 25-13 Easts (SCG)

R.McCarthy 2, R.Sait; E.Simms 6 goals

18 July   L 24-29 Balmain (SCG)

K.Edwards, P.Sait, R.McCarthy, E.Walters tries; E.Simms 5 goals and a field goal

25 July   W 18-17 St George (SCG)

R.McCarthy, D.Lee tries; E.Simms 3 goals and 3 field goals

1 August   W 29-13 Norths (Redfern)

K.Edwards, R.Branighan, R.Coote, J.O'Neill, D.Lee tries; E.Simms 7 goals

9 August   W 21-16 Cronulla (Sports Ground)

A.Branighan, R.Branighan, R.McCarthy tries; E.Simms 6 goals

16 August   W 26-7 Wests (Sports Ground)

P.Sait, R.Honan, R.Grant, R.McCarthy tries; E.Simms 6 goals

22 August   W 24-20 Manly (SCG)

P.Sait, R.Coote tries; E.Simms 6 goals and 3 field goals

5 September   W 23-15 v Manly (SCG) Major Semi-Final

M.Cleary, R.Branighan, R.Coote, J.Sattler tries; E.Simms 5 goals and 2 field goals

19 September   W 23-12 v Manly (SCG) Grand Final

R.Grant 2, R.Branighan tries; E.Simms 3 goals and 4 field goals

1971: 22 games, 17 wins, 5 losses. 499 (for) 308 (against) – 36 pts

28 March   W 26-20 v St George (SCG)
P.Smith 2, R.McCarthy 2, K.Burke, K.Edwards tries; E.Simms 4 goals

3 April   W 28-11 v Balmain (SCG)
E.Simms 2, E.Walters, P.Sait, R.Honan, Stevens tries; E.Simms 5 goals

12 April   W 16-15 v Cronulla (SCG)
K.Burke, R.Branighan tries; E.Simms 5 goals

18 April   W 40-16 v Wests (Lidcombe)
D.Pittard 2, R.McCarthy 2, K.Edwards, R.Honan, A.Heiler, R.Grant tries; E.Simms 8 goals

26 April   W 25-18 v Parramatta (Cumberland)
D.Pittard 2, R.Honan, R.McCarthy, E.Walters tries; E.Simms 5 goals

1 May   W 36-19 v Canterbury (Redfern)
R.Branighan 2, C.Williams, R.Grant, J.O'Neill, E.Simms tries; Simms 9 goals

8 May   L 7-15 v Manly (SCG)
E.Walters try; E.Simms 2 goals

16 May   W 12-10 v Penrith (Penrith)
R.McCarthy, R.Honan tries; R.Branighan 3 goals

23 May   W 17-15 v Norths (Redfern)
D.Pittard 2, R.Branighan, K.Edwards, C.Williams tries; R.Branighan goals

30 May   W 25-14 v Newtown (SCG)
R.McCarthy, G.Fraser, K.Edwards, P.Smith, C.Williams tries; Williams 5 goals

5 June   W 28-12 v Easts (SCG)
R.Branighan 2, D.Pittard 2, R.McCarthy, P.Sait tries; R.Branighan 3, Williams 2 goals

12 June   L 12-14 v St George (SCG)
R.Honan, K.Edwards tries; R.Branighan 3 goals

20 June   W 35-9 v Balmain (Sports Ground)
K.Edwards 2, D.Pittard 2, R.McCarthy, A.Heiler, R.Branighan, P.Sait, R.Coote tries; R.Branighan 4 goals

27 June   W 22-21 v Cronulla (Endeavour)
P.Brown 3, D.Pittard tries; E.Simms 5 goals
3 July   W 35-17 v Wests (Redfern)
R.McCarthy 2, P.Smith, R.Branighan, R.Grant, R.Coote, J.Sattler tries; E.Simms 7 goals
11 July   W 19-8 v Parramatta (SCG)
R.Branighan, E.Walters, R.Honan tries; E.Simms 5 goals
18 July   L 12-15 v Canterbury (Belmore)
A.Heiler, K.Edwards tries; E.Simms 3 goals
24 July   L 12-13 v Manly (SCG)
R.McCarthy, R.Coote tries; E.Simms 3 goals
1 August   L 5-12 v Penrith (Redfern)
A.Branighan try; E.Simms goal
7 August   W 40-7 v Norths (North Sydney)
D.Lee 2, S.Kosta, R.Honan, J.Withers, R.Grant, R.Coote, C.Fraser tries; E.Simms 8 goals
15 August   W 22-13 v Newtown (Redfern)
R.Coote, R.McCarthy, J.Sattler, G.Stevens tries; E.Simms 5 goals
22 August   W 25-14 v Easts (Sports Ground)
R.McCarthy 2, G.Stevens, S.Kosta, E.Walters tries; E.Simms 5 goals
4 September W 19-13 v Manly (SCG) Major Semi-Final
R.Branighan, R.McCarthy, K.Edwards tries; E.Simms 5 goals
18 September W 16-10 v St George (SCG) Grand Final
R.Branighan, R.Coote, R.McCarthy tries; E.Simms 3 goals and a field goal

SOUTH SYDNEY GRAND FINAL PLAYERS (1967-71) CAREER STATISTICS:

BRANIGHAN, *Arthur* (b.1943) (Souths 1963–71) 100 games. 21t (63pts).

BRANIGHAN, *Ray* (b.1947) (Souths 1968–71) 57 games. 26t, 31g (140pts). (Manly 1972–78) 112 games. 30t, 52g (194pts). (NSW 1970–77) 6 games. 5g (10pts). (Australia 1970–75) 17 Tests. 4t, 10g (32pts).

BURKE, *Kerry* (b.1945) (Parramatta 1964–68) 35 games. 2t, 2g (10pts). (Souths 1969–72) 36 games. 6t (18pts).

CLEARY, *Michael* (b.1940) (Souths 1962–70) 142 games. 88t, 1g (266pts). (Easts 1971) 13 games. 5t (15pts). (NSW 1962–69) 11 games. 13t (39pts). (Australia 1962–69) 8 Tests. 5t (15pts).

COOTE, *Ron* (b.1944) (Souths 1964–71) 148 games. 49t (147pts). (Easts 1972–78) 109 games. 39t (117pts). (NSW 1965–75) 15 games. 6t (18pts). (Australia 1967–75) 23 Tests. 13t (39pts).

EDWARDS, *Keith* (b.1947) (Souths 1969 75) 86 games. 28t (84pts).

GRANT, *Bob* (b.1946) (Balmain 1965) 5 games (0pts). (Souths 1966–75) 136 games. 20t, 4fg (68pts). (NSW 1971) 1 game. 1t (3pts). (Australia 1970–72) 2 Tests (0pts).

HONAN, *Bob* (b.1944) (Souths 1967–75) 90 games. 27t, 6fg (93pts).

(NSW 1969) 3 games (0pts). (Australia 1969) 2 Tests (0pts).

JAMES, Brian (b.1943) (St George 1962–65) 17 games. 5t (15pts). (Souths 1966–69) 78 games. 32t (96pts). (NSW 1968) 2 games (0pts). (Australia 1968) 1 Test (0pts).

JONES, Ivan (b.1942) (Souths 1965–69) 70 games. 13t, 6g (51pts). (Wests 1970) 1 game (0pts).

LISLE, Jimmy (b.1940 d.2003) (Souths 1962–68) 100 games. 7t (21pts). (NSW 1962–65) 11 games. 2t (6pts). (Australia 1962–65) 6 Tests (0pts).
LONGBOTTOM, Kevin (b.1939 d.1986) (Souths 1961–69) 106 games 27t, 134g (349pts).

McCARTHY, Bob (b.1944) (Souths 1963–78) 211 games. 100t, 1fg (301pts). (Canterbury 1976–77) 40 games. 19t (57pts). (NSW 1969–73) 11 games. 7t (21pts). (Australia 1969–74) 15 Tests. 7t, 1fg (22pts).
MORGAN, Jim (b.1942. d.2006) (Souths 1965–69) 58 games. 3t, 1fg (11pts). (Easts 1970–72) 52 games. 7t (21pts). (NSW 1965–74) 6 games. 1t (3pts). (Australia 1970) 2 Tests. 2t (6pts).
MOSES, Bob (b.1940) (Souths 1965–70) 99 games. 12t (36pts). (Manly 1971–73) 14 games. 5t (15pts).

NORGARD, Greg (b.1947) (Souths 1967–72) 27 games. 4t (12pts).

O'NEILL, John (b.1943 d.1999) (Souths 1965–76) 151 games. 11t (33pts). (Manly 1972–74) 51 games. 3t (9pts). (NSW 1967–71) 6 games (0pts). (Australia 1970–75) 10 Tests. 2t (6pts).

PIGGINS, George (b.1944) (Souths 1967–78) 124 games. 6t (18pts). (NSW 1974–76) 3 games (0pts). (Australia 1975) 3 Tests (0pts).
PITTARD, Denis (b.1945) (Wests 1965 67) 44 games. 14t (42pts). (Souths 1968–73) 121 games. 56t (168pts). (Parramatta 1974–75) 32

games. 11t, 28g (89pts). (NSW 1969–72) 5 games. 4t (12pts). (Australia 1969–70) 5 Tests. 1t (3pts).

SAIT, Paul (b.1947) (Souths 1968–78) 167 games. 29t (87pts). (NSW 1969–74) 4 games. 1t (3pts). (Australia 1970–74) 16 tests. 2t (6pts).
SATTLER, John (b.1942) (Souths 1963 72) 195 games. 12t (36pts). (NSW 1969) 4 games (0pts). (Queensland 1973) 3 games (0pts). (Australia 1967–71) 4 Tests (0pts).
SCOTT, Alan (b.1939) (Souths 1960–69) 29 games. 2t (6pts). (Manly 1962–64) 24 games. 4t (12pts).
SIMMS, Eric (b.1945) (Souths 1965–75) 206 games. 23t, 803g, 86fg (1841pts). (NSW 1968) 1 game. 6g, 1fg (14pts). (Australia 1968–70) 8 Tests. 1t, 39g, 3fg (87pts).
STEVENS, Gary (b.1944) (Souths 1965–76) 168 games. 11t (33pts). (Canterbury 1977–78) 25 games (0pts). (NSW 1972–75) 6 games (0pts). (Australia 1972–75) 11 Tests (0pts).

WALTERS, Elwyn (b.1943) (Souths 1967–73) 128 games. 17t (51pts). (Easts 1974–76) 64 games. 5t (15pts). (Manly 1977) 8 games (0pts). (NSW 1969–74) 12 games. 2t (6pts). (Australia 1967–74) 20 Tests. 2t (6pts).

CHURCHILL, Clive (b.1927 d.1985) (Souths 1947–58) 157 games. 13t, 77g (193pts). (NSW 1949–57) 37 games. 5t, 31g (77pts). (Australia 1948–57) 37 Tests. 10g (20pts). Coach: Souths 1967–75: 206 games. 135 wins, 68 losses, 3 draws (65.5% win rate).

BY THE SAME AUTHOR

The History of Rugby League Clubs (Second Edition)
ISBN: 9781742570105

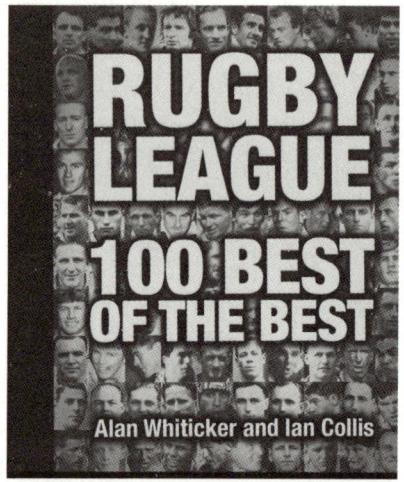

Rugby League: 100 Best of the Best
ISBN: 9781742576749

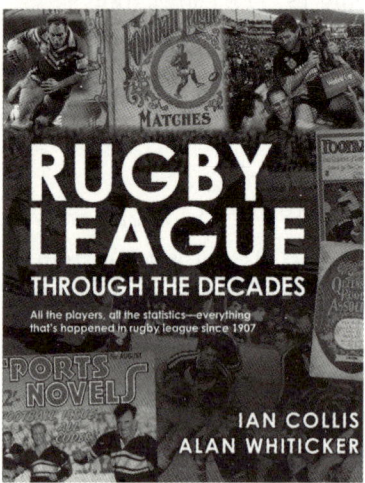

Rugby League through the Decades
ISBN: 9781742571362

St George: Eleven Golden Years of the Dragons 1956–1966
ISBN: 9781742578026